"Written with precision and attent _____, *Shabua Days* is a groundbreaking book that is about to turn biblical scholarship upside down. Paul is a thoughtful scholar, a diligent researcher, and a trusted guide. If you want a fuller picture of God's design for the universe as well as for your everyday life, this is the next book you need to pick up."

— MANDY ARIOTO
President and CEO of MOPS International

"When we understand what the Bible teaches about time, we are able to not only understand our lives, but God's nature as well. *Shabua Days* will help your work, your worship, and your appreciation for the Scriptures."

— DR. JOHN TOWNSEND
New York Times bestselling author of *Boundaries*

"*Shabua Days* by Paul Wozniak stirs my mind and spirit, and affirms my fervent conviction about the inerrancy of God's written Word. His well-written volume takes the reader on a journey through time and through Scripture—from creation to the new creation, as well as from the exodus to Christ's crucifixion and resurrection. Wozniak provides a wealth of information to which each of us needs to give adequate attention... You will grow through this experience, and you will be looking forward to Wozniak's next volume, *Shabua Years*, to continue this glorious study."

— WILLIAM D. BARRICK, TH.D.
Professor Emeritus of Old Testament at The Master's Seminary

"Paul Wozniak has put together a powerful exposition of the veracity and authenticity of the Truth! Few can pull that off. Nearly everyone else regurgitates other good writers."

— TIM RAFALOVICH
Senior Vice President at Wells Fargo Bank

"*Shabua Days* is one of the best books I have ever read. Through connecting the deep mysteries of God in the Old Testament and New Testament, the intentionality and precise nature of God are seen in new ways. Paul does a great job explaining things that are difficult to understand by repeating key understandings and linking them together time and time again. If you love being a student of deeper understanding in God's Word, this book is for you! Seeing the sovereignty of God is beautiful. When we study in this depth, trusting an omniscient God becomes easier as we see His fingerprints in each and every detail of biblical history!"

– CARMELLA HANSBERGER
Women's Pastor at Mariners Church

"Every once in a while there is a book that comes out that shakes some of the preconceived notions of the Bible. In *Shabua Days*, Paul Wozniak shows his intense effort to stretch our knowledge of the Bible when it comes to history, the geopolitical landscape, and Jewish history and culture. This book is not for the faint of heart, but for the student of the Bible who wants to chew on the meat of the Word."

– ERIC HEARD, M.DIV.
Pastor at Mariners Church

"*Shabua Days* may launch a new area of investigation that has been overlooked in the study of God's Word. It shows how the term *shabua* should play an active role in the vocabulary of anyone studying the Bible. *Shabua Days* also establishes the importance of understanding this term in order to grasp the history and flow of biblical literature. Utilizing his legal background, Paul Wozniak builds a strong case for divine creation by setting the Genesis account in the context of *shabua*. Learning about *shabua* also gives fresh insight into the Old Testament biblical feasts. *Shabua Days* will enrich every reader's understanding of Scripture."

– CARL WESTERLUND, TH.M.
Founder of Calvary Chapel School of Ministry

SHABUA DAYS

Paul Wozniak

Cru✗Press

Publishing books that matter

CONTENTS

FIGURES

CHAPTER 4

CHAPTER 5

INTRODUCTION

Can our understanding of a single word really make a difference in our understanding of the Bible? Yes, it can! The word *shabua* is just that significant. *Shabua* helps us to understand biblical timing, and that timing has relevance in the past, in the present, and for the future. Biblical timing also helps us to understand the full and intended meaning of many well-known Bible passages and topics, some that have long been an enigma. So, you might be wondering why you haven't heard the word *shabua* before, and why—if *shabua* is so important—so little is known about it even among Bible scholars and theologians.

Frankly, the meaning of *shabua* has simply faded from memory over time. If we lived thousands of years ago when Hebrew was one of the world's prominent languages, we would know that *shabua* is a term with a unique compound meaning. There is nothing hidden, nor imagined, nor mysterious about it, and it is not some sort of Bible code word. The fact that the use of *shabua* is always consistent, always predictable, and always reliable leaves no reason to speculate about its meaning. And when you know what *shabua* means, that understanding will change your perception about many things in the Bible, including the relevance of the Old Testament for us today.

Practically speaking, *shabua* links the Old Testament to the New Testament, the book of Genesis to the book of Revelation, Judaism to Christianity, and history to prophecy. In *Shabua Days* you will learn that the entire Bible is connected through the repeated use of precedent, pattern, and prophecy. These three principles occur in the Bible so often that there is no way the relationship between them could be a coincidence. So, if the recurrence of precedent, pattern, and prophecy is not a coincidence, it must have been intended; if it was intended, there must be a reason; and if there is a reason, it is incumbent on us to know that reason. After reading *Shabua Days* you will know it.

Also, whatever you have read, have heard, or currently believe about Creation, the Big Bang, and evolution, the information about each topic in *Shabua Days* is so compelling that there is a real chance it will revive the discussion—particularly among those who don't have an opinion, don't think it matters, or haven't made up their mind. To encourage open dialogue we devote equal weight to the biblical worldview and the secular worldview, and we make a concerted effort to be objective by presenting facts and avoiding opinions. You will be just as astonished to learn what secular science actually says about the Big Bang and evolution as you will be to learn what the Bible actually says about Creation.

Whether you are an atheist, skeptic, seeker, new believer, serious Bible student, or committed scholar, *Shabua Days* is a compelling read that will cause you to re-evaluate your thoughts about many topics. We encourage you to read *Shabua Days* with your Bible open and pen in hand. We are confident that you will find nuggets of information about the Bible that are guaranteed to prompt many *Aha!* moments. The companion *Shabua Days Study Guide* was designed to help you assimilate the building blocks of information as you read. The guide is a useful tool for individual and/or small-group study.

We hope to change the perception that the Old Testament is outdated and irrelevant in the twenty-first century. In *Shabua Days* we provide numerous examples to demonstrate that the full and intended meaning of many important biblical concepts and principles are rooted in the Old Testament. We hope these examples will open your eyes and inspire you to read and study God's Word in its entirety. That is the way God intended for us to experience the uncanny level of coordination between books and passages in the Bible as well as the Bible's consistency, accuracy, and attention to detail.

SHABUA AND BIBLE PRECEDENT, PATTERN, AND PROPHECY

Few people realize that the Bible contains a comprehensive timeline for all history: the timeline begins in the first chapter of Genesis and ends in the last chapter of Revelation. In fact, based solely on the absolute precision with which the Bible marks time, a compelling case can be made that the Bible is indeed—as many believe—the literal Word of God. In order to understand this biblical timeline, however, we need to know a unique method the Bible uses to measure time. This method is called *shabua*. The Bible uses *shabua* to mark past time, present time, and future time. Whether referring to a short, intermediate, or long span of time, the application of *shabua* is always consistent, predictable, and reliable.

After first defining *shabua*, we will examine various ways the Bible has used the term in the past. In the process, we will systematically evaluate some of the most widely known yet least understood passages that refer to *shabua* including the six days of Creation, Jacob's weddings to Leah and Rachel, manna, the Sabbath, the Fourth Commandment, the Feast of Passover, the Feast of Unleavened Bread, the barley sheaf firstfruits ceremony, the Feast of *Shabua*, the wheat loaves firstfruits ceremony, and Pentecost. At the same time, we will carefully scrutinize some of the most controversial secular subjects of our day, including the Big Bang theory and the theory of evolution.

THE BIBLE USES SHABUA TO PREDICT FUTURE EVENTS

In addition to examining the ways the Bible consistently uses *shabua* to measure and chronicle the historic past, we will look at ways the Bible has used *shabua* in prophecy to predict future events. As we do so, the significance and relevance of *shabua* in the New Testament will become apparent. In prophecies, for instance, *shabua* foretells the exact days of the death of Jesus, the resurrection of Jesus, and the birth of the church on the day of Pentecost. There are many, many more examples on the pages that follow.

The concept of *shabua* also helps to explain a wide range of topics for which a great diversity of opinion currently exists among Bible teachers, theologians, secular scientists, and historians. The key to these topics is an understanding of *shabua*, a Hebrew word that is not part of today's culture or vocabulary. That's why we give considerable attention to the meaning of *shabua*: we will look at Bible history, context, and terminology. Don't be discouraged if it takes some time to get a handle on *shabua*. And know that certain sections of this book may be more demanding than others as you familiarize yourself with the concept, but—guaranteed—the insights you gain will be well worth your effort.

Finally, this book relies almost exclusively on the Bible for insight regarding spiritual matters, which is why hundreds of Bible verses are quoted (in *italics*) and cited. The English Standard Version (ESV) is the primary translation used, but when a different translation better captures the intended meaning of a text, that Bible translation is quoted and cited. When a particular Hebrew or Greek word requires further analysis, you'll find a reference to the Bible research tool used. Now, let's begin this journey through time.

THE ORIGIN OF THE SEVEN-DAY WEEK

Think of your favorite childhood memories....

Most people's happy memories focus on family traditions, some of which have been passed down for many generations. In addition to strengthening family relationships, such traditions help create as well as preserve memories. Societies, communities, and even governments rely on traditions to draw people together, strengthen their bonds, and promote a love for their city and their country.

As important as such traditions are to families, societies, communities, and governments, their significance pales in comparison to religious traditions. After all, most traditions in a given religion can be traced to an individual or to an event that has become fundamental to its doctrine. Jews, for instance, remember the exodus and the Ten Commandments when they celebrate Passover and Shavuot. Christians remember Jesus' birth and resurrection when they celebrate Christmas and Easter. Muslims remember Muhammad's birth and the Qur'an when they celebrate Mawlid al-Nabi and Ramadan.

Some other traditions and practices, such as celebrating New Year's Day, are the logical result of a recurring natural phenomenon. For example, the origin of the year is naturally derived from Earth's orbit around the sun. The origin of the month is naturally derived from the moon's orbit around Earth. The origin of the day is naturally derived from Earth's rotation on its axis. The origin of the seven-day week, however, is an anomaly: no naturally occurring event repeats in a pattern of seven days. The seven-day week therefore appears to have been contrived. It is, in fact, one application of the larger biblical concept called *shabua*.

NEITHER HIDDEN, NOR IMAGINED, NOR MYSTERIOUS

Take a look at the illustration (Figure 1.1). Are the horizontal lines parallel or slanted? Are the black and white squares the same size or different sizes?

FIGURE 1.1 Optical illusion

The horizontal lines in the optical illusion are perfectly parallel, and all the black and white squares are identical in size. A ruler or straight edge can confirm that claim, but it is extremely difficult to see the lines as parallel and the squares as identical by just looking at the illustration. That is, unless you change the *way* you look at it. When you change your perspective—when your line of sight is across the horizontal plane of the page—the pattern instantly becomes crystal clear. Simply hold the book at eye level—open and flat—and instead of looking down on the illustration, look across it. You will see that the true design of the illustration is neither hidden, nor imagined, nor mysterious; it's simply a matter of having the proper perspective.

Similarly, there is nothing hidden, nor imagined, nor mysterious about the meaning and significance of *shabua* when it is used in the Bible. It is simply a matter of having the proper perspective, and that is the perspective of an individual who lived when one of the languages was Hebrew, from the time of Abraham around 2000 BCE through the destruction of Jerusalem in 70 CE. This perspective requires knowing that the Hebrew word *shabua* does not simply mean "week" or "seven" as it is typically translated.

SHABUA

SHABUA IS TRANSLATED "WEEK" OR "SEVEN"

Although the full and intended meaning of *shabua* has faded over time, the term never lost its significance or relevance. This ancient concept can be found throughout the Bible: it is not a new idea, it is not a secret, and it is certainly not a hidden code. Although Bible scholars typically translate the Hebrew word *shabua* as either "week" or "seven," neither translation adequately conveys its full and intended meaning. The goal of this chapter is to thoroughly define *shabua* because a clear understanding of that term is foundational to the chapters that follow as well as to *Shabua Years*, the sequel to this book.

As you will see, the basic meaning of *shabua* is not complicated. It is simply a matter of understanding the way the Bible uses it, and that understanding is a matter of perspective. (If there is any mystery at all, it's trying to figure out why such an important biblical concept has been overlooked for so long.) Whenever the Bible uses the word *shabua* or alludes to the concept, its use is always consistent, predictable, and reliable. *Shabua* is used to refer to both the micro (the small, as in a seven-day week) and the macro (the large, as in the sweep of history). *Shabua* helps to explain the relationship between history and prophecy, Judaism and Christianity, and the Old and the New Testaments.

After we finish defining *shabua* here in chapter 1, we will examine in subsequent chapters how the Bible used *shabua*. This review of the role it has played in the past will make evident its role in helping us understand Bible prophecy and its fulfillment. This discussion may also shed light on some of the events taking place in the world today. Again, please bear with the sections of this chapter that are a bit technical. Your comprehensive understanding of the concept of *shabua* is absolutely necessary for unpacking its astonishing historical and prophetic significance.

ALTERNATIVE DEFINITIONS AND MEANINGS

The original language of the Old Testament is primarily Hebrew, and the original language of the New Testament is primarily Greek. Both testaments contain words no longer used today. In addition, as in any language, many of the original words have alternative definitions and meanings, and these definitions and meanings continue to change over time especially as a language grows. And languages do grow. For example, Noah Webster's dictionary *An American Dictionary of the English Language* contained 70,000 words when it was first published in 1828.[1] Today, according to Merriam-Webster, "it has been estimated that the vocabulary of English includes roughly 1 million words."[2]

Due to never-ending changes in languages (particularly English), Bible translation can be challenging. Although translators may be working from the same original Hebrew or Greek text, they do not always agree on the most appropriate English word or words to use to convey the meaning; in fact, the choice may come down to their best guess. That's one reason why so many Bible translations are available, yet because virtually all originate from the same Hebrew or Greek text, they are remarkably similar. The variations are minor and do not alter the basic meaning of a word, verse, or passage.

LOST IN TRANSLATION

Sometimes, even when a word is translated correctly, it can still be difficult to convey the meaning. This gap is analogous to an individual who chooses to watch a 2019-era Blu-ray movie made in digital, THX surround sound, LED, 4K color, Ultra High-Definition, and 3D on a 1965-era black and white tube television set (a few of these are still around). The director and producer control how the movie is produced, but they cannot control the medium the viewer uses or the viewer's experience. Although the movie is the same, the dynamic picture, sound, and special effects are totally lost. According to Strong's Concordance, such would seem to be the case with the Hebrew word *shabua*.

Strong's Concordance is a reference tool that enables a reader to locate every time a specific word is used in the Bible. To facilitate biblical research, each word is assigned a number. Strong's has assigned H7620 to *shabua* and reports that it is used in the Bible a total of twenty times.[3] Nineteen times it is translated as the English word *week*; one time it is translated as the English word *seven*. As mentioned previously, neither word captures the full and intended meaning of *shabua*. Without more information, the meaning of the term would be lost in translation. Fortunately, further research leads to a more complete understanding. So then, besides "week" and "seven," what does *shabua* mean?

THE ROOT OF THE MATTER

Let's begin our analysis of *shabua* by thinking for a minute about the word *dozen*. When you see or hear the word *dozen*, what's the first thing that comes to mind? You undoubtedly think, "Twelve of something," often eggs or donuts. In the Merriam-Webster English dictionary, the primary definition of *dozen* is, in fact, "a group of twelve."[4] *Dozen* was derived from the Old

French word *dozaine*, which originated from the Latin word *duodecim*, from *duo* (two) and *decem* (ten).[5] Although we don't give it a second thought, the English term *dozen* is actually an equation $(2 + 10 = 12)$. And, yes, this is a completely unnecessary exercise if you can read, write, and speak English. A dozen means twelve.

Similarly, to understand the full and intended meaning of *shabua*, we need to have the perspective of a person who, many centuries ago, would have been as familiar with that term as we are with the word *dozen*. To gain this perspective, we need to dig down to the root of the word (also called the *word stem*). A word root is the basic foundation of a word. A root can stand alone, but most of the time it has a prefix and/or suffix attached to it. Also, the core meaning of the root is retained even as prefixes and/or suffixes are added to modify that meaning. Consider, for instance, the word *exportable*. The root word *port* means "to carry." The prefix *ex-* means "out." The suffix *-able* means "able to." So the word *exportable* means "able to carry out." This same approach is used when translating words from other languages. Finding the root of the Hebrew word *shabua* will therefore help us better understand the term's full and intended meaning.

שבע MEANS "SEVEN" AND "COMPLETE"

Strong's indicates that the three-character Hebrew root (שבע) used in *shabua* (H7620) is the foundation of nine different Hebrew words. These nine words are listed in Figure 1.2 according to the number Strong's has assigned them. They are followed by Strong's primary Hebrew to English transliteration as well as the key words used by Strong's to define them.

As Figure 1.2 reveals, the three-character Hebrew root (שבע) has two primary meanings as well as the ability to serve as a female name. In each instance, the precise definition is determined either by the way the root is slightly modified or by its context. One of the primary meanings of the root (שבע) is the cardinal number seven (7). The second primary meaning of the root (שבע) is expressed with descriptive words like *full, sufficient, satisfactory,* and *plenty* (words that suggest being total and complete). However, a closer examination of Strong's usage notes reveals an interesting correlation between the two primary meanings.

STRONG'S	TRANSLITERATION	DEFINITION
H7620	*shabua*	week, seven
H7646	*saba*	satisfy, fill, full, plenty, enough
H7647	*saba*	plenty, plenteous, abundance
H7648	*soba*	full, fullness, sufficed, satisfying
H7649	*sabea*	full, satisfied
H7650	*shaba*	swear, charge, oath, adjure
H7651	*sheba*	seven (cardinal number 7)
H7652	*Sheba*	female name
H7655	*sheba*	seven, seven times

FIGURE 1.2 Nine Hebrew words that use the root (שׁבע)

THE TWO PRIMARY MEANINGS MELD TOGETHER

According to Strong's usage notes for *shabua* (H7620), *shaba* (H7650), and *sheba* (H7651), the two primary meanings meld together. Notice in the usage notes (Figure 1.3) the way the meaning of each word is utterly dependent on related words that use the same root (שׁבע). (When Strong's Concordance is quoted and cited, the definitions, references, italics, parenthetical inserts, and usage notes are original to Strong's.)

What we learn from the usage notes is that the three-character Hebrew root (שׁבע) also has a compound meaning that incorporates both primary meanings: the cardinal number "seven" as well as "to be complete" (or "full"). In other words, the root (שׁבע) can mean both "seven" and "to be complete" at the same time. This compound meaning is relevant because of the way the Hebrew word *shabua* is used: on every occasion *shabua* appears in the Bible, it retains both of the meanings inherent in the root (שׁבע). But in addition to incorporating the number "seven" and the meaning "to be complete," *shabua* has another layer of meaning as well.

TRANSLITERATION	STRONG'S	USAGE NOTE
shabua	H7620	a "properly, passive participle of H7650 as a denominative of H7651; literally sevened, i.e. a week (specifically of years): seven, week."
shaba	H7650	"a primitive root; properly to be complete, but used only as a denominative from H7651; to seven oneself, i.e. swear (as if by repeating a declaration seven times)."
sheba	H7651	"from H7650; a primitive cardinal number; seven (as the sacred full one); also (adverbially) seven times; by implication a week."

FIGURE 1.3 Strong's usage notes for *shabua, shaba,* and *sheba*

A COMPLETE TIME PERIOD OF SEVEN

The additional layer of meaning inherent in the word *shabua* is the communication of a time period. To be specific, *shabua* appears in the Bible twenty times, and each time the context is a complete time period of seven. This time period is evident nineteen times when *shabua* is translated as the English word *week*: one week is a complete time period of seven. On the single occasion that *shabua* is translated as *seven* (Ezekiel 45:21), the context is still a complete time period of seven.

When *shabua* is used in the Bible, however, it can refer to either a complete time period of seven days or a complete time period of seven years. The word *shabua* does not differentiate between days or years. Only in Ezekiel 45:21 is the *shabua* interval specified, and in that verse *shabua* refers to an interval of days. The interval of seven is not specified as days or years in any of the other nineteen occurrences of *shabua*. However, in each instance, the context enables readers to easily determine whether the *shabua* refers to seven days or seven years.

KNOWING THE CONTEXT IS CRUCIAL

You will find it tremendously helpful to think of *shabua* as a term instead of a word with a single, one-word definition. The Hebrew word *shabua* and the English word *dozen* are similar in this regard. We understand that the term *dozen* means "a complete group of twelve," and now we know that the term *shabua* means "a complete time period of seven." But neither word makes complete sense if we don't know the context. What specific group of twelve is *dozen* referring to: eggs or donuts? Likewise, what specific time period of seven is *shabua* referring to: days or years?

When either *dozen* or *shabua* is used, the meaning is usually very obvious from the context. When you order a *dozen* at a donut shop, you are going to get twelve donuts, not twelve eggs. The context is equally unambiguous every time *shabua* is used in the Bible: it is relatively easy to discern whether *shabua* is referring to seven days or seven years. Again, the Hebrew word *shabua* always refers to a complete time period of seven, either seven days or seven years depending on the context. When the interval of time is not specified, it must be determined by the context.

But why, you may be wondering, doesn't the Bible simply state *seven days* or *seven years*? Wouldn't that be helpful? Actually, the Bible does use those exact words, but never when referring to a *shabua* of days or a *shabua* of years. *Shabua* is used alone because it has a very particular additional meaning when it is stated or even implied, and this topic will be covered in the next chapter. Until then, this fact will be sufficient: not all of the seven intervals of a *shabua* are the same. In every instance that *shabua* is either stated or implied, the 7th and final interval (the 7th day or the 7th year) differs from the previous six intervals (the previous six days or the previous six years).

PRECEDENT, PATTERN, AND PROPHECY

KEY WORDS, THEMES, AND CONCEPTS

When an infant utters that very first "Momma" or "Dada," parents react as if they have just won the lottery. This momentous occasion signals the start of a learning process that never ends. Soon, the infant is a child whose vocabulary grows and grows. Before long, the child is a student who puts words together to express thoughts. Later, the student is an employee who uses those thoughts to develop ideas and earn a living. Then the employee gets married, becomes a parent, and encourages that little person to say "Momma" and "Dada."

From the moment an infant learns the meaning of *Momma* and *Dada*, that meaning never changes. Early use nails down the correct meaning in the child's mind and creates a precedent. Subsequent use of the terms reinforces that precedent and establishes a pattern as the terms are repeated again and again. This same principle is evident in the educational process. When new material is introduced, the definitions of fundamental words, themes, and concepts set precedents. Subsequent use of these key words, themes, and concepts reinforce the precedent and establish a predictable pattern that enables greater understanding of the subject on a more advanced level.

However complicated the subject matter may eventually become, the definitions of the fundamental words, themes, and concepts will remain unchanged. For example, the number recognition learned in preschool is necessary for the college student learning calculus. Knowledge of basic mathematical principles learned in elementary school ($1 + 1$ will always be 2) provides part of the foundation and sets the precedent for building the framework—establishing the pattern—necessary to learn calculus. Teachers prepare lessons and professors write textbooks based on this movement from precedent to pattern.

BIBLE PRECEDENT

This information is relevant because the God-designed movement from precedent to pattern occurs repeatedly throughout the Bible. From the start, the Old Testament defines key words and introduces fundamental themes and concepts. Among the words, themes, and concepts introduced in the book of Genesis are God, Creation, man, woman, sin, Satan, sacrifice, judgment, forgiveness, repentance, death, salvation, *shabua*, and the Sabbath.

Like the Old Testament, the New Testament also defines key words and introduces fundamental themes and concepts at the beginning, specifically in the first four books of the New Testament. These books are called the Gospels, and their titles—Matthew, Mark, Luke, and John—are derived from the names of the four respective authors. The main subject of the Gospels is Jesus. Among the words, themes, and concepts introduced in the Gospels are Jesus' birth, life, ministry, message, miracles, suffering, death, and resurrection.

BIBLE PATTERNS BASED ON BIBLE PRECEDENT

The key words, themes, and concepts introduced in the book of Genesis are developed and expanded throughout the remaining thirty-eight books of the Old Testament. Similarly, the key words, themes, and concepts introduced in the four Gospels are developed and expanded throughout the remaining twenty-three books of the New Testament. The repeated use and the consistent application of these principles in each testament establish identifiable patterns.

But major Old Testament words, themes, and concepts are introduced, developed, and expanded without being fully resolved within the Old Testament text, making it clear that the Old Testament was never intended to stand alone as a complete work. In addition, some major patterns are only partially completed as the Old Testament concludes. Consider an artist who sketches his entire design on canvas with a graphite pencil before beginning to paint. The Old Testament can be compared to that detailed sketch. Although the drawing may be beautiful, the artist never intended the work to be complete without color.

THE OLD TESTAMENT IS 77% OF THE BIBLE

The New Testament picks up where the Old Testament leaves off by adding vibrant color. Just as it is not essential to have seen the artist's initial sketch to appreciate the finished painting, it is not essential to know the Old Testament to understand the basic message of the New Testament. While the Old Testament requires the New Testament to complete unresolved key words, themes, concepts, precedents, and patterns, the New Testament is able to stand alone. This means an individual who reads only the New Testament will find all the doctrine they need to make an informed decision about Jesus, the church, and what it means to be a Christian.

Since the New Testament can stand alone, does that render the Old Testament outdated, irrelevant, and unnecessary? If not, why is so little attention given to that 77% of the Bible? Considering the fact that it is referenced the least and titled "Old," it is easy to understand why people give it little weight or ignore it entirely. Furthermore, in addition to being chronologically older, the Old Testament is more difficult to read and understand than the New Testament because it involves knowing history and culture, subjects that many think are a waste of time.

PROPHECY IS A PREDICTION OF FUTURE EVENTS

Are there any reasons to overcome the factors that may hinder people from studying the Old Testament? Indeed, there are many compelling reasons, and you will see some of them presented on the pages that follow. As indicted earlier, the Old Testament introduces many key words, themes, concepts, precedents, and patterns that are developed and expanded without reaching final resolution. Someone who reads only the New Testament will find such Old Testament issues resolved without even knowing they were issues. These readers entirely miss some fundamentally important principles. Consider students who learn to do math only by using a calculator. Although these students will get the correct answer every time, they will never learn to work with formulas, a skill required in advanced math. But they don't know what they don't know: they only know math-by-calculator.

Similarly, New Testament readers don't know what they don't know: they don't recognize, for instance, that the understanding of many of the New Testament principles, parables, references, metaphors, and symbolism relies on knowledge of the Old Testament. In addition, these readers may not be aware that biblical precedents and patterns are—with extraordinary specificity and detail—used to predict future events. That foreshadowing of future events is called *prophecy*, which the Merriam-Webster dictionary defines as "a prediction of something to come." When that "something to come"—the future event—happens, it is called the *fulfillment* of the prophecy.

God intentionally created prophecy by weaving into His Word an Old Testament pattern based on an Old Testament precedent that predicts a future

New Testament event. If you are not aware of this interrelationship, you cannot fully appreciate the significance of the prophecy being so precisely fulfilled. To reiterate, precedents and patterns initiated in the Old Testament are often completed in the New Testament as the fulfillment of Bible prophecy, and the value of our knowing the significance and relevance of that fact cannot be overstated.

AN EXAMPLE IN THE SACRIFICIAL SYSTEM

The sacrificial system offers a striking example of an Old Testament precedent and pattern reaching its prophetic fulfillment in the New Testament.

When His people were enslaved in Egypt, God instructed each Hebrew family to slaughter an unblemished male lamb on Nisan 14 (precedent), the day before the exodus from Egypt. The lamb was a substitute for the family's firstborn male child who would now—as a result of his parents' obedience—be passed over during the plague of death. In Exodus 12:14 the people were told, "*This day shall be for you a memorial day, and you shall keep it as a feast to the LORD; throughout your generations, as a statute forever, you shall keep it as a feast.*" The annual sacrifice of an unblemished male lamb on Nisan 14 (pattern) was not only a perpetual memorial; it was a *temporary* pardon from the spiritual death penalty that is the consequence of sin.

The Old Testament sacrificial system established a precedent and a pattern that foreshadowed the New Testament sacrificial death of an unblemished male lamb on Nisan 14 (prophecy). Jesus was the unblemished male because He never sinned; He is called *the Lamb of God* in John 1:29; and He died on Nisan 14. For those individuals who recognize their need for forgiveness and who believe in Jesus, Christ's death on the cross is the *permanent* pardon for sin, eliminating completely the spiritual death penalty.

The precedent and the pattern initiated in the Old Testament were not complete until they were fulfilled in the New Testament. Again, while it is not imperative to know the history, this Old Testament background provides—in our example—the full context for Christ's death. The Old Testament describes the precedent-creating event in Egypt, validates the annually repeated pattern of sacrificing a lamb for sin, establishes the prophecy, and sets the stage for the New Testament fulfillment by Jesus.

FROM PRECEDENT... TO PATTERN... TO PROPHECY

Prophecy in the form of precedents and patterns that foreshadow actual future events—fulfillments—are found throughout the Bible. Technically speaking, the precedent, the pattern, and the fulfillment are all components of the *prophecy*. However, the word *fulfillment* can be confusing because some prophecies have been fulfilled in the past and some prophecies are still future. Therefore, for the purpose of this text, the labels *precedent, pattern*, and *prophecy* (both fulfilled and unfulfilled) are used to differentiate between the three categories (Figure 1.4).

LABEL USED	DEFINITION FOR PURPOSE OF THIS TEXT
Precedent	An actual historical event that foreshadows a prophetic future event
Pattern	The repetition of a precedent that foreshadows a prophetic future event
Prophecy	An event foreshadowed by the precedent and/or pattern that is: Fulfilled—has already happened Unfulfilled—has not yet happened

FIGURE 1.4 Precedent, pattern, and prophecy

As you will soon see, *shabua* repeatedly appears in the Bible as precedent, pattern, and prophecy. The *shabua* precedent is created at the beginning of the Bible when the concept is introduced in the book of Genesis. The subsequent and consistently repeated appearances of *shabua* reinforce the precedent and establish an identifiable pattern. These identifiable *shabua* patterns based on precedent foreshadow future events, called prophecy. When the subject of a *shabua* prophecy initiated in the Old Testament is precisely replicated in a New Testament event, the purpose of the precedent, pattern, and prophecy has been fulfilled. In the Bible, the relationship between precedent, pattern, and prophecy is not limited to *shabua*.

A PREVIEW OF COMING ATTRACTIONS

We have defined *shabua* as "a complete time period of seven." In the next chapter we will examine the initial appearance of a *shabua* in the Bible. That will lead to a more complete introduction of the concept of a *shabua* of days and a discussion of how that concept applies to the first seven biblical days, the period of time that both Moses in the Old Testament and Jesus in the New Testament called "the beginning." For ease of identification, when the Bible refers to a *shabua* of days we will use the term *shabua*-days, and when the Bible refers to a *shabua* of years we will use the term *shabua*-years.

In this chapter we defined *shabua* and introduced its use in the Bible as precedent, pattern, and prophecy. Subsequent chapters will cover a different but consistent use and application of *shabua*-days. The topics covered in *Shabua Days* are listed below (Figure 1.5).

Chapter 1	*Shabua* in the Bible as precedent, pattern, and prophecy
Chapter 2	*Shabua*-days in the beginning at the time of Creation
Chapter 3	*Shabua*-days in a biblical wedding, manna, and the Fourth Commandment
Chapter 4	*Shabua*-days in the Feast of Passover and the Feast of Unleavened Bread
Chapter 5	*Shabua*-days in the Feast of *Shabua* and on the day of Pentecost

FIGURE 1.5 Topics covered in *Shabua Days*

CREATION, THE BIG BANG, AND EVOLUTION

In chapter 1, we looked closely at the Hebrew word *shabua*. We saw that, although it is translated as "week" and "seven," neither of those words conveys the full and intended meaning. In the Bible, *shabua* is a term that refers to "a complete time period of seven." The initial appearance of a complete time period of seven in the first two chapters of the Old Testament—Genesis 1-2—establishes the biblical precedent for *shabua*. (As defined in chapter 1, a biblical precedent is an actual historical event that foreshadows a prophetic future event.) Since *shabua* can alternatively refer to an interval of seven days or seven years, it is crucial to know the context to determine the interval—days or years—that *shabua* is referring to. This precedent setting *shabua* is specified as an interval of days.

The inaugural *shabua* incorporates the biblical account of Creation. Creation is the biblical view of the beginning of everything. Needless to say, this is a hotly debated topic. Many Bible believing-Christians struggle with the Creation passage because they don't think it can be supported scientifically. Many others are afraid of appearing uninformed, weak, or foolish because the biblical view is based on faith. The goal of this chapter is to present relevant Bible verses in sufficient detail to create a greater understanding of what Scripture says about this subject matter and its timing.

TWO DISTINCT WORLDVIEWS

There are two distinct worldviews: the biblical and the secular. The biblical worldview is based on the account of Creation (the beginning of the universe and the diversity of living things). The secular worldview is based on the theories of the Big Bang (the beginning of the universe) and evolution (the diversity of living things). The two worldviews are summarized in Figure 2.1.

WORLDVIEW	THEORY	EXPLAINS
Biblical	Creation	The existence of everything, including: The beginning of the universe The diversity of living things
Secular	The Big Bang	The beginning of the universe
	Evolution	The diversity of living things

FIGURE 2.1 The biblical and secular worldviews

It is important to note that not all those who disagree with the Bible—including secular scientists—support the theories of the Big Bang and evolution. However, for the purpose of this text, when the word "science" or "scientists" is used, it refers to those who hold the secular worldview.

THE INAUGURAL SHABUA

WHETHER IN MILLISECONDS OR TRILLIONS OF YEARS...

If the first five words of the Bible are true—*In the beginning, God created* (Genesis 1:1)—God could have done so in a fraction of a millisecond, or He could have done so over the course of trillions of years. In essence, if *God created*, the length of time He took to create pales in significance next to the very fact that God *did* create. However, as will soon become abundantly clear, the time God specified for Creation is not vague, and it was not meant to be open to interpretation. As this book will reveal, the length of time it took God to create plays a very important role in our understanding of His past, present, and future plan for all mankind.

Knowing the timing of Creation is incredibly relevant since it established the *shabua* precedent that would be used repeatedly in Bible pattern and prophecy. The Bible says that after God created everything in six days, He rested on the 7th day. Although God did not need to rest on the 7th day, by doing so He established the first *shabua*—a complete time period of seven— that includes six intervals of work or activity followed by a 7th and final interval of rest (precedent). *Shabua* is not only consistently repeated throughout the Bible (pattern), but it is also used to predict future events with uncanny accuracy (prophecy). Now let's see what the Bible says about the beginning.

VARIOUS INTERPRETATIONS OF A BIBLICAL DAY

Every Bible version translates the Hebrew word *yom* in Genesis 1 as *day*. However, when defining the length of this *day*, people interpret it as a span of time that ranges from a period of 24 hours to a period of billions of years. Only a minority believes *day* in this chapter refers to a period of 24 hours. Divergent views arise primarily due to the fact that the general consensus in the scientific community is that the universe began billions of years ago. A literal interpretation of these verses is therefore in direct conflict with the general consensus, contributing to a wide disparity of opinion even among many who believe the Bible is true.

Numerous religious views have been offered in an attempt to explain the six days of Creation. The predominant interpretation is that the initial six *days* in the beginning span a period of billions of years. (This view is likely based on the prevailing scientific theory that says the universe began to form—on its own without God—in a moment of time 13.8 billion years ago.) Others interpret *day* symbolically and propose that *day* refers to an indeterminate interval of time in an increment of six. Still others believe that after the initial creation of the heavens and the earth, a gap of billions of years preceded the commencement of all remaining creation activity. Other theories exist as well because people believe that the interpretation of *day* is up for discussion.

But if the Bible does not mean *day*, then why did God direct Moses to use that specific term? Why would the Bible open with apparent ambiguity? Why doesn't the Bible specify the interval of time as billions of years if that is what is meant—and if that is the actual time frame? If *day* is a symbolic reference to something, why doesn't the text describe that interval using the words "like" or "as"? Why would the exact same language be used to describe the close of every day if each of the days is of a different but unspecified duration? Do any other Bible verses support a specific interpretation of what length of time *day* refers to in this context?

A DAY IS A PERIOD OF DARKNESS AND LIGHT

Let's start our analysis with the third verse in the Bible to see if it gives us any clues as to the meaning of a biblical *day*. In the very beginning, Genesis 1:3-5 establishes a *day* as a period of time that includes both darkness and light: *God said, "Let there be light," and there was light. And God saw that the light was good. And God separated the light from the darkness. God called the light Day, and the darkness he called Night. And there was evening and there was morning, the first day.*

In other words, a *day* did not exist until God created a period of light to follow a period of darkness. This combination of darkness and light defines the first biblical *day*. Based on a plain reading of the text, it appears that *darkness* corresponds to evening/night while *light* corresponds to morning/day in that particular order (precedent). And this combination is referred to at the conclusion of each of the six days of Creation (pattern).

EACH DAY ENDS THE SAME WAY

Each *day* ends the exact same way: *And there was evening and there was morning, the [first, second, third, fourth, fifth, sixth] day* (vv. 5, 8, 13, 19, 23, 31). So the framework for each *day* in the Bible is established by the consistent repetition of the phrase "there was evening and there was morning" at the close of each *day*. The phrase did not change on Day 4 even when God created the specific *lights*—the sun, moon, and stars—to replace the unspecified *light* He created on Day 1 (this topic will be discussed further in the sections under "The Bible's Universe").

It is noteworthy that the 24-hour day in Israel has always precisely followed this biblical model of evening-then-morning. Even today, in the twenty-first century, each new 24-hour day still commences in the evening immediately after the previous day's sunset. This manner of reckoning time was established in the beginning, literally on the first day of Creation. People living in Israel continue to recognize sunset as simultaneously the end and the beginning of every 24-hour day. For millennia, the time of sunset was determined through direct observation. Today people in Israel can determine the time of sunset (past, present, and future) through published charts that rely on computer algorithms.

CONNECTIONS TO A 24-HOUR DAY

There is other biblical support for interpreting *day* in Genesis 1 as a period of 24-hours. Exodus 20:8, for instance, makes a direct reference to a literal 24-hour day in the Fourth Commandment: "*Remember the Sabbath day, to keep it holy.*" Verse 9 continues the theme of a 24-hour day: "*Six days you shall labor, and do all your work.*" Verse 10 repeats the commandment and makes it more emphatic: "*But the seventh day is a Sabbath to the LORD your God. On it you shall not do any work.*" Then verse 11 gives the reason: "*For in six days the LORD made heaven and earth, the sea, and all that is in them, and rested on the seventh day. Therefore the LORD blessed the Sabbath day and made it holy.*"

How could the Sabbath in verse 8 be understood as anything other than one 24-hour day of rest? How could the interpretation of verse 9 be anything other than six 24-hour days of labor? These verses from Exodus unequivocally link six 24-hour days of labor to the six days of Creation. (These verses also link the Sabbath day to the seventh day when God rested.) Since they are linked, six 24-hour *days* appears to be the most natural, logical, and reasonable interpretation of both the Genesis and Exodus accounts. Any other meaning for a period of labor—as in billions of years, an indefinite period, or a gap—makes little, if any, sense. Therefore, *day* must mean the same thing in both Genesis 1 and Exodus 20.

BOOKENDS OF CREATION

On the first 24-hour day, Genesis 1:1 says, *In the beginning, God created the heavens and the earth.* On the sixth 24-hour day, *God created man in his own image... male and female he created them* (v. 27). These two days are bookends of all of God's creation activity. In the absence of additional creation activity, there must be a way to explain the continuing supply of living things on planet Earth. A natural, logical, and reasonable explanation is that God created mature living things with the ability to reproduce.

Although there has been a lot of reproducing since the six days of Creation, no *new* creation activity has taken place since the beginning: *Thus the heavens and the earth were finished, and all the host of them* (Genesis 2:1). God limited His creation activity to six 24-hour days, but He created every living thing—vegetation, birds, sea creatures, animals, and human beings—mature with the ability to reproduce. This fact is particularly evident in the human beings that God created: *male and female he created them. And God blessed them. And God said to them, "Be fruitful and multiply and fill the earth"* (Genesis 1:27-28). God told the first human beings to reproduce and populate the world—and this implies that He created them mature. Also, it is clear from this passage that God created them as a male and female pair.

JESUS WAS PRESENT AT CREATION

Jesus confirmed this understanding in Matthew 19:4: *"Have you not read that he who created them from the beginning made them male and female?"* This statement by Jesus is significant because the Bible teaches that He was present in the beginning when God created the heavens and the earth. Referring to Jesus, for instance, the apostle John wrote: *In the beginning was the Word, and the Word was with God, and the Word was God. He was in the beginning with God. All things were made through him, and without him was not any thing made that was made* (John 1:1-3). John tells us "the Word" in the beginning refers to Jesus: *And the Word became flesh and dwelt among us, and we have seen his glory, glory as of the only Son from the Father, full of grace and truth... [For] grace and truth came through Jesus Christ* (vv. 14-17).

A similar passage written by the apostle Paul says: *[Jesus] is the image of the invisible God, the firstborn of all creation. For by him all things were created, in heaven and on earth, visible and invisible, whether thrones or dominions or rulers or authorities—all things were created through him and for him. And he is before all things, and in him all things hold together* (Colossians 1:15-17). The apostles John and Paul both teach that all things were created in the beginning by and through Jesus. Therefore, since Jesus created all things, He certainly ought to know every detail about what He did and when He did it.

JESUS AND THE BEGINNING

Jesus—who was there *in the beginning, [when] God created the heavens and the earth* (Genesis 1:1)—said *he who created them from the beginning made them male and female* (Matthew 19:4). Jesus used the identical phrase—*the beginning*—to link the creation of male and female human beings (Day 6) to the same period of time that the heavens and the earth were created (Day 1). Both the Genesis and Matthew passages call this six-day interval of time *the beginning* (Day 1 through Day 6). All God's creation activity took place over the course of these six days, and all six days occurred in *the beginning*.

What we learn from this is that *the beginning* has a very specific meaning, "the first six days of Creation as a unit," in addition to a general meaning, "the start of it all." So the Genesis 1:1 and Matthew 19:4 words *the beginning* do not appear to be at all figurative or subjective. And that means the heavens, the earth, light, Heaven, Earth, Seas, vegetation, plants, trees, lights, living creatures, birds, sea creatures, livestock, creeping things, beasts, and male and female human beings were all created during the same finite six-day interval of time that both Genesis and Jesus call "the beginning."

NO NEW CREATION UNTIL THE ETERNAL STATE

It is noteworthy that the Bible uses the words "created" and "made" a total of nine times in describing "the beginning." Repetition such as this is used to emphasize a point. The first chapter in the Bible ends with this statement:

God saw everything that he had made, and behold, it was very good. And there was evening and there was morning, the sixth day (Genesis 1:31). So, as the six days of Creation concluded, God looked over everything that He had created and made and saw that "it was very good." The next verse adds, *Thus the heavens and the earth were finished, and all the host of them* (2:1). These verses not only reveal that God was satisfied with everything He had created in six days, they indicate that the heavens, Earth, and everything in them were finished.

After the account of Creation opens the Bible, no new creation activity is mentioned until the very end of the Bible, where Revelation 21:1 says, *Then I saw a new heaven and a new earth, for the first heaven and the first earth had passed away, and the sea was no more.* At the end of this age, the presently existing heaven and earth—defiled by Satan, sin, death, and evil—will be eliminated: *the heavens shall pass away with a great noise, and the elements shall melt with fervent heat, the earth also and the works that are therein shall be burned up* (2 Peter 3:10 KJV). For believers entering the eternal state, God said "*For behold, I create new heavens and a new earth, and the former things shall not be remembered or come into mind*" (Isaiah 65:17).

THE 7TH AND FINAL DAY OF THE SHABUA

Whatever your opinion regarding the interpretation of the initial six *days* described in Genesis 1, the fact remains that the Hebrew word *yom* is always translated as *day*. In cases where the *shabua* interval is not specified, it is determined by the context, which in the creation account is unequivocally defined as days. In Genesis 2 the Bible introduces one additional day to complete the first *shabua*. This 7th and final day immediately follows the six days of Creation and establishes the *shabua* precedent: 6 days + 1 day = 7 days.

The last day of the inaugural *shabua* is described in Genesis 2:2-3: *On the seventh day God finished his work that he had done, and he rested on the seventh day from all his work that he had done. So God blessed the seventh day and made it holy, because on it God rested from all his work that he had done in creation.* The 7th and final day of this *shabua* differs from the first six days in that there is no creation activity whatsoever.

SHABATH DESCRIBES THE ACTION OF RESTING

Not only is there a complete absence of creation activity on the 7th and final day of this *shabua*, but Genesis 2:2-3 adds on that particular day *God rested*. In fact, the word *rested* is used twice—which indicates emphasis—in reference to what God did on the 7th and final day of this inaugural *shabua*.

Rested is the English translation of the Hebrew word *shabath* (Strong's H7673), which is "a primitive root; to repose, i.e. desist from exertion; used in many implication relations (causative, figurative or specific):–(cause to, let, make to) cease, celebrate, cause (make) to fail, keep (sabbath), suffer to be lacking, leave, put away (down), (make to) rest, rid, still, take away." In essence, *shabath* is a verb that expresses the action of resting. Strong's indicates that *shabath* is translated forty-seven times as "to cease" and eleven times as "to rest."

THE INAUGURAL SHABUA IS SHABUA-DAYS

Like *shabua*, the word *shabath* also has a double meaning, both "to cease" and "to rest." God chose the 7th and final day of the first *shabua* to both cease and rest from the work of creating. Six intervals of work followed by a 7th and final interval of rest establish a biblical *shabua*. Like every subsequent *shabua*, this first complete time period of seven—in Genesis 1-2—began with six intervals of work or activity and concluded with a 7th and final interval of rest (precedent).

Since a *shabua* interval can be comprised of either seven days or seven years, the time period must be determined by the context when it is not directly specified. In the case of the inaugural *shabua*, the interval is specified as days. Since this *shabua* is a complete time period of seven days, we refer to it as "*shabua*-days" in this text. (A *shabua* does not extend to an eighth day [or an eighth year]; instead, a new *shabua*-days [or *shabua*-years] begins immediately after each respective *shabua* ends.) It was during this inaugural *shabua*-days that, the Bible says, God created everything from nothing.

CREATION OR THE BIG BANG?

Creation cannot be proved because it cannot be replicated and nobody saw it happen. On the other hand, there is no way to disprove it. On one of the six days of the inaugural *shabua*-days, the Bible says God created the universe, but even among Bible-believing Christians a wide range of opinions exists about this subject matter and its timing. This topic is hotly debated because we human beings want to be able to explain our existence—including the origin of the universe—and our two choices are an explanation that is consistent with the Bible or one that is distinct and different from it.

The alternative to biblical Creation is the theory of the Big Bang. Like Creation, there is no way to prove the Big Bang theory because it cannot be replicated and nobody saw it happen. On the other hand, there is no way to disprove it. Whether you are inclined to believe in Creation or the Big Bang, in this chapter you will see that the differences between these two mutually exclusive views are so great they cannot be reconciled. In other words, both cannot be true. Before we examine what the Bible says about the universe, it is important to understand some basics of the Big Bang, the prevailing secular theory regarding the beginning.

THE BIG BANG'S UNIVERSE

THE SUN, THE STARS, AND THE MILKY WAY GALAXY

For millennia, the belief in a Supreme Being-created universe was the prevailing worldview. But eager to find a secular alternative to the Bible's explanation that God created everything from nothing, scientists and philosophers have continued to advance the distinct and different theory of the Big Bang. Since 1931, the idea that the universe began with the Big Bang has gradually gained acceptance, and it eventually supplanted Creation as the prevailing worldview. The origin and development of this theory might surprise you.

Let's begin our discussion of the Big Bang with what we know about the universe at the present time. The visible universe contains galaxies (among other things), and each galaxy consists of a cluster of stars. Our sun is one such star located in our Milky Way Galaxy. Astronomers' opinions regarding the number of stars in the Milky Way Galaxy differ. For example, "Astronomers estimate that there are *100 billion to 400 billion* stars contained within our galaxy, though some estimates claim there may be as many as a trillion."[1]

GALAXIES AND THE HUBBLE SPACE TELESCOPE

Similarly, astronomers' opinions regarding the number of galaxies contained in the universe also differ. For many years scientists estimated that the universe contained up to 200 billion galaxies. A more recent estimate has increased this number "by a factor of 10, from 200 billion to 2 trillion."[2] The point is, the number of stars in our Milky Way Galaxy is difficult to ascertain, and the number of galaxies in our universe is also difficult to ascertain, but with each advance in technology, the numbers always seem to increase rather than decrease.

Current estimates are primarily based on interpolating data from telescopes on Earth as well as from the very powerful Hubble Space Telescope (HST). The HST orbits the Earth in space outside of the atmosphere in order to avoid any distortion of the images captured by its large 2.4-meter (7 feet, 10.5 inch) primary mirror.[3] To get an idea of just how rapidly advances in technology are improving the field of astronomy, let's look at three HST surveys within a period of twenty years: Hubble Deep Field North, Hubble Ultra Deep Field, and eXtreme Deep Field.

HUBBLE DEEP FIELDS

Deep Field North: In 1995, astronomers directed the HST toward a tiny—seemingly empty—void in space within the constellation Ursa Major. (The relative size of this HST field of view from our vantage point on Earth can be compared to looking—with the naked eye—at a tennis ball 100 meters away.) This region was called the Hubble Deep Field North (HDF-N). To the astonishment of astronomers, this void in space contained an estimated 3,000 galaxies.[4]

Ultra Deep Field: NASA launched a twelve-day servicing mission of the HST in 2002 that included five spacewalks. One of the major technological upgrades to its instruments was the Advanced Camera for Surveys. Two years later, in 2004, using this advanced camera, the HST was directed toward a new speck in the universe within the constellation Fornax (the Furnace). This region became known as the Hubble Ultra Deep Field (HUDF). Astronomers initially observed an estimated 10,000 galaxies in this region.[5]

eXtreme Deep Field: After compiling ten years of HUDF images (2004-2014), astronomers made a composite photograph of a small center section—within the already small HUDF—and named this region the eXtreme Deep Field (XDF). According to an article by NASA, "the photo was assembled by combining 10 years of NASA Hubble Space Telescope photographs taken of a patch of sky at the center of the original Hubble Ultra Deep Field." NASA went on to explain that "the new full-color XDF image is even more sensitive, and contains about 5,500 galaxies even within its smaller field of view."[6]

MEASURING DISTANCES AT LIGHT SPEED

The Hubble surveys confirm the universe is indeed an immeasurably vast expanse containing an unfathomable number of galaxies. The scale is beyond the capacity of the human mind to comprehend. In fact, distances in space are so incredibly large that they must be measured by the speed that light travels. A *light-second* is the distance that light travels in one second, which is 299,792 kilometers (186,282 miles), or the equivalent of 7.5 trips around Earth at 670,616,629 mph.[7] A *light-year* is the distance that light travels in one year, which is 9.5 trillion kilometers (5.9 trillion miles).[8] Since distances in space are hard to imagine, consider the amount of time it takes light to travel between destinations we are familiar with (Figure 2.2).

TRAVEL DESTINATION	TRAVEL DISTANCE	LIGHT SPEED TIME
Moon to Earth	385,000 kilometers (240 thousand miles)	1.3 seconds
Sun to Earth	149,000,000 kilometers (93 million miles)	8.3 minutes
Pluto (when closest) to Earth	4.4 billion kilometers (2.7 billion miles)	5.5 hours
Proxima Centauri to Earth	40.2 trillion kilometers (25 trillion miles)	4.2 years
Span of Milky Way Galaxy	1 quintillion kilometers (.62 quintillion miles)	100 thousand years
Adromeda Galaxy to Earth	The closest galaxy to the Milky Way	2.5 million years

FIGURE 2.2 Distances measured at the speed of light

Out of the hundreds of billions of stars (some say up to one trillion stars) in our Milky Way Galaxy, Proxima Centauri is the closest star to Earth, yet it is still 4.2 light-years away.[9] Now consider this: out of the hundreds of billions of galaxies (some say up to two trillion galaxies) in the universe, the Andromeda Galaxy is the closest galaxy to our Milky Way Galaxy, yet it is a staggering 2.5 million light-years away! Can you see why the size of the universe is beyond the capacity of the human mind to comprehend? And data compiled from decades of observations indicate our already massive universe continues to expand. Since there is no disputing the fact that the universe is big and continues to get bigger, the inevitable question is "How did it all begin?"

ERASMUS DARWIN'S EXPLOSIVE BEGINNING

Few people realize that the Big Bang theory originated as an abstract idea in a poem written by Erasmus Darwin in 1791. (Erasmus Darwin is the grandfather of Charles Darwin.) Erasmus was a brilliant philosopher, physician, botanist, naturalist, and writer. He often expressed his thoughts and ideas in poetry. In Canto 1 of his poem "The Economy of Vegetation," Erasmus suggested that the universe of suns ("stars") and earths ("planets") had an explosive beginning:

Through all his realms the kindling ether runs,
And the mass starts into a million suns;
Earths round each sun with quick explosions burst,
And second planets issue from the first;
Bend, as they journey with projectile force.

In Canto 2, Erasmus continued to develop the notion of an explosive beginning, but with a narrower focus. Here, Erasmus suggested that the Earth was born when the Sun violently expelled a flaming ball of gas into a void of vaporous cold air that apparently extinguished the fire and created the oceans:

Gnomes! Your bright forms, presiding at her birth,
Clung in fond squadrons round the new-born earth;
When high in ether, with explosion dire,
From the deep craters of his realms of fire,
The Whirling Sun this ponderous planet hurled,
And gave the astonished void another world.
When from its vaporous air, condensed by cold,
Descending torrents into oceans rolled;
And fierce attraction, with relentless force,
Bent the reluctant wanderer to its course.[10]

THE "PRIMORDIAL PARTICLE" OF EDGAR ALLAN POE

The extensive writings of Erasmus Darwin influenced many people. Two well-known individuals likely influenced by Erasmus include his grandson Charles Darwin (more on Charles later) and the American writer Edgar Allan Poe. In 1848, fifty-seven years after Erasmus published "The Economy of Vegetation" suggesting that the universe had an explosive beginning, Edgar Allan Poe wrote an essay on the material and spiritual universe titled "Eureka." The subject matter and Poe's terminology are strikingly similar to that of Erasmus. According to Poe, the universe began when a single "primordial Particle" fragmented, and the particles spread out in all directions from a center:

The assumption of absolute Unity in the primordial Particle includes that of infinite divisibility. Let us conceive the Particle, then, to be only not totally exhausted by diffusion into Space. From the one Particle, as a centre, let us suppose to be irradiated spherically—in all directions—to immeasurable but still definite distances in the previously vacant space.[11]

ALEKSANDR FRIEDMANN AND GEORGES LEMAÎTRE

Decades after Erasmus Darwin and Edgar Allan Poe, ideas about the universe were still generally limited to thoughts expressed in poetry. Things did not begin to change until after Albert Einstein published his general theory of relativity in 1915. In 1922-24, the Encyclopædia Britannica says a Russian scientist and mathematician named Aleksandr Friedmann "used Einstein's general theory of relativity to formulate the mathematics of a dynamic (time-dependent) universe... Friedmann also calculated the time back to the moment when an expanding universe would have been a mere point, obtaining tens of billions of years; but it is not clear how much physical significance he attributed to this speculation."[12]

In 1927, a Belgian priest, astronomer, and physicist named Georges Lemaître proposed a theory "in which he stated that the expanding universe was the same in all directions—the same laws applied, and its composition was the same—but it was not static. He had no data to prove this, so many scientists ignored it."[13] Without supporting data, Lemaître's theory about an expanding universe was not remarkably different from that of Friedmann. (Both men arrived at their conclusions using mathematics.) In fact, we probably wouldn't be talking about Lemaître today if it weren't for what happened next that gave him and his idea credibility as well as worldwide exposure.

ASTRONOMER EDWIN HUBBLE AND HUBBLE'S LAW

In 1929, Edwin Hubble—an astronomer who was not aware of Lemaître's calculations—proved the universe was expanding by measuring incremental movements of galaxies. (Lemaître is usually given credit for originating the concept because he had accurately calculated the rate of universe expansion in 1927, two years before Hubble confirmed it through his observations in 1929.) Evidence that the universe is expanding led to the development of Hubble's Law:

> Hubble's Law, which is an empirical relationship, was the first concrete evidence that Einstein's theory of General Relativity applied to the universe as a whole, as proposed only two years earlier by Lemaître (interestingly, Lemaître's paper also includes an estimate of the Hubble constant!); the universal applicability of General Relativity is the heart of the Big Bang theory, and the way we see the predicted expansion of space is as the speed at which things seem to be receding being proportional to their distance, i.e. Hubble's Law.[14]

To picture an expanding universe—the essence of Hubble's Law—mark a deflated balloon with dots to represent galaxies. When the balloon is inflated, each dot is uniformly spread out or stretched out at a rate that is proportional to the distance from the center and each other.

REDSHIFTS PROVE THE UNIVERSE IS EXPANDING

An expanding universe means that from any vantage point on Earth—or from satellites in space—we observe galaxies moving farther away from Earth, and the rate of recession is proportional to its distance. Analyzing the light waves (called *shifts*) is one way to determine the direction galaxies are moving. *Redshifts* occur when light from a galaxy is moving *away* from the observer: the elongated wavelengths (elongated because of the increasing distance) are shifted toward the red end of the color spectrum. Conversely, *blueshifts* occur when light from a galaxy is moving *toward* the observer: the compressed wavelengths (compressed because of the decreasing distance) are shifted toward the blue end of the color spectrum.

Virtually every galactic survey since 1929 has validated Hubble's Law: light from distant galaxies is redshifted, not blueshifted. Redshifts of galaxies prove the universe is expanding, which is why this phenomenon is called Hubble's Law (not Hubble's Theory). Vision Learning (a science website supported by the National Science Foundation and the U.S. Department of Education) says, "Laws *describe* phenomena, often mathematically." They further define a *scientific law* as "an expression of a mathematical or descriptive relationship observed in nature."[15] Hubble's Law is an integral component of the Big Bang theory; however, that does not mean the Big Bang is a scientific law.

LEMAÎTRE'S INITIAL QUANTUM AND PRIMEVAL ATOM

The Big Bang is a *theory* that uses Hubble's Law to speculate about how the universe began. Lemaître began to speculate about the beginning of the universe in 1931, only two years after his mathematical calculations— confirmed by Hubble—brought Lemaître prestige and a voice. In an article in the science journal *Nature* on May 9, 1931, Lemaître suggested that if the world began with an "initial quantum" (he also called it a "unique quantum" and "original quantum"), then "the beginning of the world happened a little before the beginning of space and time."[16] (Merriam-Webster defines *quantum* as "any of the very small increments or parcels into which many forms of energy are subdivided.") A few months later, on September 29, 1931, during a presentation at the prestigious British Association for the Advancement of Science in London, Lemaître said:

> At the origin, all the mass of the universe would exist in the form of a unique atom; the radius of the universe, although not strictly zero, being relatively very small. The whole universe would be produced by the disintegration of this primeval atom…Whether this is wild imagination or physical hypothesis cannot be said at present, but we may hope that the question will not wait too long to be solved.[17]

In other words, Lemaître suggested the whole universe began when a "primeval atom" disintegrated. The terminology that Lemaître used was significant because the atom was the smallest known particle in physics at that time. Also, Merriam-Webster defines *primeval* as "of or relating to the earliest ages (as of the world or human history)." Did you notice that the language and concept are similar to Edgar Allan Poe's "primordial Particle" in "Eureka?" To this day, whether Lemaître's idea is "wild imagination or physical hypothesis" has still not been solved.

A COSMIC CATACLYSM CALLED THE BIG BANG

Notwithstanding the fact that there is still no data to back up Lemaître's idea that the universe began when a primeval atom disintegrated, this theory continues to be the leading explanation for how the universe began. According to National Geographic, this cosmic cataclysm—called the Big Bang—occurred with explosive force:

> The most popular theory of our universe's origin centers on a cosmic cataclysm unmatched in all of history—the big bang. This theory was born of the observation that other galaxies are moving away from our own at great speed, in all directions, as if they had all been propelled by an ancient explosive force.

> Before the big bang, scientists believe the entire vastness of the observable universe, including all of its matter and radiation, was compressed into a hot, dense mass just a few millimeters across. This nearly incomprehensible state is theorized to have existed for just a fraction of the first second of time.[18]

A SINGULARITY OF INFINITE DENSITY

The Big Bang is described as "the leading explanation about how the universe began. At its simplest, it talks about the universe as we know it starting with a small singularity, then inflating over the next 13.8 billion years to the cosmos that we know today."[19] Once again, notice that the concept of a singularity inflating is similar to Darwin's notion of an explosive beginning;

Poe's "primordial Particle"; Friedmann's "mere point"; and Lemaître's "initial quantum" and "primeval atom." An article in Universe Today says a singularity "can occur when matter is forcibly compressed to a point, causing the rules that govern matter [the laws of physics] to break down."[20] Another Universe Today article states:

> According to the Hawking-Penrose singularity theorem, if the universe truly obeyed the models of general relativity, then it must have begun as a singularity. This essentially meant that, prior to the Big Bang, the entire universe existed as a point of infinite density that contained all of the mass and space-time of the universe, before quantum fluctuations caused it to rapidly expand....

> Inflation theory – which had been proposed by Alan Guth that same year – posits that following the Big Bang, the universe initially expanded very rapidly before settling into to a slower rate of expansion.[21]

THE ORIGIN OF THE SINGULARITY IS AN ENIGMA

In reality, a singularity is sheer speculation on a universe-sized scale; it is a proposed condition that is purely hypothetical. This uncertainty is evident in the following quote: "What existed before the big bang? It's still an open question. Perhaps nothing. Perhaps another universe or a different version of our own. Perhaps a sea of universes, each with a different set of laws dictating its physical reality."[22] The origin of the singularity is a paradox for Big Bang proponents, and there is a lack of consensus about it among scientists. As a result, the origin of the singularity continues to be an unresolved issue.

Some scientists do not believe a singularity existed at all before the Big Bang because that belief would require them to explain how it got there, and that might imply the singularity was created. For them, the singularity was apparently nothing and nowhere but suddenly became something and somewhere without a cause. Other proponents believe that a singularity existed before the Big Bang, but they aren't able to explain its origin. No viable theories have been put forth to explain the origin of the singularity—the supposed origin of everything—that is essential to the Big Bang's bang.

Where did the singularity come from? How did it get there? What caused it to suddenly explode? Since the Big Bang theory has no answers for such questions, the entire issue is simply ignored or hedged. (To personally witness the way the origin of the singularity is ignored or hedged, just ask a scientist to explain it.) A monumental problem for Big Bang proponents is that the theory is based on a singularity that expanded, but its origin is strictly hypothetical.

THE SIZE OF THE SOLAR SYSTEM IN .00001 SECONDS

Although scientists say the universe "expanded" or "inflated" from the singularity, it seems "exploded" is a more appropriate way to describe the velocity of the singularity's growth at a rate a quadrillion (10^{15} or 1,000,000,000,000,000) times *faster* than the speed of light. According to *LHC the Guide*, a brochure by the European Organization for Nuclear Research (CERN), the universe grew from a mere point to the size of the solar system in .01 milliseconds[23] (also expressed as 10^{-5} seconds). The Large Hadron Collider (LHC) guide gives the sizes of the universe at this and various other times, which are listed in Figure 2.3. (It also says the LHC exploration range is 10^{-12} seconds after the Big Bang. The significance of this will be discussed is the section titled "The LHC does not test the initial Big Bang.")

SIZE OF THE UNIVERSE	TIME AFTER THE BIG BANG
The singularity	.0000000000000000000000000000000000000000001 (10^{-43}) seconds
Size of an apple	.00000000000000000000000000000001 (10^{-32}) seconds
Radius of 300 million kilometers	.000000000001 (10^{-12}) seconds (LHC exploration range)
Size of the solar system	.00001 (10^{-5}) seconds

FIGURE 2.3 The universe after the Big Bang

CERN's calculations are consistent with a National Geographic article that describes the Big Bang theory as follows:

> The theory maintains that, in the instant—a trillion-trillionth of a second—after the big bang, the universe expanded with incomprehensible speed from its pebble-size origin to astronomical scope. Expansion has apparently continued, but much more slowly, over the ensuing billions of years.

> Scientists can't be sure exactly how the universe evolved after the big bang. Many believe that as time passed and matter cooled, more diverse kinds of atoms began to form, and they eventually condensed into the stars and galaxies of our present universe.[24]

THE ACCELERATING RATE OF UNIVERSE EXPANSION

So how did we go from a fact that has scientifically been proven true—the universe is expanding—to the inference that the universe was once an extremely small particle? Hubblesite says, "Because all of the galaxies in the universe are generally moving apart, we infer that they must all have been much closer together sometime in the past. Knowing the current speeds and distances to galaxies, coupled with the rate at which the universe is accelerating, allows us to calculate how long it took for them to reach their current locations."[25] (In the next section we will discuss why the theory that the universe is expanding at an *accelerating* rate is an enigma for scientists.)

This inference—that the universe was once a very small singularity—is based on the assumption that the universe has always expanded at the same rate, and scientists rewind the entire expansion back to the supposed beginning when the universe would have been a mere point. According to an article by the BBC, "Detailed measurements of the expansion rate of the universe place this moment at approximately 13.8 billion years ago, which is thus considered the age of the universe."[26] In other words, scientists compute the age of the universe mathematically: assuming the universe was a mere point that exploded and expanded at certain rate, they then calculate how long it would take to rewind its present vast size back to that mere point. The problem is, there is no data—and there never has been any data—that supports this conclusion. In addition, scientists do not believe the rate of expansion has always been the same.

NEWTON'S FIRST AND SECOND LAWS OF MOTION

Now let's discuss the fact that astronomers have observed distant galaxies receding—moving away from Earth—at a velocity that is increasing with time, not decreasing or staying constant. National Geographic says Nobel Prize-winning scientists Saul Perlmutter, Adam Riess, and Brian Schmidt "contributed to the discovery that the universe is not only expanding but also speeding up."[27] Do the laws of physics support the notion that—since the Big Bang—the universe has always expanded at a rate that has continued to accelerate? A NASA article that quotes Sir Isaac Newton's First and Second Laws of Motion says this:

> [First Law of Motion] "A body at rest will remain at rest unless an outside force acts on it, and a body in motion at a constant velocity will remain in motion in a straight line unless acted upon by an outside force. If a body experiences an acceleration (or deceleration) or a change in direction of motion, it must have an outside force acting on it. Outside forces are sometimes called net forces or unbalanced forces. The property that a body has that resists motion if at rest, or resists speeding or slowing up, if in motion, is called inertia."

> [Second Law of Motion] "If an unbalanced force acts on a body, that body will experience acceleration (or deceleration), that is, a change of speed."[28]

Scientists know the universe is expanding at an accelerating rate, and they know the First and Second Laws of Motion require an outside force to cause acceleration (or deceleration). Since established laws in physics cannot explain the acceleration, scientists assume an unknown force—they call it "dark energy"—must be causing the increase in the speed of the expansion. This is how the National Geographic article describes *dark energy*: "a mysterious force that repels gravity... But more than a decade after the Nobel-worthy find, scientists are still trying to pin down exactly what dark energy is and thus solve what some experts call 'the most profound problem' in modern physics."[29]

ONLY ONE POINT OF VIEW IS PRESENTED

Although the universe beginning as the Big Bang from a singularity is conjecture, it is the only point of view that is offered in public schools to explain the origin of everything. This particular point of view is presented in textbooks that students are required to read and taught by teachers whom students are required to respect. As a result, a student is left with the impression that the Big Bang from a singularity must be a proven fact that is therefore true.

This way of thinking is problematic for a number of reasons. According to Vision Learning, "A common misconception in science is that science provides facts or 'truth' about a subject. Science is not a collection of facts; rather, it is a process of investigation into the natural world and the knowledge generated through that process."[30] Should the Big Bang from a singularity be presented in such a manner that a student is left with the impression that it is supported by facts and that it is true?

THE DEFINITION OF A SCIENTIFIC THEORY

Vision Learning also says, "One of the challenges in understanding scientific terms like *theory* is that there is not a precise definition even within the scientific community." Nevertheless, they go on to define a *scientific theory* as "an explanation inferred from multiple lines of evidence for some broad aspect of the natural world and is logical, testable, and predictive."[31] Does the universe beginning with the Big Bang fall within this definition of a scientific theory? Is the universe beginning with the Big Bang an explanation that is "logical, testable, and predictive"?

There is plenty of evidence that the universe is expanding outward in every direction from our vantage point on Earth; astronomers have repeatedly validated what Edwin Hubble confirmed in 1929. Based on solid evidence of an expanding universe, the scientific community inferred that the universe must have been the size of a singularity 13.8 billion years ago. (Friedmann and Lemaître suggested this idea before they had evidence.) This conclusion, however, is not supported by facts or evidence. Does the existence of a singularity fall within Vision Learning's definition of a scientific theory? Is the existence of a singularity an explanation that is "logical, testable, and predictive"?

"LOGICAL, TESTABLE, AND PREDICTIVE"

Let's examine each of the three criteria—logical, testable, and predictive—used by Vision Learning to define a scientific theory to see how the two key components of the Big Bang theory—an expanding universe and a singularity—measure up.

Logical: The theory of an expanding universe is logical. There is significant evidence of expansion and no meaningful evidence of recession. But what about a singularity? Is it logical to assume—based on less than one hundred years of observations—that 13,800,000,000 years ago the universe was exceedingly small; or that the whole universe can be rewound back to a pinpoint epicenter; or that an entire universe of energy, matter, particles, and space originated as a primordial particle, mere point, primeval atom, initial quantum, or singularity?

Testable: The theory of an expanding universe is testable. It has been tested by thousands of astronomers with increasingly sophisticated instruments for many decades. (For example, Cosmic Microwave Background Radiation testing is done with a detector the size of a two story house that looks like a giant ear.) And in the future this theory will continue to be tested by many more astronomers who will have even more precise instruments. But what about a singularity? How do scientists test for the one-time existence of a singularity that defies all known laws of physics; or that supposedly existed in a moment of time 13.8 billion years ago; or that has the potential energy to explode with a velocity a quadrillion times faster than the speed of light? (As the next section explains, the Large Hadron Collider does not test the singularity.)

Predictive: The theory of an expanding universe is predictive. The movement of a galaxy can be measured using a variety of instruments and techniques to determine the speed of expansion. A technician with a computer can use that data to predict incremental movements of that galaxy in the future. But what about a singularity? Can a singularity be predictive when it is merely an assumption that is impossible to analyze; or when there is no evidence of anything like it in nature; or when scientists are not able to replicate it?

In summary, an expanding universe and a singularity are the two key components of the Big Bang theory. An expanding universe meets the criteria for Vision Learning's definition of a scientific theory because it is based on evidence that is logical, testable, and predictive. Whether or not the one-time existence of a singularity is logical, testable, and predictive is a matter of opinion.

THE LARGE HADRON COLLIDER

Scientists think they will one day prove what happened at the time of the Big Bang by replicating certain conditions in the laboratory. The European Organization for Nuclear Research (CERN) is the organization coordinating the effort. More than 10,000 scientists from around the world have invested over $13.25 billion to construct and maintain a massive subatomic particle accelerator to—theoretically—simulate a Big Bang type of event.[32] This highly sophisticated machine is called the Large Hadron Collider (LHC), and according to *LHC the Guide*, that name is significant:[33]

Large: The 27-kilometer (17-mile) circular machine is housed in a subterranean circular tunnel that straddles the France-Switzerland border at a mean depth of 100 meters (328 feet).

Hadron: The circular machine accelerates hadrons. *Hadrons* are particles composed of quarks. The Encyclopædia Britannica says a *quark* is "any member of a group of elementary subatomic particles that interact by means of the strong force and are believed to be among the fundamental constituents of matter... Quarks appear to be true elementary particles; that is, they have no apparent structure and cannot be resolved into something smaller. In addition, however, quarks always seem to occur in combination with other quarks or with antiquarks, their antiparticles, to form all hadrons."[34]

Collider: An extremely powerful network of electromagnets sends and accelerates two hadron particle beams around the circular machine in opposite directions. The two beams travel toward each other in separate tubes. When each particle beam reaches 99.9999991% of the speed of light, they are forced to collide. (The LHC cannot accelerate particles to 100%—or greater—than the speed of light.) Picture two high-speed train engines at full throttle in a head-on collision on the same track. Scientists plot and analyze the properties and distribution of the particle debris field produced by the collision.

THE LHC DOES NOT TEST THE INITIAL BIG BANG

Regardless of how many scientists, the amount of money, or the number of man-hours invested in particle acceleration and collision research, the LHC does not test the initial Big Bang. *LHC the Guide* says this: "The energy density and temperature that are produced in the collisions at the LHC are similar to those that existed a few moments *after* the Big Bang. In this way physicists hope to better understand how the Universe evolved"[35] (italics added). This means that the LHC collisions are an attempt to mimic the conditions that supposedly existed *after* the Big Bang (10^{-12} seconds in Figure 2.3). This might not sound like much, but it is a quantum leap from the conditions that supposedly existed *prior to* and *at* the Big Bang. In other words, the LHC does not test—and therefore cannot prove—the moment *before* or *concurrent with* the Big Bang. The LHC does not test and therefore cannot prove:

The origin of the singularity or that something can come from nothing.

A singularity existed in a stationary and stable state of equilibrium.

An entire universe of energy and matter was once the size of a mere point.

The "energy density and temperature" prior to or at the time of the Big Bang.

The catalyst that caused the singularity to become unstable and explode.

The conditions that existed up to 10^{-12} seconds after the Big Bang event.

A force that travels a quadrillion times faster than the speed of light.

These monumental issues—all at the heart of the Big Bang—are not tested by the LHC. The LHC accelerates hadron particles in order to produce a violent collision. This cannot compare to a singularity existing in a stationary and stable state—with universe-sized potential—that suddenly exploded without a catalyst. In addition, the LHC requires something that exists: hadron particles. This perspective on the origin of the universe stands in stark contrast to the point of view that nothing existed in the beginning. If an argument were made that the singularity is *nothing*, it would create a circular reasoning problem because *something* (the universe) can't come from *nothing*. Therefore, the singularity must be considered *something*, and *something* that existed cannot be considered *nothing*.

PHASES OF THE UNIVERSE AFTER THE BIG BANG

The properties and composition of the singularity cannot be explained or tested, and scientists do not address the issue of its origin. Nevertheless, the singularity is the leading explanation for an entire universe of energy, matter, space, and time. Without the singularity, the Big Bang does not bang, and all subsequent assumptions about the universe are called into question. This is relevant because scientists believe the universe developed in phases following the Big Bang. *LHC the Guide* provides the following phases[36] (Figure 2.4).

TIME AFTER THE BIG BANG	PHASE OF THE UNIVERSE
.000000000001 seconds	Quark-gluon plasma
.00001 seconds	Protons and neutrons
3 minutes	Light nuclei
380 thousand years	Light atoms
200 million years	Stars and galaxies
9.2 billion years	The solar system
Unknown	Life on Earth
13.8 billion years	The universe today

FIGURE 2.4 Phases of the universe after the Big Bang

FAITH IN THE BIG BANG OR CREATION

There is no disputing that the Big Bang is a theory that attempts to explain the natural world's very existence. A dispute arises when the Big Bang is presented as a proven fact that is therefore true. This implied authenticity is the clear message when the Big Bang is taught without offering complete information; without indicating there is no empirical data to support it; without explaining that the theory is based on massive assumptions; without discussing the many unresolved issues; and without mentioning an alternative point of view.

As indicated earlier, we human beings want to be able to explain the origin of the universe, and the two primary choices are either the Big Bang or Creation. Both require a measure of *faith*, as in the "firm belief in something for which there is no proof."[37] The Big Bang requires the belief in a singularity that somehow existed and then exploded, expanded, and is accelerating in its rate of expansion. Creation requires belief in God. Now that we know what science says about the universe, let's take a closer look at what the Bible says about the universe.

THE BIBLE'S UNIVERSE

THE INAUGURAL SHABUA-DAYS

Earlier in this chapter we introduced the inaugural *shabua*—a complete time period of seven—as an interval of days. Genesis 1 is a step-by-step account of Creation; it describes all of the creation activity that took place during each of the first six days of the *shabua*-days. Genesis 2 completes the *shabua*-days by describing the 7th and final day. The Bible passages for each of the days are listed in the first column of Figure 2.5. That column is followed by the Hebrew-to-English transliteration; the English translation; and a brief description of the creation activity that took place.

GENESIS	TRANSLITERATION	ENGLISH	DESCRIPTION OF CREATION ACTIVITY
1:1-5	*Yom Ehad*	First Day	*The heavens* (undefined waters), *the earth* (without form and void), *light* (unspecified)
1:6-8	*Yom Sheni*	Second Day	*An expanse (Heaven) in the midst of the waters (waters under the expanse/waters above the expanse)*
1:9-13	*Yom Shelishi*	Third Day	*Earth, Seas, vegetation, plants, trees* (after God gathered the *waters under the expanse*)
1:14-19	*Yom Rebii*	Fourth Day	*Lights* ([specific] when God filled the *waters above the expanse* with the sun, moon, and *stars*)
1:20-23	*Yom Hamishi*	Fifth Day	*Living creatures, birds, sea creatures* (to fill Earth's empty sky and Seas with life)
1:24-25	*Yom Shishshi*	Sixth Day (Part 1)	*Livestock, creeping things, beasts* (to fill Earth's empty dry land with life)
1:26-31	*Yom Shishshi*	Sixth Day (Part 2)	*Man* ([*male/female/them*] to *be fruitful and multiply and fill the earth* with human beings)
2:1-3	*Yom Shebia*	Seventh Day	*[God] rested on the seventh day from all his work that he had done* (no creation activity)

FIGURE 2.5 The inaugural *shabua*-days

"IN THE BEGINNING, GOD CREATED"

Genesis 1:1-3 says: *In the beginning, God created the heavens and the earth. The earth was without form and void, and darkness was over the face of the deep. And the Spirit of God was hovering over the face of the waters. And God said, "Let there be light," and there was light.* These three verses are impossible for human beings to understand because they contain terms and refer to activities and materials that no person has experienced.

It might help to consider the materials God created on Day 1 as equivalent to a six-day supply of water and clay that a potter would procure before getting to work. Just as a potter molds and shapes beautiful pots using these raw materials, God molded and shaped His creation—over a period of six days—primarily from the elements He made on Day 1. The heavens, the earth, and the light that God made on Day 1 (Figure 2.6) are components of Creation in their most elementary form. As you will see, the events of Day 2 (Figure 2.7), Day 3 (Figure 2.8), and Day 4 (Figure 2.9) are more detailed and specific.

DAY 1

The heavens: On Day 1, God initially created "the heavens" in their most elementary form: *God created the heavens... And the Spirit of God was hovering over the face of the waters* (Genesis 1:1-2). Although "the heavens" and "the waters" are vague and nebulous terms, they nevertheless clearly refer to something that God literally created. The Bible says God formed three separate and distinct entities from the waters of the heavens: Heaven (Day 2), the Seas (Day 3), and the universe (Day 4).

The earth: On Day 1, God initially created "the earth" in its most elementary form: *God created... the earth. The earth was without form and void, and darkness was over the face of the deep* (Genesis 1:1-2). Although "the earth" is a vague and nebulous term, it nevertheless clearly refers to something that God literally created. The Bible says God formed six separate and distinct entities from the earth: planet Earth (Day 3), vegetation (Day 3), birds (Day 5), sea creatures (Day 5), land creatures (Day 6), and human beings (Day 6).

Light: On Day 1, God initially created "light" in its most elementary form: *God said "Let there be light," and there was light. And God saw that the light was good. And God separated the light from the darkness. God called the light Day, and the darkness he called Night. And there was evening and there was morning, the first day* (Genesis 1:3-5). Although "light" is a vague and nebulous term, it nevertheless clearly refers to something that God literally created. The Bible says the unspecified light ("Day") that God created on

Day 1 offset the darkness ("Night") for three days—Days 1-2-3—until God formed the specific lights (the sun, moon, and stars) on Day 4.

DAY 2

An expanse called Heaven: On Day 2, *God said, "Let there be an expanse in the midst of the waters, and let it separate the waters from the waters." And God made the expanse… And God called the expanse Heaven* (Genesis 1:6-8). In the midst of the waters, God made the expanse called Heaven.

The waters are separated: On Day 2, *God made the expanse and separated the waters that were under the expanse from the waters that were above the expanse* (Genesis 1:7). God partitioned the waters He created on Day 1 into two sections: "the waters that were *under* the expanse" of Heaven would become the Seas that God gathered to reveal Earth (Day 3), and "the waters that were *above* the expanse" of Heaven would become the universe that God filled with the sun, moon, and stars (Day 4).

DAY 3

Seas: On Day 3, God gathered *the waters that were* under *the expanse* of Heaven to form the Seas: *"Let the waters under the heavens be gathered together into one place"… and the waters that were gathered together he called Seas* (Genesis 1:9-10). The vague and nebulous waters (Day 1) that were under Heaven (Day 2) became the Seas (Day 3).

Earth: On Day 3, God gathered *the waters that were* under *the expanse* of Heaven to reveal Earth: *"Let the waters under the heavens be gathered together into one place, and let the dry land appear"… God called the dry land Earth* (Genesis 1:9-10). The formless and void earth (Day 1) became the dry land we call Earth (Day 3).

DAY 4

Lights: On Day 4, in *the waters that were* above *the expanse* of Heaven, God formed separate and distinct lights: *"Let there be lights in the expanse of*

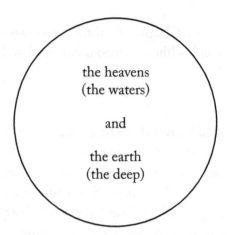

Genesis 1:1-2 *In the beginning, God created the heavens and the earth. The earth was without form and void, and the darkness was over the face of the deep. And the Spirit of God was hovering over the face of the waters.*

FIGURE 2.6 Day 1: The heavens and the earth

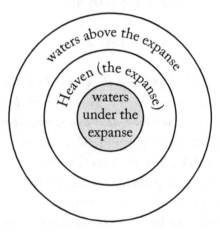

Genesis 1:6-8 *And God said, "Let there be an expanse in the midst of the waters, and let it separate the waters from the waters." And God made the expanse and separated the waters that were under the expanse from the waters that were above the expanse. And it was so. And God called the expanse Heaven.*

FIGURE 2.7 Day 2: Heaven (the expanse)

[handwritten annotations: "God created an Earth centered universe → Earth was first!", "Olivet discourse", "Math 24", "Mark 13", "Luke 17", "Sun + Moon came AFTER earth"]

Genesis 1:9-10 *And God said, "Let the waters under the heavens be gathered together into one place, and let the dry land appear." And it was so. God called the dry land Earth, and the waters that were gathered together he called Seas.*

FIGURE 2.8 Day 3: Earth and Seas

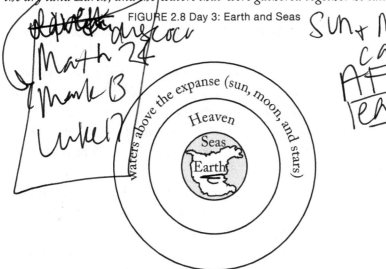

Genesis 1:14-16 *And God said, "Let there be lights in the expanse of the heavens to separate the day from the night...for signs and for seasons, and for day and years, and...to give light upon the earth." And it was so. And God made the two great lights–the greater light to rule the day and the lesser light to rule the night–and the stars.*

FIGURE 2.9 Day 4: Sun, moon, and stars (the universe)

[handwritten at bottom: "earth earth"]

the heavens to separate the day from the night. And let them be for signs and for seasons, and for days and years, and let them be lights in the expanse of the heavens to give light upon the earth" (Genesis 1:14-15). The elementary form of light that God created on Day 1 lasted for three days. Then, on Day 4, God formed the specific "lights." These *lights* performed the same function that *light* had on Days 1-2-3: these specific lights continued the 24-hour cycle of separating light from darkness on planet Earth.

To achieve this result, *God made the two great lights—the greater light to rule the day and the lesser light to rule the night—and the stars. And God set them in the expanse of the heavens to give light on the earth, to rule over the day and over the night, and to separate the light from the darkness* (Genesis 1:16-18). God made the greater light (the sun) to rule the day, the lesser light (the moon) to rule the night, and the stars.

GOD CREATED THE UNIVERSE WITH HIS WORD

The Bible says, *By faith we understand that the universe was created by the word of God, so that what is seen was not made out of things that are visible* (Hebrews 11:3). In other words, the universe ("what is seen") was created when God literally spoke it ("by the word of God") into existence from something that human beings are not able to see ("not made out of things that are visible").

And we know from Genesis 1 that God created the waters on Day 1 (Figure 2.6), God separated the waters into waters under Heaven and waters above Heaven on Day 2 (Figure 2.7), and God filled the waters above Heaven with the sun, the moon, and the stars on Day 4 (Figure 2.9). This means the universe did not exist until Day 4 when God spoke it into being.

To believe the universe began in this manner—with God speaking the sun, the moon, and the stars into existence in the waters above Heaven—is conceptually hard to understand, but it offers a biblical explanation for the presence of ice (frozen water) on comets, asteroids, and planets in outer space. However, the fact that water on Earth is often associated with organic life (living things) does not mean organic life exists elsewhere. There is no evidence of life on comets, asteroids, or planets in outer space.

THE EPICENTER OF THE UNIVERSE

As we have learned, the prevailing theory in science—the Big Bang—says the universe began when a somehow existing singularity suddenly exploded from a stable state of equilibrium… somewhere out there. If this were true, Earth is nothing more than a tiny speck located at some random spot in the cosmos. Furthermore, if the Big Bang happened, somewhere out there one would expect to find trace evidence of its epicenter, the pinpoint location in the universe from which everything emanated from the (hypothetical) singularity. Astrophysicists have not, however, been able to identify such a location. And they may not like what some of their own findings do suggest.

Consider that astrophysicists are not able to identify the location of the epicenter of the singularity that exploded, but they will not even consider the possibility that Earth—within the Milky Way Galaxy—is in the vicinity of the epicenter. After all, the universe is so incredibly large that the (prideful?) assertion that Earth occupies such an incredibly prominent position does seem a bit ridiculous. It's hard to imagine how the tiny microscopic speck called Earth could be the center of hundreds of billions of galaxies. So it is understandable that astrophysicists scoff at the mere suggestion. But should they? Does the Bible give us any possible clues about Earth's place in our vast universe?

THE FOUNDATION OF THE EARTH

First, let's begin our discussion with Isaiah 48:13: "*My hand laid the foundation of the earth.*" Merriam-Webster defines *foundation* as "something (such as an idea, a principle, or a fact) that provides support for something." An earth "without form and void" is one of the very first things God created on Day 1. This nebulous earth set the stage for planet Earth, and planet Earth is the foundation for everything else that God created. Earth is God's center stage on which His power, majesty, and creativity are displayed. The prominent role of the nebulous earth as well as planet Earth is evident in all six days of Creation (Figure 2.10).

Day 1	The earth was created *without form and void, and darkness was over the face of the deep.*
Day 2	The *waters under the heavens* were set apart to prepare the nebulous earth for the next day.
Day 3	The *waters under the heavens* were gathered to form Seas; reveal Earth; and allow for vegetation.
Day 4	The sun, moon, and stars were made to shine their *lights* on Earth for signs, seasons, days, and years.
Day 5	Living creatures, birds, and sea creatures were made to multiply and fill Earth's sky and Seas.
Day 6 (Part 1)	Livestock, creeping things, and beasts were made to multiply throughout Earth's dry land.
Day 6 (Part 2)	Human beings were made to multiply on Earth, fill the Earth, and have dominion over all the Earth.

FIGURE 2.10 Earth's prominent role during Creation

GOD STRETCHED/SPREAD OUT THE UNIVERSE

Knowing that Earth has a prominent role in God's Creation helps us to understand the universe better. Isaiah 40:22 says, *It is he who sits above the circle of the earth… who stretches out the heavens like a curtain, and spreads them like a tent to dwell in.* This verse implies that Earth is the epicenter from which God "stretches out the heavens." In the Bible, the word *heavens* is used in a general sense (as in all Creation) and in the specific sense (as in Heaven, the sky, and the universe). Here *heavens* is used in the specific sense—the universe. The following twelve verses in Figure 2.11 indicate God "stretched out" and "spread out" the heavens (the universe).

Job 9:8	*[God] alone stretched out the heavens and trampled the waves of the sea.*
Job 37:18	*Can you, like him, spread out the skies, hard as a cast metal mirror?*
Psalm 8:3	*I look at your heavens, the work of your fingers, the moon and the stars, which you have set in place.*
Psalm 104:2	*[God, you are] covering yourself with light as with a garment, stretching out the heavens like a tent.*

Isaiah 40:22	*It is he…who stretches out the heavens like a curtain, and spreads them like a tent to dwell in.*
Isaiah 42:5	*Thus says God, the* L*ORD,* *who created the heavens and stretched them out.*
Isaiah 45:12	*"I made the earth and created man on it; it was my hands that stretched out the heavens."*
Isaiah 48:13	*"My hand laid the foundation of the earth, and my right hand spread out the heavens."*
Isaiah 51:13	*"[I am] the* L*ORD,* *your Maker, who stretched out the heavens and laid the foundations of the earth."*
Jeremiah 10:12	*It is he… who established the world by his wisdom, and by his understanding stretched out the heavens.*
Jeremiah 51:15	*It is he… who established the world by his wisdom, and by his understanding stretched out the heavens.*
Zechariah 12:1	*Thus declares the* L*ORD,* *who stretched out the heavens and founded the earth.*

FIGURE 2.11 God stretched out/spread out the universe

GOD FORMED EARTH BEFORE THE UNIVERSE

The sequence of *what* was created *when* is highly significant. As indicated in Figures 2.8 and 2.9, the Bible says God made the distinct Earth before He filled the waters above the expanse with specific "lights" (sun, moon, and stars). In other words, God formed planet Earth (Day 3) before He formed the universe (Day 4). Obviously, the biblical account of Creation cannot be reconciled with the Big Bang theory that says the universe (13.8 billion years old) began to take shape about 9.2 billion years prior to Earth (about 4.6 billion years old). The earth/Earth is featured in all six days of Creation, and the universe is only featured on one of those six days. And the Bible says God formed the universe—after Earth—to separate day from night; to mark signs, seasons, days, and years; and to provide light on Earth (Figure 2.10).

So, when Isaiah 40:22 says, *It is he who sits above the circle of the earth… who stretches out the heavens like a curtain, and spreads them like a tent to dwell in*, it literally means that Earth was round when God created it and that Earth existed before God stretched out the heavens. This verse is consistent with the biblical timing from Genesis 1: God created the distinct Heaven—a literal place that is also called "the expanse"—in the midst of the waters on Day 2 (Figure 2.7); God revealed Earth in the waters under Heaven on Day 3 (Figure 2.8); and God created the universe in the waters above Heaven on Day 4 (Figure 2.9).

STRETCHED OUT LIKE A CURTAIN, SPREAD LIKE A TENT

The prophet Isaiah used two metaphors in the same verse (Isaiah 40:22) to describe how God formed the universe. In the first metaphor, God *stretches out the heavens like a curtain.* To be stretched out implies that the heavens were compressed. Picture a fully collapsed shower curtain. As you draw the curtain, each previously compressed fold is stretched out at a rate that is proportional to its distance—as in Hubble's Law—from the fixed side (Figure 2.12). The way these folds expand as they open can be compared to observed redshifts of galaxies.

According to NASA, the "'redshift appeared to be larger for faint, presumably further, galaxies. Hence, the farther a galaxy, the faster it is receding from Earth.' The galaxies are moving away from Earth because the fabric of space itself is expanding."[38] This is what Hubble's Law means

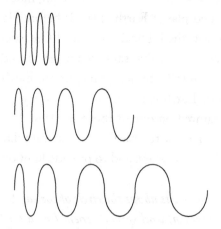

FIGURE 2.12 Stretched-out curtain folds   FIGURE 2.13 Spread-out tent folds

when it says that galaxies are receding at a rate that is proportional to their distance from our vantage point on Earth. If the curtain folds contained galaxies, the galaxies in the folds that are farther away from the fixed side would have a larger redshift than the galaxies in the folds that are closer to the fixed side. The similarity between this curtain metaphor and Hubble's Law is uncanny.

In the second metaphor, God *spreads [the heavens] like a tent to dwell in*. Since people in biblical times lived in tents, they certainly would have been familiar with the ridges, peaks, and troughs that appear when tent material—such as canvas—is spread over the top of a rectangular tent frame (Figure 2.13).

THE TWO VIEWS CANNOT BE RECONCILED

Now, having looked at both views, we clearly see that the Bible's universe cannot be reconciled with the Big Bang's universe. The two views completely contradict each other in regard to both the order and the timing. To reiterate, scientists believe the universe began to form *first* 13,800,000,000 years ago, and Earth began to form *second* 4,500,000,000 years ago. On the other hand, the Bible says God formed Earth *first* on Day 3 of Creation—about 6,000 years ago—and He formed the universe *second* on Day 4. (This book's sequel, *Shabua Years*, will address the year of Creation based exclusively on Scripture.)

Science and the Bible diverge on matters regarding the universe, but many aspects of Earth's geological history suggest that science and the Bible are more in sync than one might expect. For example, the contiguous landmass that scientists call Pangaea could have been the dry land that appeared on Day 3 when God gathered the waters to reveal Earth (Genesis 1), and it is possible that shifting tectonic plates broke up Pangaea to form our existing seven continents.

Another example is found in many geological features on Earth that scientists believe were formed by floodwaters. It is entirely possible that a single catastrophic flood—like that described in the days of Noah (Genesis 7-8)—was the primary cause. The compatibility between Earth

Science and the Bible is both compelling and credible. This interesting and relevant topic, however, is beyond the scope of this work, so it will be addressed in a future publication.

THE SEQUENCE AND TIMING DIFFER

Figure 2.14 summarizes what we have covered so far about the Seas, Earth, and universe, and it also introduces the upcoming discussion regarding living things. In addition, it highlights the differences between the biblical worldview and the secular worldview in regard to what happened when. The Bible says the events happened in a matter of days approximately 6,000 years ago. Science says the events happened gradually over a span of billions, millions, and hundreds of thousands of years. (BBC is the source of the scientific information.[39])

BIBLICAL WORLDVIEW		SEQUENCE	SECULAR WORLDVIEW	
WHEN	WHAT		WHAT	WHEN
6,000: Day 3	Seas	1st	Universe	13,800,000,000
6,000: Day 3	Earth	2nd	Earth	4,500,000,000
6,000: Day 3	Vegetation	3rd	Seas	Unspecified
6,000: Day 4	Universe	4th	Microorganisms	3,800,000,000
6,000: Day 5	Sea creatures	5th	Sea creatures	530,000,000
6,000: Day 5	Birds	6th	Vegetation	475,000,000
6,000: Day 6	Land creatures	7th	Land creatures	200,000,000
6,000: Day 6	Human beings	8th	*Homo sapiens*	200,000

FIGURE 2.14 Sequence and timing of the biblical vs. secular worldviews

Now, let's turn our attention to living things. Before we examine what the Bible says about living things, let's examine what science says. Then we'll compare these two views just as we compared the two views regarding the beginning of the universe.

EVOLUTION'S DIVERSITY

ERASMUS DARWIN'S HYPOTHESIS OF EVOLUTION

Any discussion about living things on Earth would be incomplete without mentioning Erasmus Darwin and his grandson Charles Darwin. After Erasmus Darwin published *The Botanic Garden* concerning the explosive beginning of the universe and Earth, Erasmus began to speculate about the development of organic life on planet Earth. In 1794, three years after he published *The Botanic Garden*, Erasmus published a two-volume set titled *Zoonomia*, which the Dictionary of Scientific Biography called the "first consistent, all-embracing hypothesis of evolution."[40] Erasmus Darwin died six years after publishing *Zoonomia*.

Although Charles Darwin (1809-1882) is considered by many to be the father of evolutionary thought, it seems that designation properly belongs to his pioneer grandfather Erasmus Darwin (1731-1802). However, it was Charles who refined the hypothesis of evolution—promulgated by Erasmus in *Zoonomia*—and brought it to the attention of the world. Although Charles was not born until seven years after Erasmus died, both the life and the career of Charles were profoundly influenced by the extensive writings and stellar reputation of his famous grandfather.

THE PROGRESSION OF CHARLES DARWIN'S THEORIES

In college, Charles studied medicine at the prestigious University of Edinburgh, but he quit after only a couple of years. Charles's father, Robert Darwin, made arrangements for him to attend Christ's College in Cambridge where he completed his schooling and obtained a bachelor's degree in 1831. After graduation, twenty-two-year-old Charles embarked on the *HMS Beagle* for his first natural history voyage, and it lasted almost five years. As he traveled, Charles observed layers of strata on land and discovered among seashells some huge fossils and bones of extinct mammals. Then, upon seeing the indigenous inhabitants of Fuego, Charles wrote this in a letter on March 30, 1833:

We here saw the native Fuegian; an untamed savage is I really think one of the most extraordinary spectacles in the world.—the difference between a domesticated & wild animal is far more strikingly marked in man.—in the naked barbarian, with his body coated with paint, whose very gestures, whether they may be peacible or hostile are unintelligible, with difficulty we see a fellowcreature. No drawing or description will at all explain the extreme interest which is created by the first sight of savages.[41]

Eight weeks later, on May 23, 1833, Charles wrote these words:

In Tierra del I first saw bona fide savages; & they are as savage as the most curious person would desire.—A wild man is indeed a miserable animal, but one well worth seeing.[42]

Aligning these statements with his other writings suggests that Charles believed the native inhabitants of Fuego had not yet completed the transition from wild animals to domesticated human beings.

CHARLES DARWIN'S *ON THE ORIGIN OF SPECIES*

During the journey, Charles spent time on land collecting specimens, investigating geology, and studying different species of plants, birds, mammals, and reptiles. He spent time at sea studying marine invertebrates like plankton. He routinely sent his notes and specimens back to England where some of his findings were published while he was still at sea. By the time the *HMS Beagle* returned to England in 1836, a number of scholars were already interested in the work of the now twenty-seven-year-old Charles Darwin. Information he gathered on the voyage prompted the development of his many ideas. In the years that followed, Charles continued to expand those ideas, and more and more often they were published in journals, essays, and books.

In 1859, sixty-three years after Erasmus Darwin published his ideas about organic life and evolution in *Zoonomia*, and twenty-three years after the *HMS Beagle* docked at Cornwall, Charles Darwin published his most famous work titled *On the Origin of Species*. This book was different from his earlier publications that were more academic and scholarly: those were therefore read primarily by specialists in the various disciplines. *On the Origin of Species*, however, used terminology that was easier for the general public to understand. As a result, the book attracted widespread interest. In the decades that followed, this idea of evolution continued to garner interest and acceptance as an alternative to the biblical explanation of the existence of diverse living things on planet Earth.

THE THEORY OF EVOLUTION

Encyclopædia Britannica says that evolution is a "theory in biology postulating that the various types of plants, animals, and other living things on Earth have their origin in other preexisting types and that the distinguishable differences are due to modifications in successive generations."[43] (Charles Darwin called this "descent with modification."[44]) In other words, "the central idea of biological evolution is that all life on Earth shares a common ancestor."[45] When the term "evolution" is used in this chapter, it refers to this type of broad scale transitioning from a common ancestor.

Scientists believe the common ancestor from which every living thing evolved was a single-celled microorganism called a prokaryote. (The prokaryote is assumed to be the first living thing on planet Earth.) Over the course of billions of years, they say the prokaryote went through an evolutionary process of "mutation, migration (gene flow), genetic drift, and natural selection as mechanisms of change."[46] Scientists say the diversity of living things is the result of these mechanisms of change.

THE BIG BANG, EVOLUTION, AND A PROKARYOTE

Most people are not aware that the existence of the first living thing on planet Earth is not addressed by either the theory of the Big Bang or evolution; neither theory resolves the origin of the prokaryote. The Big Bang begins with a singularity that exploded to form an entire universe of energy and matter; the Big Bang does not explain how energy and matter (inorganic/nonliving) developed into a prokaryote (organic/living). Evolution begins with a pre-existing prokaryote that evolved into every diverse and complex living thing that has ever inhabited Earth; evolution does not explain the origin of the prokaryote.

Although neither the Big Bang nor evolution addresses the origin of organic life on Earth, various theories try to bridge the gap. But before we evaluate those theories, we need to discuss the origin of water. Knowing the theories regarding the origin of water is relevant because water is essential for life. Understanding how water might have arrived on Earth requires knowing the prevailing theory regarding the development of the solar system.

THE SOLAR SYSTEM, SUN, PLANETS, AND EARTH

Scientists believe our solar system developed out of a massive rotating disk of interstellar dust and gas 9.2 billion years after the Big Bang (Figure 2.14): "Approximately 4.6 billion years ago, the solar system was a cloud of dust and gas known as a solar nebula. Gravity collapsed the material in on itself as it began to spin, forming the sun in the center of the nebula." (Picture a spinning CD or DVD collapsing into its hollow center to form a small plastic marble.) As the article continues, it says that Earth began to form when "the remaining material began to clump up. Small particles drew together, bound by the force of gravity, into larger particles."[47]

As more particles drew together and primitive Earth continued to grow in size, scientists say that its ability to attract more dust, gas, particles, and pieces of rock also increased. (The greater the mass of an object, the greater its gravitational pull.) And this became a self-perpetuating reaction: as the size of the sphere increased, the gravitational pull became stronger; more dust, gas, particles, and pieces of rock were added; the size of the sphere increased; and on and on. Earth's gravitational pull eventually became such a powerful force that it created extreme compression, generated tremendous heat, melted the particles and the rock, caused the heavier metals—iron and nickel—to sink to the center, and became a molten fireball.

EARTH WAS AND STILL IS A MOLTEN FIREBALL

Even though scientists say Earth slowly cooled in thick concentric layers, evidence that our planet was once a molten fireball still exists just under Earth's crust. (This is apparent every time a volcano erupts and spews magma.) A relatively thin outer crust wraps around the thick hot molten layer called the mantle. At the center of the inner Earth—encompassed by the mantle—is an extremely dense super-heated core. A hard-boiled egg can help illustrate Earth's composition: the egg yolk compares to the core, the egg white compares to the mantle, and the shell compares to the thin outer crust.

Although the hottest temperatures are within Earth's core, the mantle remains exceedingly hot all the way from its boundary with the core to its boundary with the crust. Because the inner Earth is inaccessible, scientists can only speculate about the temperature. National Geographic says this about the mantle: "The temperature of the mantle varies greatly, from 1000° Celsius (1832° Fahrenheit) near its boundary with the crust, to 3700° Celsius (6692° Fahrenheit) near its boundary with the core."[48] They say the temperatures of the core "range from about 4,400° Celsius (7,952° Fahrenheit) to about 6,000° Celsius (10,800° Fahrenheit)."[49]

332,519,000 CUBIC MILES OF WATER ON EARTH

If you think the inner Earth is hot now, scientists say it was much hotter in the past. And that raises the question at hand: how did water accumulate on a molten fireball? It might help to know how much water exists on Earth before we introduce the most popular theory on how it could have accumulated. The surface of Earth is approximately 71% water and 29% dry land. Although that is a very large surface area, it does not help us understand the volume of water because it does not account for depth.

Fortunately, the U.S. Geological Survey provides statistics on water volume: "There are over 332,519,000 cubic miles of water on the planet. A cubic mile is the volume of a cube measuring one mile on each side. Of this vast volume of water, NOAA's National Geophysical Data Center estimates that 321,003,271 cubic miles is in the ocean. That's enough water to fill about 352,670,000,000,000,000,000 gallon-sized milk containers!"[50] Now that we know how much water is on Earth, we can look at ideas about how it might have come into existence.

WATER ON EARTH FROM ICE IN COMETS

One theory suggests the water came from ice in comets that melted after impacting Earth. NASA says comets "consist mostly of ice coated with dark organic material. They have been referred to as 'dirty snowballs.'... Comets may have brought water and organic compounds, the building blocks of life, to the early Earth."[51] Since comets are composed of porous materials that vaporize, it is hard to find evidence that they ever impacted Earth.

According to NASA, comets are diffused into space: "The nucleus contains icy chunks, frozen gases with bits of embedded dust. A comet warms up as it nears the sun and develops an atmosphere, or coma. The sun's heat causes the comet's ices to change to gases so the coma gets larger."[52] A comet's coma and its long luminous tail are evidence that the ice, gas, and dust are diffused into space. If comets—that disintegrate—are the source of water on Earth, how was all that water able to accumulate? The idea that water arrived on Earth in comets at any stage of Earth's development—whatever the state of the atmosphere—is problematic. (Held in place by gravity, the atmosphere is the protective layer of gases that shield Earth from comets, meteors, asteroids, intense heat from the sun, and deadly radiation.)

If, for instance, comets arrived on a primitive Earth when the surface was molten, wouldn't the porous comets have vaporized as soon as they struck the exposed mantle? If Earth had a crust but little to no atmosphere (like the moon), the side exposed to the sun would have been extremely hot. ("The temperature [of the moon] reaches about 260 degrees Fahrenheit [127 degrees Celsius] when in full sun."[53]) So wouldn't any water from the comets have evaporated without an atmosphere to protect it from the intense heat of the sun? If Earth had an atmosphere, wouldn't the comets have diffused into space when they passed through that atmosphere and well before they impacted Earth? (This is precisely what happens to comets today.) Finally, if comets were the source of water, how many comet strikes were needed to deliver 332,519,000 cubic miles of water to Earth?

THE SOURCE OF EARTH'S WATER IS UNRESOLVED

A related theory suggests water came from asteroids. However, asteroids not only face the same issues as comets, but asteroids present additional complications: they are primarily large pieces of rock (there is little evidence to indicate they contain a significant quantity of ice), and most are located a long way from Earth in the asteroid belt between Mars and Jupiter. Yet another theory suggests that "Earth's huge store of water might have originated via chemical reactions in the mantle, rather than arriving from space through collisions with ice-rich comets."[54] This idea—that intense pressure and extreme heat can create water—is relatively new and lacks supporting data.

As Smithsonian.com acknowledges, the source of water on Earth is a conundrum: "Water is so vital to our survival, but strangely enough, we don't know the first thing about it—literally the first. Where does water, a giver and taker of life on planet Earth, come from?"[55]

In summary, although scientists aren't sure how it happened, they say Earth was molten, it cooled, it formed a crust, and it accumulated a lot of water. Again, how and when water appeared on Earth is relevant because the presence of water is one of the conditions necessary for life to begin and to be sustained. In essence, a discussion regarding living things on Earth begins with a discussion regarding the existence of water. So let's turn our attention to a discussion about the origin of living things.

SEVEN THEORIES ON THE ORIGIN OF LIFE

The evolutionary process requires an already existing living thing—a prokaryote—so how do scientists explain its origin? According to Diana Northup, a cave biologist at the University of New Mexico, "many theories of the origin of life have been proposed, but since it's hard to prove or disprove them, no fully accepted theory exists."[56] (To see for yourself that no fully accepted theory exists regarding the origin of life, ask a scientist to explain how nonliving things became living things, or do a search on the "origin of life.")

One perspective says that "life on Earth began more than 3 billion years ago, evolving from the most basic of microbes into a dazzling array of complexity over time. But how did the first organisms on the only known home to life in the universe develop from the primordial soup?" As the "7 Theories on the Origin of Life" article continues, the following seven theories are presented (labels added). It is noteworthy that some form of water is a component of all seven theories.

> **Lightning:** Electric sparks can generate amino acids and sugars from an atmosphere loaded with water, methane, ammonia and hydrogen… Lightning might have helped create the key building blocks of life on Earth in its early days.

> **Clay:** The first molecules of life might have met on clay… These surfaces might not only have concentrated these organic compounds together, but also helped organize them into patterns much like our genes do now.

> **Hydrothermal Vents:** The deep-sea vent theory suggests that life may have begun at submarine hydrothermal vents spewing key hydrogen-rich molecules. Their rocky nooks could then have concentrated these molecules together and provided mineral catalysts for critical reactions.

> **Ice:** Ice might have covered the oceans 3 billion years ago, as the sun was about a third less luminous than it is now, scientists say. This layer of ice, possibly hundreds of feet thick, might have protected fragile organic compounds in the water below from ultraviolet light and destruction from cosmic impacts.

> **RNA:** DNA and proteins need each other to form. They may have been helped by RNA, which can store information like

DNA, serve as an enzyme like proteins, and help create both DNA and proteins.... [and act] as an on-off switch for some genes. The question still remains how RNA got here in the first place.

Reactions: Life might have begun with smaller molecules interacting with each other in cycles of reactions. These might have been contained in simple capsules akin to cell membranes, and over time more complex molecules... could have evolved.

Panspermia: Perhaps life did not begin on Earth at all, but was brought here from elsewhere in space, a notion known as panspermia... Meteorites have been found on Earth that some researchers have controversially suggested brought microbes over here... Other scientists have even suggested that life might have hitchhiked on comets from other star systems. However, even if this concept were true, the question of how life began on Earth would then only change to how life began elsewhere in space.[57]

THE ORIGIN OF LIFE IS UNRESOLVED

Of the seven theories, the most popular one used to explain the origin of life on Earth is Panspermia: life was contained in icy comets or asteroids that came to Earth from outer space. This theory is popular because it suggests both life and water could have arrived on Earth at virtually the same time. However, even if comets or asteroids were the source of life on Earth, Panspermia does not explain the origin of that life found on the icy comets or asteroids in outer space. In other words, Panspermia deflects the problem regarding the origin of life away from Earth, but it does not solve the new problem regarding the origin of life in outer space.

How life began and whether it began on Earth or in outer space remains an open question. Secular scientists seem sure that life began as a prokaryote, but they are not sure how this primitive single-celled microorganism formed itself or where it came from. As indicated earlier, neither the Big Bang nor evolution addresses the origin of the prokaryote. The Big Bang is used to explain the formation of energy and matter (inorganic/nonliving), and evolution is used to explain how things evolved after the prokaryote (organic/living) had already appeared on Earth.

EVOLUTION ADDRESSES DIVERSITY, NOT ORIGIN

Although evolution does not deal with the origin of life, it treats this enigma as if it has been fully and completely resolved. In essence, life had to exist before it could begin to evolve. So, beginning with a primitive single-celled microorganism that already existed, the theory of evolution proposes this prokaryote increased in number and complexity through a gradual process of reproduction, mutation, combination, and selection. Scientists believe this explains the great diversity of living things on planet Earth, including all vegetation, plants, trees, living creatures, birds, sea creatures, livestock, creeping things, beasts, and people.

The theory of evolution rests upon the notion that, given enough time (billions of years), a primitive single-celled microorganism randomly evolved into everything else, including the most highly complex living things (human beings) that have ever existed on planet Earth. Evolution has not been proved, yet it is the theory regarding the diversity of life that is taught in public schools in America. The problem is, evolution is not presented as a theory, but as if it is a proven fact that is therefore true.

If evolution on such a broad scale is true, shouldn't there be credible evidence that living things are still evolving from one biological classification to another? Also, shouldn't there be evidence in the fossil record that conclusively demonstrates that living things evolved in the past? In other words, if the incomprehensible number of transitions took place, shouldn't a plethora of examples—of transitions in process from one biological classification to another—be preserved in sedimentary rock? If not a plethora, shouldn't there be at least some examples of such transitions that are not so speculative, and therefore more widely accepted by the scientific community?

1 GRAM OF DNA = 1,000,000,000 TERABYTES

Now, to get an idea of the degree of complexity that does exist in every living thing, let's look at DNA (deoxyribonucleic acid). DNA is contained in every cell of every living organism, from a prokaryote to people. It encodes and stores complex genetic instructions that are unique to its host. (Only identical twins share the same DNA.) The storage capacity of DNA is so incredible that Microsoft is purchasing DNA "to investigate the use of genetic material to store data. The data density of DNA is orders of magnitude higher than conventional storage systems, with 1 gram of DNA able to represent close to 1 billion terabytes (1 zettabyte) of data."[58] Since a typical computer today has about 1 terabyte of storage, 1 gram of DNA can be compared to 1 billion computers.

The complexity of human DNA as well as its capacity for storing and retrieving information is hard to imagine. What are the odds that human DNA—a powerful microscopic supercomputer with 1,000,000,000 terabytes of storage capacity—evolved by happenstance? Scientists say we don't see transitions because they happen gradually over a long period of time, but knowing what we know about the complexity of human DNA, is evolution of such magnitude even possible in an infinite amount of time? What is the probability that DNA occurred as a result of random transitions?

PROBABILITY IS A MEASURE OF THE ODDS

Probability is "the chance that a given event will occur."[59] To teach probability teachers often have students calculate the odds of a monkey just happening to type out the 30,557 words in William Shakespeare's play *Hamlet*. Well, the odds are so great it's hard to calculate and even harder to imagine. So—greatly simplifying the assignment—what are the odds of the monkey correctly typing the 6 letters that spell the word "Hamlet"? On a keyboard with 50 keys for letters, capitalization, and punctuation, "the chance of the monkey typing the word 'Hamlet' correctly is one in 15,625,000,000."[60]

The probability that six events (in this case, keystrokes) happened in a particular sequence by chance is very low. The reason is, odds increase exponentially with each added event. The more complex something is, the more unlikely it is to have happened by chance. Regardless of time, increased complexity quickly tips the scales from highly unlikely to virtually impossible. Could something as complex as DNA have occurred as a result of random transitions over the course of billions of years? Is it even possible if time weren't a factor? But if evolution is an exception to the odds of something happening by chance, is evolution an exception to the laws of physics as well?

THE SECOND LAW OF THERMODYNAMICS AND ENTROPY

An important principle in the science of physics is the Second Law of Thermodynamics. Vision Learning says, "The Second Law is commonly referred to as the Law of Increased Entropy. During the conversion of energy from one form to another... a portion becomes unusable as it increases disorder and randomness within the system."[61] Entropy is the measure of the disorder and randomness in a system. As energy and matter change in form, entropy increases, resulting in greater disorder and greater randomness.

Encyclopædia Britannica says this: "The principal deduction from the second law of thermodynamics... is that, when an isolated system makes a transition from one state to another, its entropy can never decrease."[62] In other words, natural processes in an isolated system—such as the universe—always result in an increase in disorder and randomness. "An isolated system does not exchange energy or matter with its surroundings,"[63] but energy and matter can change in form within the system. (The First Law of Thermodynamics "explains that energy cannot be created or destroyed, only transformed from one form to another."[64])

IMPECCABLE ORDER AND METICULOUS DESIGN

What we learn from physics is that natural processes do not result in a more meaningful order or design, yet throughout the universe both impeccable order and meticulous design are found everywhere and in everything. The design of a United States coin might help to illustrate the likelihood of a natural process resulting in order and design. If you closely examine the back of a Lincoln Memorial penny, you will observe a highly detailed image. Upon closer examination, you will even notice a tiny statue of Abraham Lincoln sitting on a chair between the center columns of the Lincoln Memorial.

Even though we may not be familiar with all the steps required to produce that copper penny, its unique characteristics tell us it was designed and manufactured. In fact, after artists collaborated on the coin's design and after a decision was made to make the penny out of copper, an eighteen-step process—in a very particular order—was required to produce it. In addition, the copper ore itself must go through eight stages before it is even purchased by the U.S. Mint. "These eight stages include: mining, grinding, concentrating, roasting, smelting, conversion, anode casting, and electro-refining."[65] Next, after the U.S. Mint buys the copper in coils that are 13 inches wide and 1,500 feet long, it puts the copper through ten stages of its own: blanking, annealing, washing, drying, upsetting, striking, inspecting, counting, bagging, and shipping.[66]

Now, the raw element copper (Cu) is found on Earth embedded in ore, but would you believe someone who said that a copper penny formed itself from the ore as a result of natural processes? Does the credibility change if that process was said to have taken a billion years or even an infinite amount of time? This same principle—natural processes do not result in a more meaningful order or design—applies to everything in our world, especially living things.

A PROKARYOTE'S DESIGN IS INTRICATE AND COMPLEX

The smallest living microorganism that scientists have been able to observe—a prokaryote—is a single cell, yet its design is still infinitely more intricate and complex than the detailed image on a penny that must go through eighteen stages before we are able to hold it in our hand. (Furthermore, a penny cannot reproduce itself or become a nickel, dime, quarter, half dollar, or dollar coin.) Would you believe someone who said energy and matter (nonliving) became a prokaryote (living) through natural processes?

Secular scientists say that after the nonliving became living, this primitive single-celled microorganism began to evolve into other living things, exhibiting progressively more elaborate designs with ever increasing complexity. As we asked earlier, if it is true that all living things evolved over billions of years, wouldn't there have been a plethora of transitions, and wouldn't evidence of those transitions exist throughout the fossil record, and wouldn't we be able to observe ongoing transitions—between biological ranks—of living things today? If such transitions occurred, why is there continuous debate—even among secular scientists—about the credibility of the few fossil and bone fragments used to support evolution?

HUMAN BODY SYSTEMS, ORGANS, AND TISSUES

Now let's consider the exquisite order, microscopic detail, and meticulous design of the human body. Encyclopædia Britannica says the human body is "the physical substance of the human organism, composed of living cells and extracellular materials and organized into tissues, organs, and systems."[67] A fully functioning human body requires an integrated network of body systems all working simultaneously, and each body system further requires multiple organs and tissues all working simultaneously. If one single tissue or organ is not functioning properly, a body system is affected; and if one single body system is not functioning properly, the entire body is affected.

Because the body is such a highly integrated network, to function properly, every tissue, organ, and body system needs to function at the same time. So did each tissue, organ, and body system randomly develop at the same time and then randomly begin to function as a system? If not, did each tissue and organ randomly develop independently, then did each tissue and organ randomly combine with the other tissues and organs to form each body system, and then did each body system randomly combine with other body systems to form a fully functioning human body? Scientists say it took human beings 3.8 billion years to evolve from a prokaryote, but—again—is this level of design and degree of coordination possible even if time were infinite?

Adding to the complexity, tissues and organs can be shared by multiple body systems. Figure 2.15 is a chart of the twelve different body systems and sixty-four of the different organs and tissues that comprise those body systems.[68] It is not a complete list of all of the tissues and organs used by each body system, and although tissues and organs can be shared by multiple systems, they are only listed once within their primary system.

BODY SYSTEM	PRIMARY TISSUES AND ORGANS OF EACH BODY SYSTEM
Circulatory	Arteries, capillaries, heart, veins
Digestive	Esophagus, gall bladder, large intestine, liver, rectum, small intestine, stomach
Endocrine	Adrenals, hypothalamus, pancreas, parathyroid, pineal, pituitary, thyroid
Immune	Adenoids, bone marrow, thymus
Integumentary	Hair, nails, oil glands, skin, sweat glands
Lymphatic	Nodes, vessels, spleen, tonsils
Muscular	Joints, muscles, tendons, tissues
Nervous	Brain, nerves, sensory organs, spinal cord
Reproductive (M)	Epididymis, penis, prostate, scrotum, testes, vas deferens
Reproductive (F)	Cervix, fallopian tubes, mammary glands, ovaries, uterus, vagina
Respiratory	Bronchi, diaphragm, larynx, lungs, nose, pharynx, trachea
Skeletal	Bones, cartilage, ligaments
Urinary	Bladder, kidneys, ureters, urethra

FIGURE 2.15 Human body systems, organs, and tissues

THE EYE HAS THIRTEEN ANCILLARY PARTS

As outlined in Figure 2.15, each organ and tissue has a dedicated purpose and function and must work simultaneously with other organs and tissues within its particular body system. In addition, some organs are comprised of ancillary parts. Consider that the sensory organs—within the nervous system—are used to see, smell, taste, touch, and hear. Each sense requires numerous ancillary parts all working simultaneously. The eye, for example, cannot see without these thirteen major ancillary parts all working simultaneously: the aqueous humor, choroid, ciliary muscle, cones, cornea, iris, lens, optic nerve, pupil, sclera, retina, rods, and vitreous humor.[69] If one ancillary part of the eye is not functioning properly, the sense of sight is adversely affected.

Did all thirteen ancillary parts of the eye randomly develop at the same time and then randomly begin to function as an organ system to enable the eye to see? If not, did each ancillary part randomly develop itself, then did each ancillary part randomly combine with the other twelve, and then did all thirteen ancillary parts randomly begin to function as an organ system that resulted in an eye that is able to see? Did all the ancillary parts necessary for the senses of smell, taste, touch, and hearing also randomly develop and then randomly combine? And did each of these parts form independent organ systems to enable a nose to smell, a tongue to taste, a hand to feel, and an ear to hear?

THE MALE AND FEMALE REPRODUCTIVE SYSTEMS

In addition to body systems, organs, tissues, and ancillary parts all working together in a fully functioning human being, two distinct sexes are required for reproduction (Figure 2.15). Biologists classify the sexes of human beings by the pairing of the sex chromosomes: XY for male and XX for female. This pairing happens at the moment of fertilization and determines whether the person is male or female. Encyclopædia Britannica says, "The differences between a male and a female are genetically determined by the chromosomes that each possesses in the nuclei of the cells. Once the genetic sex has been determined, there normally follows a succession of changes that will result, finally, in the development of an adult male or female."[70]

These chromosome pairs determine the distinct and different reproductive systems for male and female human beings, and the combination of those two systems enable human beings to multiply. Encyclopædia Britannica says the human reproductive system is an "organ system by which humans reproduce and bear live offspring... For this biological process to be carried out, certain organs and structures are required in both the male and the female."[71] Human reproduction requires both a mature male (to produce the sperm) and a mature female (to produce the egg).

Helping to remind us of the need for a mature male and mature female for reproduction is to pose this age-old question: "Which came first, the chicken or the egg?" The answer cannot be a single chicken or a single egg because it is impossible for a single chicken or a single egg to reproduce itself. In order to produce baby chicks, both a mature female hen and a mature male rooster are required to come together to produce eggs that develop and hatch male and female baby chicks.

DEVELOPMENT AND DIVISION OF THE SEXES

This requirement of a mature male and a mature female for reproduction applies to a broad spectrum of living creatures on land, in the skies, and in the seas, including some types of vegetation. There is no disputing the fact that two different sexes exist; the question is when those sexes appeared. Did both sexes evolve at the same time in one body and then separate into male and female? Or did each sex evolve independently with distinct and different but complementary parts?

This question as to whether the sexes evolved together and then split or each sex evolved independently applies to every branch on evolution's Tree of Life—from a prokaryote to people. Again, male and female sexes exist in a broad spectrum of living things. If a living thing evolved with both sexes, when did it separate into male and female? If two living things evolved separately as male and female, when did they develop their complementary reproductive systems and find each other?

CELLS, DNA, AND NUCLEOTIDES

Every part of the body (skin, bones, organs, muscles, blood, etc.) is comprised of a network of cells that is intricately designed to serve a specific purpose and function. The adult body is estimated to have 37.2 trillion cells.[72] In addition, Encyclopædia Britannica says "there are some 200 different types of cells in the body."[73] Furthermore, "virtually every single cell in the body contains a complete copy of the approximately 3 billion DNA base pairs, or letters."[74] DNA is the genetic blueprint that provides crucial instructions that enable the body to automatically repair and replace old cells that die with new cells that perform the same function.

DNA is unique to each particular individual (and their identical twin). And each individual's DNA can be distinguished from the DNA of every other living thing on planet Earth (including vegetation, living creatures, and other human beings). DNA is an organized network of nucleotides, and nucleotides are comprised of a molecule of sugar, a molecule of phosphoric acid, and a base (adenine, thymine, guanine, or cytosine). DNA's double helix structure—which resembles a twisted ladder—is made up of two strands of nucleotides held together by hydrogen bonds. As mentioned previously, 1 gram of DNA can store and retrieve an estimated 1 billion terabytes of coded information. Before we go even smaller into particle physics, remember that evolution cannot explain the origin of the DNA contained in the first single-celled microorganism.

ATOMS, PROTONS, NEUTRONS, ELECTRONS, QUARKS, AND LEPTONS

Every cell within the human body is comprised of even smaller particles called atoms. (Atoms exist in every cell of every living and nonliving thing on Earth.) Every atom has a dedicated purpose and function, and every atom is comprised of a unique system of component parts that all must function simultaneously. The three parts of every atom are protons, neutrons, and electrons. These three parts function as a system when the negatively charged electrons orbit a core nucleus of positively charged protons and electrically neutral neutrons. The atom is the antithesis of the universe: just as the universe is unimaginably vast, an atom is unimaginably small.

Consider the exaggerated proportions used by the European Organization for Nuclear Research (CERN) to illustrate an atom's size: "If the protons and the neutrons were 10 centimeters (3.9 inches) across, then the quarks and electrons would be less than 0.01 millimeters (.0004 inches) in size and the entire atom would be about 10 kilometers (6.2 miles). More than

99.99% of the atom is empty space." Regarding quarks and electrons (leptons), CERN goes on to say, "Quarks and leptons are the building blocks of matter, and forces act through carrier particles exchanged between the particles of matter."[75]

At the present time, quarks (discovered in 1968) and leptons (discovered in 1936) are the very smallest subatomic particles of matter that scientists have been able to observe. Even though these particles are exceedingly small, scientists have been able to identify six types of quarks and six types of leptons.[76] Every one of the six types of quarks (up, down, charm, strange, top, and bottom) has a dedicated purpose and function, and every one of the six types of leptons (electron, electron neutrino, muon, muon neutrino, tau, and tau neutrino) has a dedicated purpose and function. Someday scientists may even discover that quarks and leptons have component parts that all function properly and simultaneously.

RANDOM TRANSITIONS INCREASING IN COMPLEXITY

In summary, from the smallest subatomic particles to a fully functioning human body, we find exquisite order, microscopic detail, and meticulous design. The relevant question is not whether order, detail, and design exist—we ourselves are evidence that they do—but how did this happen? Evolution says the human body resulted from a gradual process of reproduction, mutation, combination, and selection. Can the fortuitous alignment of cells in the human body be explained as random transitions of ever increasing complexity? Consider these supposedly random transitions that eventually resulted in a human being:

Quarks and leptons developed as elementary building blocks.

Protons, neutrons, and electrons arranged themselves into atoms.

Atoms organized themselves into elements and chemicals.

Elements and chemicals formed a nucleotide.

Two nucleotides bonded together to form DNA.

DNA contained itself within a protective shell called a cell.

A single cell of DNA became the first living thing (prokaryote).

The prokaryote evolved into different multicellular organisms.

Multicellular organisms developed organs and tissues.

Organs and tissues arranged themselves into body systems.

Body systems began to function together in one physical body.

THE HUMAN MIND IS A MYSTERY

Evolution maintains that human beings defied astronomical odds and randomly evolved from disorder to order, from randomness to design, and from a prokaryote to people who developed into the male and the female sexes somewhere in the process. This scenario might explain the biology of the human body, but it does not explain the existence of the human mind and emotions. Our ability to learn, think, reason, understand, create, express emotions, and speak cannot be explained by biomechanics. Evolution cannot explain the *how* or the *why* of the human mind or emotions.

Needless to say, every human being has an absolutely unique and exceedingly complex mind, and it is the human mind that sets people apart from every other living thing on Earth. Our minds enable us human beings to compile data, evaluate facts, make decisions, and form opinions. Everybody, for instance, seems to have an opinion regarding the origin of life on this planet. It is up to each individual to weigh the facts in his or her own mind before deciding what to believe. The problem is, most people will never hear all the facts necessary to make an informed decision.

In summary, neither the theory of the Big Bang nor evolution addresses the origin of life, nor are there any fully accepted scientific theories that align the Big Bang and evolution. But now that we know what evolution says about the development of living things on Earth, let's compare it to what the Bible says about living things on Earth. In the account of living things—like the account of the universe—the biblical chronology of *what* happened *when* cannot be reconciled with the scientific chronology (Figure 2.14).

THE BIBLE'S DIVERSITY

ALL LIVING THINGS CAME FROM EARTH'S SOIL

The Bible says God made the first living things from the ground on the same day that He gathered the waters together to form the Seas and reveal Earth's dry land (Day 3). In fact, the Bible says that it was "out of the ground" that God made: all vegetation, plants, and trees (Day 3); every winged creature that flies in the air (Day 5); and every living creature and creeping thing that moves on the land (Day 6). Genesis 2:9 and 19 say: *Out of the ground the* LORD *God made to spring up every tree that is pleasant to the sight and good for food… [and] out of the ground the* LORD *God had formed every beast of the field and every bird of the heavens.*

In addition to these living things, the Bible also says God made human beings "from the ground" (Day 6): *The* LORD *God formed the man of dust from the ground and breathed into his nostrils the breath of life, and the man became a living creature* (Genesis 2:7). In essence, three days after revealing Earth's dry land (Day 3), God molded the first human being (Adam) from that dry land and breathed life into him (Day 6). In fact, scientific evidence supports the biblical account that the human body is composed of elements found in the soil on Earth as well as in the atmosphere. (See the online article "Building Blocks of Life" with its periodic table that identifies the major elements found in the human body.[77])

"ACCORDING TO THEIR KINDS"

So, according to the Bible, life began when God made every living thing from Earth's dry land. Now let's look at the development and the multiplication of living things inhabiting Earth from a biblical perspective. The Bible indicates that every living thing that God made was created to be self-replicating. In other words, God designed every living thing—on Day 3, Day 5, and Day 6—with the naturally ability to reproduce its own kind.

Vegetation, plants, and trees: On Day 3, *God said, "Let the earth sprout vegetation, plants yielding seed, and fruit trees bearing fruit in which is their* *seed, each according to its kind, on the earth." And it was so. The earth brought forth vegetation, plants yielding seed according to their own kinds, and trees bearing fruit in which is their seed, each according to its kind.* (Genesis 1:11-12). God designed the vegetation, plants, and trees that He created with the natural ability to reproduce their own kind. These two verses repeat the phrase "according to their own kinds" (also "its kind") three times, the repetition indicating emphasis.

Living creatures, birds, and sea creatures: On Day 5, *God created the great sea creatures and every living creature that moves, with which the waters swarm, according to their kinds, and every winged bird according to its kind. And God saw that it was good. And God blessed them, saying, "Be fruitful and multiply and fill the waters in the seas, and let birds multiply on the earth"* (Genesis 1:21-22). God designed the living creatures, birds, and sea creatures that He created with the natural ability to reproduce their own kind. These two verses repeat the phrase "according to their kinds" (also "its kind") two times, the repetition again indicating emphasis.

Livestock, creeping things, and beasts: On Day 6 (part 1), *God said, "Let the earth bring forth living creatures according to their kinds—livestock and creeping things and beasts of the earth according to their kinds." And it was so. And God made the beasts of the earth according to their kinds and the livestock according to their kinds, and everything that creeps on the ground according to its kind* (Genesis 1:24-25). God designed the livestock, creeping things, and beasts of the earth that He created with the natural ability to reproduce their own kind. These two verses repeat the phrase "according to their kinds" (also "its kind") five times, yet again indicating emphasis.

Human beings: On Day 6 (part 2), *God created man in his own image, in the image of God he created him; male and female he created them. And God blessed them. And God said to them, "Be fruitful and multiply and fill the earth and subdue it, and have dominion over the fish of the sea and over the birds of the heavens and over every living thing that moves on the earth"* (Genesis 1:27-28). Although "according to their kinds" is not repeated here in reference to human beings, the current world population—about 7.5

billion people[78]—is evidence that human beings have the natural ability to reproduce their own kind.

CREATED MATURE WITH THE ABILITY TO REPRODUCE

Remember, if it is true that God created everything from nothing, then absolutely anything is possible. Thus, whether we're talking about vegetation, plants, trees, living creatures, birds, sea creatures, livestock, creeping things, beasts, or people, the Bible says God designed every living thing that He created with the natural ability to reproduce its own kind. We cannot ignore the fact that "according to their kinds" (also "own kinds" and "its kind") is clearly repeated ten times in a span of just eight verses.

Although not directly stated—since only mature things are able to reproduce their own kind—the creation account implies that God created everything mature. Only mature vegetation, plants, and trees can produce similar vegetation, plants, and trees. Only mature living creatures, birds, and sea creatures can produce similar living creatures, birds, and sea creatures. Only mature livestock, creeping things, and beasts can produce similar livestock, creeping things, and beasts. And only mature male and female human beings can produce similar male and female human beings.

IF NOT CREATED MATURE, THEN WHAT?

The only natural, logical, and reasonable assumption based on a plain reading of Genesis is that God created a mature Adam and then took one of Adam's ribs to form a mature Eve: *"the rib that the LORD God had taken from the man he made into a woman"* (Genesis 2:22). Although the Bible does not say God created Adam and Eve as mature human beings, any other conclusion is problematic because God commanded them to "be fruitful and multiply and fill the earth." From a biblical perspective, there are no other viable alternatives to explain the existence of human beings on this planet. Again, the only logical conclusion is that God created two mature human beings: one male and one female.

If Adam and Eve were not mature when God created them, at what life stage could they have been? Major problems are encountered when we consider any other life stage as a possibility. Every alternative actually presents more problems than solutions. For example, how would Adam and Eve have survived in the garden if God had created them as a sperm and an egg, or as zygotes (sperm-fertilized eggs), or embryos, or infants, or toddlers, or young children? Survival at any of these life stages would not be possible without a massive amount of assistance, and nothing of the sort is mentioned.

EACH KIND CONTAINED A COMPREHENSIVE GENOME

So it appears that God created Adam and Eve as the first mature male and female pair of human beings. In the same way, it appears that God also made a mature pair—male and female—of other living creatures as well. Although God did not create anything after the first six days, every original pair that He initially created was capable of producing a wide range of similar *types* within its particular *kind*. Biblical taxonomy (classification) is drastically different from today's scientific taxonomy. However, a biblical *kind* seems most similar to the biological rank *family* or *genus*, and a *type* seems most similar to the biological rank *species*.

When God commanded the living things He created in Genesis 1 to be fruitful, multiply, and fill Earth "according to their own kinds," His words imply that every living thing that has ever existed can be traced back to a particular kind that God created in the beginning. Technically speaking, this means each initial created *kind* (family/genus) contained a comprehensive genome that enabled it to produce every *type* (species) within its own kind. Consider this definition from the field of molecular biology:

A genome contains all of a living organism's DNA. It is the complete set of genetic instructions for building, running, and maintaining that organism. Virtually every single cell in the body carries a complete copy of all of the DNA that makes up the genome. All living things, from bacteria to plants to animals, have genomes.[79]

HUMAN BEINGS ARE A CREATED KIND

This comprehensive genome of each created *kind* is the same throughout its own *kind*, and this includes human beings. Adam and Eve possessed a comprehensive genome that enabled them to produce every race (*type*) of human beings (*kind*) that has ever existed. Technically speaking, every race of the human being kind possesses a genome with almost identical DNA: "In any two humans, 99.9% of their DNA is identical. However, the entire set of genetic instructions is so large that the 0.1% variation allows for millions of possible differences. This tiny fraction of DNA where variations occur leads to the enormous diversity that makes each of us unique."[80]

At the same time, the human genome is different from the genome of every other *kind*. For example, human being kinds have a genome that is different from Equidae (horses, donkeys, zebras). And Equidae have a genome that is different from Canidae (wolves, dogs, jackals, foxes). And Canidae have a genome that is different from Ursidae (bears, giant pandas). And Ursidae have a genome that is different from Felidae (cats, lions, cheetahs, leopards). And Felidae have a genome that is different from... This distinction—the genome of each kind is unique—is replicated throughout every living thing.

THE ARK AT THE TIME OF THE FLOOD

Understanding biblical kinds may help to explain what happened at the time of the flood. God said to Noah "*of every living thing of all flesh, you shall bring two of every sort into the ark to keep them alive with you. They shall be male and female*" (Genesis 6:19). To execute His plan to preserve a pair of each and every kind before the deluge began, God gave Noah instructions to build a three-deck ark with an estimated capacity of 630 standard 40-foot rectangular shipping containers. This cargo capacity is based on the measurements specified in the Bible: 300 cubits in length, 50 cubits in width, and 30 cubits in height.

The length of a cubit in the historical records varies. It is generally believed to be the distance from the elbow to the tip of the finger. The biblical cubit is most likely the Egyptian royal cubit that measures 52.3 centimeters

(20.6 inches).[81] More conservative dimensions for a cubit measure 45.7 centimeters (18 inches).[82] Based these dimensions, the ark was approximately 137 meters (450 feet) long, 23 meters (75 feet) wide, and 14 meters (45 feet) high.

KINDS AT THE TIME OF THE FLOOD

Though massive, the ark would not have been large enough to preserve every pair of every *type* (species) that would have existed at that time. But the ark would have been able to hold—and therefore preserve—pairs of each and every *kind* (family/genus), especially if each pair were young and still small in stature. (Remember, each *kind* or family/genus on the ark would have contained a comprehensive genome with the ability to produce various *types* or species after the flood.)

The identical terminology used to describe God's *creation* of kinds in Genesis 1 is used to describe God's *preservation* of kinds at the time of the flood in Genesis 6. God instructed Noah to bring into the ark a male and female pair of each and every kind: *"Of the birds according to their kinds, and of the animals according to their kinds, of every creeping thing of the ground, according to its kind"* (Genesis 6:20). Here, the same phrase "according to their kinds" (also "its kind") is repeated three times in the same verse. And just as the repetition of "kinds" indicated emphasis at the time of Creation, the repetition here indicates emphasis at the time of the flood. In other words, a male and female pair of every kind (not species) of bird, animal, and creeping thing made it onto the ark with Noah, his wife, their three sons, and their wives.

LIVING THINGS ARE DIVERSE AND SIMILAR

It is impossible to factually prove what happened in the beginning and therefore confirm Creation (or evolution), but certain aspects of the creation account are replicated every moment of every day: living things produce more living things. Although reproduction alone does not factually prove what happened at the very beginning, it is at least consistent with the biblical account that repeatedly states that God created kinds to "be fruitful and multiply and fill the earth" (also "the waters") according to their own kinds.

In addition, consider as overwhelming evidence the exquisite order, microscopic detail, and meticulous design of every living thing. This reality is consistent with the biblical view of the origin of life: God was orderly and organized in His creation process, He paid attention to the microscopic details, and everything He created exhibits meticulous design. Living things are diverse because God made multiple different kinds (families/genera) under the broad classifications of vegetation, birds, sea creatures, and land creatures. At the same time, living things are similar because God gave each particular kind the ability to produce various types (species) within its own kind.

THE BIBLE'S KINDS VS. EVOLUTION

Now that we have looked at both views of the origin, development, and diversity of living things, it is clear that the Bible's kinds (God-created diversity) cannot be reconciled with the theory of evolution (serendipity-created diversity). The only way the two views can be merged is if Genesis 1 does not mean what it says but is open to interpretation. The problem is, extremely detailed and specific language is consistently used, and it is repeated over and over for emphasis. Under these circumstances, if the Bible does not mean what it says, then what it says does not mean a thing.

Just like the Bible and the Big Bang views of the universe, the Bible and evolution are contradictory in regard to substance as well as timing (Figure 2.14). Rather than explain the origin of life, evolution merely states that life began 3,800,000,000 years ago with a primitive single-celled microorganism that formed itself on Earth (or elsewhere in the universe) and subsequently evolved into every diverse form of life that has ever existed. On the other hand, the Bible does explain the origin of life: it says about 6,000 years ago God made different kinds from Earth's dry land and gave each and every kind the natural ability to reproduce according to its own kind.

THE REASON EVOLUTION IS SO DOMINANT

As mentioned previously, evolution is the only theory about living things taught in America's public schools. This is the result of a Supreme Court ruling that teaching religious ideology—such as Creation—in science classrooms is prohibited under the Establishment Clause of the First Amendment to the U.S. Constitution.[83] Since only evolution may be taught, most children will only hear this one explanation of how living things came to be. That would still be acceptable if some of the theory's prominent weaknesses (mentioned earlier) were discussed and not ignored. Instead, evolution is generally presented as if it is based on proven facts that are true.

No wonder surveys indicate that as students advance through each grade level in school, their belief in evolution increases at the same rate that their belief in Creation—if there ever was any—decreases. Since the theory of evolution is so prevalent in public school classrooms during a child's formative years, it is no surprise that students continue to embrace this understanding after they graduate. Given the school system and its curriculum, it is also no surprise that evolution is the prevailing worldview today. While this may be a reason most people think evolution explains the diversity of life, most are not aware that the theory has a myriad of unresolved issues. Although these issues are not publicized, any one of them casts doubt on the entire theory.

THE BIBLE VS. SECULAR SCIENCE

TODAY'S WORLDVIEW IS INCOMPATIBLE WITH THE BIBLE

The secular worldview begins with the Big Bang of a singularity that exploded and produced nonliving things, which became the universe, galaxies, solar system, and Earth. This secular worldview continues with the evolution of all living things from a primitive single-celled microorganism that formed on Earth or came to Earth from elsewhere in the universe; that went through a gradual process of reproduction, mutation, combination, and selection; that developed into sea creatures, vegetation, land creatures, and birds with male and female sexes; that evolved into human beings with an exceedingly complex mind that has the ability to learn, think, reason, understand, and express emotions.

This is not only the prevailing worldview, but because these secular theories are so pervasive, it is also the view held by many who read the Bible. Even so, while two people reading the Bible may not always agree on how to interpret certain passages, it is hard to imagine how an individual can reconcile the theory of the Big Bang with Genesis 1, which says God formed Earth before He formed the universe. And it's hard to imagine how an individual can reconcile the theory of evolution with Genesis 1, where the statement that God "created" or "made" everything "according to their kinds" (also "own kinds" or "its kind") appears ten times.

FAITH IN SOMEONE, SOMETHING, OR A PROCESS

Any discussion regarding the inaugural *shabua*-days is incomplete without an examination of the six days of Creation. And any discussion regarding the six days of Creation is incomplete without an examination of both the Big Bang and evolution. What we have learned from this examination is that there does not seem to be any way to reconcile either the Big Bang or evolution with the Bible. In other words, the Big Bang and evolution are incompatible with the biblical account of Creation. Despite the overwhelming conflicts between the Bible and secular science, these different perspectives have one aspect in common. Belief in Creation, belief in the Big Bang, and belief in evolution all require *faith*.

A general dictionary definition of *faith* is the "firm belief in something for which there is no proof."[84] Creation requires faith in Some*one*: God created everything (the universe and all living things) in six days and gave all living things the natural ability to reproduce their own kind. The Big Bang requires faith in some*thing*: the explosion of a singularity 13.8 billion years ago was the origin of the universe and everything in it. Evolution requires faith in a *process*: every diverse and complex living thing evolved from a primitive single-celled microorganism whose origin 3.8 billion years ago—on Earth or elsewhere in the universe—cannot be explained.

SHABUA-DAYS HAVE A MEANING AND PURPOSE

In conclusion, the first chapter in the Bible describes each of the six days of Creation, a finite period of time that the Bible calls "the beginning." Although there is disagreement regarding the interpretation of "day" in Genesis 1, there is no disputing the fact that there are six of them, and each of them ends in an identical way: "and there was evening and there was morning." The six days of Creation in Genesis 1 are immediately followed by a 7th and final day of rest in Genesis 2. This complete time period of seven establishes the inaugural *shabua* in an interval of days that we call *shabua*-days.

Despite the conflict with the Big Bang and evolution, and despite the fact that some believe the word *day* in Genesis 1 is open to interpretation, everything written in the Bible has meaning and purpose. The inaugural *shabua*-days establishes a method that is used to mark time; it sets the precedent for every subsequent *shabua* (expressed or implied; either days or years); and it is used repeatedly in Bible pattern and prophecy. Beginning in this book—and continuing in the sequel *Shabua Years*—you will learn the important role that *shabua* has in our understanding of God's past, present, and future plan for all mankind.

THE WORD OF GOD HAS BEEN PRESERVED

If it is true that God created, the length of time it took Him to create might seem irrelevant, but it is not. God chose to create for six days and rest on the 7th and final day of the *shabua*, that is why those words were written, that is why those words have been preserved, and that is why we are able to read them today. As Jesus promised: "*Truly, I say to you, until heaven and earth pass away, not an iota, not a dot, will pass from the Law until all is accomplished*" (Matthew 5:18). *Shabua* has been an integral part of God's plan from the very beginning, and it will continue to be an integral part of God's plan until the very end.

In the next chapter we will examine other instances where the Bible uses *shabua*-days to mark time. This discussion will also include ways in which the Bible consistently and repeatedly uses *shabua*-days in pattern and prophecy. In addition, we will take a closer look at the Hebrew word *Shabbat*, which is translated as *Sabbath* in English. Since *Shabbat* (Sabbath) is derived from *shabath*—the word used for to "cease/rest" on the 7th and final day of the inaugural *shabua*-days—it naturally has a very similar meaning. Furthermore, you will also learn that the Sabbath uniquely, specifically, and exclusively involves the people of Israel.

CHAPTER 3

A BIBLICAL WEDDING, MANNA, AND THE FOURTH COMMANDMENT

A *shabua* is a complete time period of seven that includes six intervals of work or activity followed by a 7th and final interval of rest. The overall span of time covered in Genesis 1 and 2 is widely disputed, but there is no disputing the fact that the Bible consistently and repeatedly calls that interval of time "days." Accordingly, this first *shabua* cycle is a complete time period of seven days, which we call *shabua*-days. Thus the *shabua*-days precedent was established. As indicated in chapter 1, a pattern is established only when a precedent is consistently repeated.

Nothing in Genesis 1 or 2 explains or implies how often—or even if—this precedent is to be repeated. The Bible simply reports the things that God specifically did during those first seven days. Genesis 1 specifies what God created during the first six days. Genesis 2 indicates that God finished His work and rested on the 7th and final day, the day He blessed and made holy. The *shabua*-days precedent of six days of work or activity followed by a 7th and final day of rest is not repeated until Genesis 29, where it provides the framework for a biblical wedding. In order to establish the context of that wedding, a brief overview of the book of Genesis is helpful.

A BIBLICAL WEDDING

ABRAHAM, ISAAC, AND JACOB

The first eleven chapters of Genesis span a 2,083-year period that begins in the year of Creation and concludes with the death of Abram's father, Terah, in the city of Haran in the land of Aram. When Terah died, God called Abram to leave his home and relatives in Aram and go to the land of Canaan. Abram's act of faith and obedience marked a turning point in God's plan of redemption, and God changed his name from *Abram* ("exalted father") to *Abraham* ("father of a multitude"). The last thirty-nine chapters of Genesis chronicle the sojourning of Abraham, of his son Isaac, and of his grandson Jacob. The Bible often refers to these three great Hebrew men of God as the patriarchs or fathers of the nation of Israel. Genesis concludes with an account of Jacob, his twelve sons, and their children and grandchildren dwelling in the land of Egypt.

Genesis also tells of a special covenant that God made with Abraham, a covenant that God affirmed with Abraham's son Isaac as well as with Isaac's son Jacob. On the occasion that God affirmed the covenant with Jacob, God changed his name from *Jacob* ("supplanter") to *Israel* ("God prevails"). After that, the physical descendants of Abraham through Isaac and Jacob (Israel) are variously referred to as *the children of Israel, the people of Israel,* or simply *the Israelites.* Each patriarch sojourned (lived like a nomad without a permanent home) in various places, including the land of Canaan. (The name of the land was not changed to Israel until after the people of Israel conquered the land, and that conquest did not begin until after Moses died.)

JACOB SERVED SEVEN YEARS FOR RACHEL

One of the places that the patriarch Jacob sojourned was Haran, the place where his grandfather Abraham had lived before going to Canaan. Naturally, many of Jacob's relatives still lived there, including his Uncle Laban (the brother of Jacob's mother, Rebekah). A love story begins in Genesis 29: *Now Laban had two daughters. The name of the older was Leah, and the name of the younger was Rachel.... Jacob loved Rachel. And he said, "I will serve you seven years for your younger daughter Rachel." Laban said, "It is better that I give her to you than that I should give her to any other man; stay with me"* (vv. 16, 18-19). Jacob stayed with Laban and served him because of his deep love for Rachel.

After faithfully serving Laban seven years, *Jacob said to Laban, "Give me my wife that I may go in to her, for my time is completed." So Laban gathered together all the people of the place and made a feast* (Genesis 29:21-22). That evening/night—when the bride would have been veiled and it would have been dark—Laban took his older daughter, Leah, to the room where Jacob would have been waiting for Rachel. (A bride and groom would not have had a physical relationship prior to their wedding day.) *And in the morning, behold, it was Leah! And Jacob said to Laban, "What is this you have done to me? Did I not serve with you for Rachel? Why then have you deceived me?"* (v. 25).

COMPLETE THE WEEK = COMPLETE THE SHABUA

Laban had an answer for Jacob: *"It is not so done in our country, to give the younger before the firstborn. Complete the week of this one"* (Genesis 29:26-27). The statement "complete the week of this one" has nothing to do with Jacob serving Laban before or after the wedding. The Hebrew word translated as "week" in verse 27 is *shabua*. On the morning of the first day of Jacob's surprise wedding to Leah (the wedding ceremony took place earlier that same day—biblical days begin in the evening), when Jacob realized that Laban had deceived him and protested, Laban commanded Jacob to "complete the *shabua* of Leah." Although Jacob had already completed the agreed-upon seven years of service for Rachel, Laban added two new conditions before he gave Rachel to Jacob to be his wife. The first condition required Jacob to complete the remaining six days of Leah's wedding *shabua*-days.

The second condition required Jacob to agree to serve Laban for an additional seven years: *"Complete the [shabua] of [Leah], and we will give you [Rachel] also in return for serving me another seven years"* (v. 27). The additional seven years of service did not begin until after Jacob completed Leah's wedding *shabua*-days and was then given Rachel. Verses 28 and 30 say that after Jacob completed Leah's *shabua*-days, *then Laban gave him his daughter Rachel to be his wife.*... *So Jacob went in to Rachel also, and he loved Rachel more than Leah, and served Laban for another seven years.* Notice that it was not until after Jacob married Rachel that he "served Laban for another seven years." (It appears that Laban required seven years of service for each daughter, seven years were served before the two weddings, and seven years were served after the two weddings.) The following is a synopsis of the weddings of Leah and Rachel in Genesis 29:

> Jacob completed seven years of service to marry Laban's younger daughter, Rachel.
>
> Laban deceived Jacob by giving him his older daughter, Leah, instead of Rachel.
>
> Jacob protested about the deception on the first day of Leah's wedding *shabua*-days.
>
> Laban told Jacob to complete the remainder of Leah's wedding *shabua*-days.
>
> After Jacob completed Leah's wedding *shabua*-days, Laban gave Rachel to Jacob.
>
> Rachel's wedding *shabua*-days immediately followed Leah's wedding *shabua*-days.
>
> Jacob served Laban for seven additional years after Rachel's wedding *shabua*-days.

A BIBLICAL WEDDING IS A SHABUA

Did you know that a biblical wedding is a *shabua*? The Bible uses the term *shabua* in Genesis 29:27-28 to describe Leah's wedding without specifying the interval of time. Therefore, it must be determined from the context. Since it is inconceivable that any wedding celebration would span seven years, it is obvious that Leah's wedding *shabua* is a complete time period of seven days. (Confirmation that a biblical wedding lasts seven days is evident in the marriage celebration of Samson and Delilah in Judges 14:10-20.) The concept of *shabua*-days—introduced in Genesis 1 and 2 (precedent)—is repeated here in Genesis 29 (pattern).

The prophetic significance and relevance of a biblical wedding is incredible. In addition, many of today's wedding traditions and practices are rooted in the Bible. However, further examination of this topic is beyond the scope of this book. Biblical weddings will be covered in future publications. For now, it will suffice to simply know that a biblical wedding is a complete time period of seven days, and it incorporates each distinct element of a *shabua*.

MANNA

JACOB AND HIS 69 DESCENDANTS

The next reference to *shabua*-days comes in the book of Exodus. Before examining that narrative, we need the context from Genesis. After the deaths of Abraham and Isaac, there was a severe famine throughout the region. At that time, Jacob had sixty-nine children, grandchildren, and great-grandchildren by his four wives: Leah, Rachel, Bilhah, and Zilpah. Sixty-six of Jacob's descendants were sojourning in the land of Canaan when the famine began; the other three were already in Egypt. After exhausting their food supply in Canaan, the sixty-six fled with Jacob to Egypt where they were united with the other three. Although the seven-year famine also affected Egypt, that nation was able to not only survive but actually thrive because they had stored up massive quantities of grain during a seven-year bounty.

The book of Genesis closes with the Pharaoh of Egypt treating Jacob and his descendants generously, allowing them to settle in the extremely fertile Nile Delta region called Goshen. The book of Exodus picks up there, and in the first chapter we learn that Jacob and his twelve sons all died in Egypt without ever returning to the land of Canaan. The Pharaoh who had shown favor to God's people had also died. Nevertheless, the descendants of Jacob remained in Egypt, and the *people of Israel were fruitful and increased greatly; they multiplied and grew exceedingly strong, so that the land was filled with them* (Exodus 1:7). When a new Pharaoh came to power, he was very troubled by the enormous—and increasing—number of Israelites inhabiting his land.

GOD REMEMBERED HIS COVENANT

To manage this burgeoning mass of people, the Pharaoh *set taskmasters over them to afflict them with heavy burdens…. But the more they were oppressed, the more they multiplied and the more they spread abroad. And the Egyptians were in dread of the people of Israel…. [The Egyptians] made [the Israelites'] lives bitter with hard service, in mortar and brick, and in all kinds of work in the field. In all their work they ruthlessly made them work as slaves*

(Exodus 1:11-12, 14). When the Israelites cried out for help, *their cry for rescue from slavery came up to God. And God heard their groaning, and God remembered his covenant with Abraham, with Isaac, and with Jacob* (2:23-24). God sent Moses to deliver the Israelites from slavery in Egypt and thereby fulfill a promise He had made to bring His people back to the land of Canaan. God made that promise when Abraham was sojourning in the land of Canaan (also the home of the Amorites). This promise is recorded in Genesis 15:16: *They shall come back here in the fourth generation, for the iniquity of the Amorites is not yet complete.* In this verse, "they" literally and exclusively refers to the descendants of Jacob. Not all of the descendants of Abraham and Isaac are considered the children of Israel, the people of Israel, or the Israelites. The Bible expressly excludes Abraham's offspring through his seven other sons, including Abraham's firstborn son, Ishmael. Also excluded are Isaac's offspring through his firstborn son, Esau.

THE ISRAELITES WERE PASSED OVER

We read in the Bible that Moses went to the Pharaoh of Egypt ten times to request the release of the enslaved people of Israel. Each time Moses appealed to Pharaoh, the ruler of Egypt adamantly refused to free the Israelites. Following each of Pharaoh's refusals, God afflicted the land with a plague. The ten plagues were: water turned to blood, frogs, gnats, flies, livestock disease, boils, hail, locusts, darkness, and death. In that final plague, the firstborn male child of every household in Egypt was killed. But every Israelite household that had marked the doorframe of their home with the blood of a sacrificed lamb was literally passed over by this plague (precedent). Annually, on Nisan 14, Jews since then and even today still remember this landmark event when they celebrate Passover (pattern).

In this first Passover, the Jewish families killed a lamb and roasted it over a fire. Blood from the sacrificed lamb was poured into a basin. The basin was either a bowl set in the doorway or a depression carved into the threshold that normally contained water to wash feet prior to entering the home. Blood from the basin was applied—with a hyssop branch—to the doorframe's horizontal top beam (the lintel) as well as to the right and left vertical side supports (the doorposts). Exodus 12:22 contains the instructions: *Take a bunch of hyssop and dip it in the blood that is in the basin, and touch the lintel and the two doorposts with the blood that is in the basin.* Naturally, droplets of blood from the lintel fell into the basin. The four areas in the doorway marked in blood form a cross pattern (Figure 3.1). Centuries later the design of many doors incorporates this cross pattern (Figure 3.2).

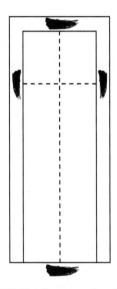

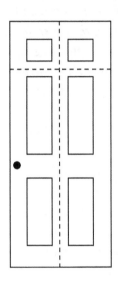

FIGURE 3.1 Passover doorframe   FIGURE 3.2 Cross panel design

THE EXODUS FROM EGYPT

Each year on the evening of Nisan 15, faithful Jews still eat the Passover lamb in an elaborate ceremonial meal. This feast is a reminder of the meal their ancestors ate in haste in Egypt just prior to the final plague: shortly after the meal, the Israelites began their exodus out of Egypt and slavery. An important element of this feast is the retelling of the exodus story, just as God commanded through Moses in Exodus 13:8-10: *You shall tell your son on that day, "It is because of what the LORD did for me when I came out of Egypt"... You shall therefore keep this statute at its appointed time from year to year.* This ritual feast is called the *Passover Seder*, which means "order of Passover."

After the Israelites had departed and the Egyptians had buried their dead, the Pharaoh regretted his decision: *What is this we have done, that we have let Israel go from serving us?* (Exodus 14:5). At the Pharaoh's command, *the Egyptians pursued them, all Pharaoh's horses and chariots and his horsemen and his army* (v. 9). When the Egyptians caught up with the Israelites, God's people found themselves trapped between the army and the Red Sea. So God parted the waters, and *the people of Israel went into the midst of the sea on dry ground, the waters being a wall to them on their right hand and on their left* (v. 22). The pursuing Egyptian army followed the Israelites only to be drowned when *the sea returned to its normal course* (v. 27), and the walls of water collapsed on them.

30 DAYS AFTER LEAVING EGYPT

After crossing the Red Sea on dry land, *all the congregation of the people of Israel came to the wilderness of Sin…on the fifteenth day of the second month after they had departed from the land of Egypt* (Exodus 16:1). This was thirty days after leaving Egypt, and the seven-day supply of unleavened bread that they had taken with them would have run out long before. Hungry, they yearned for the food they had eaten while they were enslaved in Egypt. Even though every single one of them had witnessed the ten plagues in Egypt, even though they had seen God part the Red Sea and wipe out the Egyptian army, and even though they continued to see God miraculously lead them with a pillar of cloud by day and a pillar of fire by night, they complained bitterly to Moses and Aaron that God was going to let them die.

Despite hearing the people whine, complain, and say they would rather have died in Egypt as slaves than starve to death in the desert, the merciful and gracious Lord told Moses, *"Behold, I am about to rain bread from heaven for you"* (v. 4). The Lord even acknowledged, *"I have heard the grumbling of the people of Israel. Say to them…'In the morning you shall be filled with bread. Then you shall know that I am the* LORD *your God'"* (v. 12). Despite the people's grumbling, that morning *when the dew had gone up, there was on the face of the wilderness a fine, flake-like thing, fine as frost on the ground….*

It was like coriander seed, white, and the taste of it was like wafers made with honey (vv. 14, 31).

40 YEARS OF BREAD FROM HEAVEN

As promised, God literally provided "bread from heaven" in the form of a fine white flake-like thing that the people called *manna*, which means "What is it?" Moses told them it *is the bread that the LORD has given you to eat* (Exodus 16:15). However, manna was no ordinary bread: it provided the people of Israel with all the nutritional sustenance they needed to survive in the desert for forty years. Also, at the end of their sojourning, Moses reminded the people that *your foot did not swell these forty years* (Deuteronomy 8:4). Swollen feet indicate malnutrition, so this verse makes it clear that the people of Israel were well nourished. Years later, in a time of worship and praise, Levites reminded a gathering of God's people of His great provision: *Forty years you sustained them in the wilderness, and they lacked nothing. Their clothes did not wear out and their feet did not swell* (Nehemiah 9:21).

It is noteworthy that forty years—to the day—after the Israelites made their last meal from the crops in Egypt, they made their first meal from the crops in Canaan. They prepared unleavened bread in Egypt on Nisan 14—the first day of Passover—shortly before departing from Egypt on Nisan 15. For the next four decades the Israelites ate manna instead of the produce of the land. After they arrived in the Promised Land, the people prepared unleavened bread on Nisan 14 from the crops in Canaan. On Nisan 15, precisely forty years to the day after they left Egypt, they ate their first meal from the crops in Canaan: *The day after the Passover, on that very day, they ate of the produce of the land… And the manna ceased the day after they ate of the produce of the land. And there was no longer manna for the people of Israel* (Joshua 5:11-12).

AN OMER OF MANNA EACH DAY

For forty years in the wilderness, *when the dew fell upon the camp in the night, the manna fell with it* (Numbers 11:9), and the people were told,

"Gather of it, each one of you, as much as he can eat. You shall each take an omer, according to the number of the persons that each of you has in his tent" (Exodus 16:16). As if its arrival is not unusual enough, manna had several other notable characteristics. One of those became evident after the people *gathered, some more, some less. But when they measured it with an omer, whoever gathered much had nothing left over, and whoever gathered little had no lack. Each of them gathered as much as he could eat* (vv. 17-18).

God made sure that each person had an *omer* (approximately two liters) of manna. That was the precise amount that each person needed for the day; it was neither too much nor too little. After each person had gathered an omer, Moses gave these additional instructions: *"Let no one leave any of it over till the morning." But they did not listen to Moses. Some left part of it till the morning, and it bred worms and stank. And Moses was angry with them* (vv. 19-20). God provided exactly enough bread from heaven to feed them for a day, but some disobeyed God by saving a portion of manna overnight. Yet another characteristic of manna is the people of Israel had to gather it in the morning before the sun melted it away: *Morning by morning they gathered it, each as much as he could eat; but when the sun grew hot, it melted* (v. 21).

MANNA IN PRECEDENT, PATTERN, AND PROPHECY

In this wilderness test, God wanted the Israelites to believe His promise that He would continue providing them with manna. God was trying to teach the people of Israel to have faith, to trust Him each day for their daily omer of manna—the bread from heaven. But some did not have faith: these doubters put aside a portion of the manna just in case it did not appear the next morning. When that portion "bred worms and stank," they knew they had made the wrong decision. God's gift of manna brings to mind Jesus' model prayer for us believers. In Matthew 6:11, Jesus instructed believers to pray to our Father who is in heaven, *"Give us this day our daily bread"* and then to trust that He will provide. Also unique about manna is that this God-given food points to Jesus (Figure 3.3).

Precedent	In the wilderness, Moses said that manna *is the bread that the LORD has given you to eat.*	Exodus 16:15
Prophecy	In Israel, at the Lord's Supper, *Jesus took bread... and said, "Take, eat; this is my body."*	Matthew 26:26
Analysis	Jesus is the bread of life.	

Precedent	In the wilderness, God *opened the doors of heaven, and he rained down on them manna.*	Psalm 78:23-24
Prophecy	In Israel, Jesus said, *"I am the bread that came down from heaven."*	John 6:41
Analysis	Jesus came down from heaven.	

Pattern	In the wilderness, God provided bread from heaven, and *morning by morning they gathered it.*	Exodus 16:21
Prophecy	In Israel, Jesus taught us to pray, *"Our Father in heaven... Give us this day our daily bread."*	Matthew 6:9,11
Analysis	Jesus is our daily bread.	

Pattern	In the wilderness, God gave His people bread to prevent hunger: *Forty years you sustained them.*	Nehemiah 9:21
Prophecy	In Israel, *Jesus said to them, "I am the bread of life; whoever comes to me shall not hunger."*	John 6:35
Analysis	Jesus provides everything we need.	

FIGURE 3.3 Manna in precedent, pattern, and prophecy

A DOUBLE PORTION ON THE SIXTH DAY

Another unique characteristic of manna is mentioned in Exodus 16:22-23: *On the sixth day they gathered twice as much bread, two omers each.... [Moses said to them,] "Bake what you will bake and boil what you will boil, and all that is left over lay aside to be kept till the morning."* Unlike the first five days when any manna left overnight would spoil, manna left over on the sixth day *did not stink, and there were no worms in it* (v. 24).

Consider now the parallels between the six days of Creation (precedent) and the six days of manna (pattern). During the first six days of Creation in the beginning, God created everything that exists, and He was completely satisfied (precedent). During the first six days of manna in the wilderness, the Israelites gathered all they would need, and they were completely satisfied (pattern).

After creating the living creatures (livestock, creeping things, and beasts) on the sixth day, *God saw that it was good* (Genesis 1:25). But the sixth day was not yet over: *Then God said, "Let us make man in our image, after our likeness"* (v. 26). On the sixth day God created a double portion: living creatures and human beings. On the sixth day the Israelites gathered a double portion: two omers of manna. This double-portion-on-the-sixth-day parallel between the six days of Creation (precedent) and the six days of manna (pattern) is unmistakable.

SHABUA-DAYS OF MANNA

Now read Exodus 16:21-27 in its entirety:

Morning by morning they gathered it, each as much as he could eat; but when the sun grew hot, it melted. On the sixth day they gathered twice as much bread, two omers each. And when all the leaders of the congregation came and told Moses, he said to them, "This is what the LORD has commanded: 'Tomorrow is a day of solemn rest, a holy Sabbath to the LORD; bake what you will bake and boil what you will boil, and all that is left over lay aside to be kept till the morning.'" So they laid it aside till the morning, as Moses commanded them, and it did not stink, and there were no worms in it. Moses said, "Eat it today, for today is a Sabbath to the LORD; today you will not find it in the field. Six days you shall gather it, but on the seventh day, which is a Sabbath, there will be none." On the seventh day some of the people went out to gather, but they found none.

In the book of Genesis, when God created everything in six days and rested on the 7th and final day, the *shabua*-days precedent was established: 6 days + 1 day = 7 days. This precedent is evident in the gathering of manna in the book of Exodus. In the *shabua*-days of manna, the people worked to gather the bread for six days and rested on the 7th and final day. This pattern was consistently and repeatedly practiced for forty years, the length of time the Israelites wandered in the wilderness before they entered the Promised Land.

THE 7TH AND FINAL DAY IS THE SABBATH

Although the Genesis and Exodus statements about that special 7th day are remarkably similar, they are not identical. The passage in Genesis uses a Hebrew verb—*shabath*—to indicate that God rested on the 7th and final day of the *shabua*. The passage in Exodus uses a Hebrew proper noun—*Shabbath*—as the title for the 7th and final day of the *shabua*. The following five verses from the Exodus passage (Figure 3.4) refer to the 7th and final day of the *shabua*.

EXODUS	VERSE
16:23	*This is what the LORD has commanded: "Tomorrow is a day of solemn rest, a holy Sabbath to the Lord."*
16:25	*Moses said, "Eat it today, for today is a Sabbath to the Lord; today you will not find it in the field."*
16:26	*Six days you shall gather it, but on the seventh day, which is a Sabbath, there will be none.*
16:29	*See! The LORD has given you the Sabbath... Remain each of you in his place; let no one go out of his place on the seventh day.*
16:30	*So the people rested on the seventh day.*

FIGURE 3.4 First appearance of the word Sabbath

This is the first time that *Sabbath* appears in the Bible. The fact that it is used four times in this passage highlights its importance. *Sabbath* is the English translation of the Hebrew word *Shabbath* (Strong's H7676). Notice that the spelling of *Shabbath* is very similar to the Hebrew word *shabath* (Strong's H7673) that is used in Genesis 2 to describe what God did on the 7th day: God rested. The only spelling difference between *shabath* and

Shabbath is an extra "b." This is not a scribal error; the Bible is making an important distinction that becomes readily apparent once an individual understands the context.

SHABBATH AND SHABATH HAVE SIMILAR MEANINGS

The *shabua*-days introduced in the book of Genesis (precedent) is repeated here in the book of Exodus (pattern). Both passages describe the 7th and final day as distinct and different from the previous six. Since *shabath* and *Shabbath* both originate from the same Hebrew word root, it should come as no surprise that they have a very similar meaning. In Genesis, *shabath* means "to cease or rest" on the 7th day. In Exodus, *Shabbath* means "the Sabbath" and refers to the 7th and final day of rest.

In Genesis *shabath* solely and exclusively refers to what God did on the 7th day, which was to cease and rest from His work of Creation. This *shabath* precedent of ceasing from work and then resting on the 7th day is passed on to the people of Israel via the Sabbath. God said to Moses, "*See! The LORD has given you the Sabbath; therefore on the sixth day he gives you bread for two days"… So the people rested on the seventh day* (Exodus 16:29-30). Here, God gave the people of Israel two things: the Sabbath and a double portion of manna on the sixth day so they would have food to eat on the Sabbath without having to work.

THE SABBATH IS GOD'S GIFT OF REST TO ISRAEL

Resting on the 7th and final day of the *shabua* was not optional for the people of Israel. In Exodus 16:23 Moses said, *This is what the LORD has commanded.* In the twenty-first century, commands are generally viewed with disfavor because they can inhibit our personal freedom, but this particular command has only positive connotations. Consider a father who desires to bless his son with a gift. If the son does not accept the gift, he will not receive the benefits his father intended, and the gift will be meaningless. Similarly, the Israelites needed to accept their heavenly Father's gift of the Sabbath. They did so by ceasing from work and resting on the 7th and final day of every *shabua*.

The reason this is significant is because there is no indication that people living around 1500 BCE regarded one day above another. So singling out the 7th day to be distinct and different from the preceding six was counter-cultural. But God chose to single out this 7th day as a blessing for His people: His gift of the Sabbath is entirely and exclusively designed to benefit the people of Israel. God never intended to burden His people in any way. Not only did God command the people of Israel to not work on the Sabbath, but He also commanded them to rest. To facilitate that rest, God even spared them the work of gathering a meal: God permitted His people to gather an extra portion of manna on the sixth day so they would have food for the Sabbath.

The wilderness journey and God's provision of manna only lasted for a period of forty years, but the Sabbath—formalized by the Fourth Commandment—would remain an integral part of Israel's culture and society.

THE FOURTH COMMANDMENT

THE FOURTH COMMANDMENT FORMALIZED THE SABBATH

Soon after both receiving manna for the first time and being given the instructions regarding the Sabbath, the Israelites departed from the wilderness of Sin. Twenty-one days later (three *shabua*-days), as the people of Israel stood at the foot of Mount Sinai, they heard God speak:

"Remember the Sabbath day, to keep it holy. Six days you shall labor, and do all your work, but the seventh day is a Sabbath to the LORD your God. On it you shall not do any work, you, or your son, or your daughter, your male servant, or your female servant, or your livestock, or the sojourner who is within your gates. For in six days the LORD made heaven and earth, the sea, and all that is in them, and rested on the seventh day. Therefore the LORD blessed the Sabbath day and made it holy." (Exodus 20:8-11)

This passage—the Fourth Commandment—ratifies the command that God had given to the people of Israel twenty-one days earlier: gather manna for six days and rest on the 7th and final day, the day God called the Sabbath. In addition, this passage expands the application of *shabua*-days by not limiting it to gathering manna, but by expressly extending it to all work: *"Six days you shall labor, and do all your work, but the seventh day is a Sabbath to the LORD your God. On it you shall not do any work"* (vv. 9-10). When the children of Israel eventually entered the land of Canaan after forty years of wandering in the wilderness, the supply of manna ceased. But the people continued to obey the Fourth Commandment to rest on the Sabbath, an observance that remains fundamental to the practice of Judaism today.

A NATURAL, LOGICAL, AND REASONABLE CONCLUSION

The Fourth Commandment pattern $(6 + 1 = 7)$ replicates the Creation precedent $(6 + 1 = 7)$. God created for six days; Israel is to work for six days. God rested (*shabath*) on the 7th and final day of the *shabua*; Israel is to rest on the 7th and final day of the *shabua* (the Sabbath). This parallelism offers clarity about the length of each day in Genesis 1. Since each day in Exodus is unquestionably a 24-hour period, the most natural, logical, and reasonable interpretation is that each day of Creation in Genesis is also a 24-hour period. Furthermore, if it is true that the Lord made heaven and earth, the sea, and all that is in them as the Bible says, it is really not a stretch to think that He did it in six literal 24-hour days.

Again, God's miraculous act of Creation is no less and no more a miracle if it happened in six 24-hour days or six centillion years (10^{303} years). And God certainly could have created everything in an attosecond (10^{-18} or one quintillionth of one second) and then rested long enough for things to evolve, but that is not what the Bible says happened. The Bible says God created everything in six days and rested on the 7th and final day. Similarly, God certainly could have given *shabua*-days and the Sabbath to everyone, but that is not what the Bible says happened. The Bible says God chose to give them to all of the generations of Israel as an everlasting sign of His goodness and His faithfulness. God established *shabua*-days and the Sabbath to both memorialize the work He did in the beginning as well as to bless Israel.

A SIGN FOREVER BETWEEN GOD AND ISRAEL

The keeping of the Sabbath and the Creation story are linked again in Exodus 31. Here God repeated His command regarding Sabbath observance while emphasizing the fact that it is for the people Israel: *"The people of Israel shall keep the Sabbath, observing the Sabbath throughout their generations, as a covenant forever. It is a sign forever between me and the people of Israel that in six days the LORD made heaven and earth, and on the seventh day he rested and was refreshed"* (Exodus 31:16-17).

This passage unequivocally indicates that *shabua*-days and the Sabbath are unique aspects of God's relationship with the "people of Israel." This relationship is described with such inclusive phrases as "throughout their generations," "covenant forever," "sign forever," and "between me and the people of Israel." Deuteronomy 5:15 explains why the people of Israel were commanded to observe the Sabbath: *"You shall remember that you were a slave in the land of Egypt, and the LORD your God brought you out from there with a mighty hand and an outstretched arm. Therefore the LORD your God commanded you to keep the Sabbath day."* (Israel is the only nation in history that was enslaved in Egypt and subsequently set free.)

THE SABBATH IS FUNDAMENTAL TO JUDAISM

Numerous Bible passages confirm and repeat *shabua*-days and the Sabbath, and in the Bible, repetition always indicates emphasis. (Among those passages are Exodus 20:8-11, 23:12, 31:15-17, 34:21, 35:2-3; Leviticus 23:3; and Deuteronomy 5:12-14.) As mentioned, *shabua*-days and the Sabbath continue to be honored by faithful Jews to this very day. Throughout the land of Israel, everything—the government, stores, businesses, restaurants, transportation services, etc.—shuts down for a full 24-hour period of rest on the 7th and final day of every *shabua*. In Israel the Sabbath begins Friday evening after sunset and ends Saturday evening at sunset. During this 24-hour period Israel honors God by keeping a solemn day of rest.

Honoring the Sabbath on the day and in the manner commanded in the Bible is one of the most revered practices in Judaism. "Other days of rest, such as the Christian Sunday and the Islamic Friday, owe their origins to the Jewish Sabbath."[1] Before examining the different Christian views on this subject, let's take a brief look at Islam. The Qur'an does not require Muslims to observe a 7th day of solemn rest. However, at noon every Friday—the sixth day of the week—Muslims generally gather at their local mosque for a sermon and congregational prayer called Jumu'ah. After Jumu'ah, many Muslims take the rest of the day off from work. Arab countries today differ in how they treat Fridays: some consider it entirely a day of rest, some consider it half a day of rest, and others do not consider it a day of rest at all.

CHRISTIAN OPINIONS REGARDING THE SABBATH

Today, Bible-believing Christians hold varying opinions about the Sabbath. A minority believes the Old Testament command to Israel applies to the New Testament church without exception, including the requirement to rest on Saturday, the 7th day. They find support for this position in the fact that Jesus observed Jewish feasts, festivals, and holy days, including the Sabbath. For this reason, Seventh-day Adventist churches—a Christian denomination— meet on Saturday, the 7th day. In addition, Messianic Jewish Christian churches—predominantly attended by ethnic Jews who have accepted Jesus as the Messiah—also meet on Saturday to honor the 7th day of the *shabua*.

The Saturday evening mass is a relatively recent practice; particularly for the Catholic Church. For many centuries the celebration of the obligatory weekly mass was limited to Sunday morning. It wasn't until 1967 that the Sacred Congregation of Rites said; "permission has been granted by the Apostolic to fulfill the Sunday obligation on the preceding Saturday evening." However, this accommodation had nothing to do with the fact that Saturday is the 7th and final day of the *shabua* (the Sabbath); "The purpose of this concession is in fact to enable the Christians of today to celebrate more easily the day of the resurrection of the Lord" (Sunday).[2]

REST ON THE SABBATH VS. MEETING ON SUNDAY

Christians today generally believe they keep the Fourth Commandment and honor the Sabbath by meeting in churches on Sunday. (The Saturday evening service or mass is generally viewed as an extension of Sunday.) The Fourth Commandment, however, does not say anything about gathering together in community. The commandment's one and only requirement is for the people of Israel to rest on the 7th and final day of the *shabua*, and observing a solemn day of rest on the Sabbath has been a continuous Jewish practice for more than 3,500 years. Very few Christians rest *on the day* (the Sabbath) and *in the manner* (by ceasing work and activity) described in the Bible and still practiced by Jews.

Furthermore, the Christian tradition of gathering in community on Sunday honors the first day of the week, not the 7th and final day of a *shabua* (the Sabbath). Two landmark New Testament events happened on Sunday—the first day of the week—that set that day apart from the other six. Jesus was resurrected from the dead on a Sunday, and the church was born on a Sunday when the Holy Spirit arrived at Pentecost. Sunday likely became the most highly regarded day of the week for the church because of the unequaled significance of these two events for everyone who believes in Jesus. In addition, the Roman emperor Constantine made Sunday an official day of rest in 321 CE when he introduced civil legislation that "decreed that all work should cease on that day."[3]

TWO ADDITIONAL REFERENCES TO SUNDAY

It may surprise most Christians to learn that not one single verse or passage in the entire Bible commands believers to either meet or rest on Sunday. Twice in the New Testament, though, believers seem to have gathered on Sunday. In one passage, the apostle Paul gathered with fellow believers on the first day of the week (Sunday) to share a meal: *On the first day of the week... we were gathered together to break bread* (Acts 20:7). In the other passage, a Sunday gathering is implied when Paul asked fellow believers to set aside an offering (tithe) *on the first day of every week* (1 Corinthians 16:2).

In these verses we see that, on Sunday, believers shared a meal and set aside an offering.

In neither of these two New Testament references to Sunday is the Fourth Commandment mentioned: we read nothing about rest nor the Sabbath. Furthermore, the Jewish practice of gathering in synagogues on the Sabbath was not instituted until after the destruction of the temple in Jerusalem in 586 BCE. And that happened more than 900 years after God gave the Ten Commandments to the people of Israel at Mount Sinai. To reiterate, the Fourth Commandment does not mention meeting or gathering on the first day of the week (Sunday); the only mandate is for Israel to rest on the 7th and final day of the *shabua* (the Sabbath).

GATHERING IS NOT A SUBSTITUTE FOR REST

One reason Israel was exiled to Babylon was for their failure to honor the Sabbath requirement to rest. So in order to make sure Israel kept this commandment from that point on, the leaders created hundreds of extrabiblical Sabbath rules, requirements, and restrictions to specifically define prohibited activities that violate rest. Gathering in the synagogues was definitely *not* a substitute for rest, but doing so provided faithful Jews with a place for teaching and community while they were living in exile without a temple. The Jewish tradition and practice of gathering in synagogues on the Sabbath continued after the exiles returned to Jerusalem. The people of Israel continued to meet in synagogues even after the Second Temple was rebuilt, and this practice continues throughout the world today.

The Bible certainly stresses the importance of gathering in community: *Let us consider how to stir up one another to love and good works, not neglecting to meet together, as is the habit of some, but encouraging one another, and all the more as you see the Day drawing near* (Hebrews 10:24-25). But nothing in the Old or New Testament commands Jews or Christians to regularly meet on a particular day of the week. There is, however, a very specific command that God gave to the people of Israel: they are to cease work and rest on the 7th and final day of every *shabua*. The Bible calls that day the Sabbath, and the Hebrew word for *Sabbath* is *Shabbath*.

THE HEBREW WORD FOR SABBATH

Strong's Concordance indicates that the basic form of the three-character Hebrew root (שבת) used in *Shabbath* (H7676) is incorporated in six different Hebrew words. These are listed below in the order of the number that Strong's has assigned each of them, and those numbers are followed by the Hebrew-to-English transliteration and Strong's Hebrew Dictionary definition (Figure 3.5). Notice how the concept of ceasing and resting is embedded in the meaning of these words that use the Hebrew root (שבת).

STRONG'S	TRANSLITERATION	DEFINITION
H7673	*shabath*	cease, rest
H7674	*shebeth*	cease, sit still
H7675	*shebeth*	seat, place
H7676	*Shabbath*	Sabbath
H7677	*Shabbathown*	rest, Sabbath
H7678	*Shabbethay*	Male name

FIGURE 3.5 Six words that use the Hebrew root (שבת)

THE TWO PRIMARY MEANINGS OF SABBATH

The two primary meanings of *Shabbath* are complementary ("cease" and "rest"), but the two primary meanings of *shabua* (discussed in chapter 1) are completely different ("seven" and "complete"). The similar appearance of *Shabbath* and *shabua* is noteworthy. That similarity is indicative of the fact that the Hebrew word roots used in *Shabbath* (שבת) and *shabua* (שבע) are indeed very similar. It should therefore come as no surprise that the people of Israel are commanded both to cease work and to rest on the Sabbath. Simply put, the proper noun *Sabbath* means "rest," and it is the title for the 7th and final interval of a *shabua*, which is a complete time period of seven.

The primary language of the Old Testament is Hebrew, and the primary language of the New Testament is Greek. The Greek word *sabbatismos* (G4520) means "rest" and is from a derivative of *Sabbaton*. The Greek word

Sabbaton (G4521) means "the Sabbath (i.e. *Shabbath*), or day of weekly repose from secular avocations" and its root comes from the Hebrew word *shabbath* (H7676). As you can see in Figure 3.6, the definitions in Greek are similar to the Hebrew.

STRONG'S	TRANSLITERATION	DEFINITION
G4520	*sabbatismos*	rest
G4521	*Sabbaton*	Sabbath, repose

FIGURE 3.6 Greek words for rest and Sabbath

CONSEQUENCES FOR VIOLATING THE SABBATH

God said the Sabbath is *a sign forever between me and the people of Israel* (Exodus 31:17). It is neither a suggestion nor an option for the physical descendants of Abraham, Isaac, and Jacob. The Bible says it is a command, and this command was to continue *throughout their generations* (v. 16). The Sabbath has never waned in significance since the time of the exodus, and it remains fundamental to the practice of Judaism to this very day. Observance of the Sabbath also sets the people of Israel apart from every other nation and people in history. Although the essence of the Sabbath is simply to rest, it is nevertheless a command to rest.

When the people of Israel disobeyed God's command to rest on the Sabbath, the consequences were truly catastrophic. Failure to keep the Sabbath was one cause of the wholesale slaughter of many Jews, the destruction of the city of Jerusalem and the First Temple, and the carrying off of the Jewish remnant to Babylon in 586 BCE. In fact, the seventy-year exile in Babylon was a direct consequence of violating seventy Sabbath years in the land of Israel (more on those seventy Sabbath years in *Shabua Seventy*, the third book in this series). The people of Israel had seventy years in Babylon to think about the ramifications of not honoring God's command to rest on the Sabbath. At that time the Jewish religious sect called the Pharisees developed the myriad of extrabiblical laws regarding the Sabbath.

THE EXTRABIBLICAL SABBATH LAWS OF THE PHARISEES

Noble intentions prompted and guided the development of these extrabiblical laws: since Israel had suffered horrifying consequences after willfully violating the Sabbath, the Pharisees set out to prevent that from ever happening again. To that end, they imposed stringent Sabbath rules, requirements, and restrictions on the people of Israel. The Sanhedrin (the Jewish people's Supreme Court) enforced these extrabiblical Sabbath laws. For instance, a repeat Sabbath offender who had been officially warned was executed on the testimony of two competent witnesses.

Extrabiblical Jewish law outlines thirty-nine *melachot* (categories of activities) that are forbidden on the Sabbath (Figure 3.7), and each category lists additional prohibitions as well as detailed instructions to ensure compliance. For example, "extinguishing" includes diminishing the intensity of a flame or fire. The prohibited acts in this category range from snuffing out a candle, to turning off a light by flipping a switch, to putting water on a fire even when not doing so will result in great property damage. The only exception to the extrabiblical Sabbath rules, requirements, and restrictions is when breaking one is deemed necessary to save a life.

Building	Burning	Carrying	Chain-stitching
Combing	Cooking	Demolishing	Dyeing
Erasing	Extinguishing	Finishing	Grinding
Harvesting	Kneading	Knotting	Marking
Planting	Plowing	Reaping	Selecting
Sewing	Shaping	Shearing	Sifting
Skinning	Slaughtering	Smoothing	Spinning
Tanning	Tearing	Threshing	Trapping
Unraveling	Untying	Warping	Washing
Weaving	Winnowing	Writing	

FIGURE 3.7 The 39 categories of activities forbidden on the Sabbath

JESUS OUTRAGED THE PHARISEES ON THE SABBATH

By the time of Jesus in the first century CE, keeping the Sabbath had become such a burden to the people of Israel that the concept of rest was completely lost. The Pharisees had turned the Sabbath into a day of impossible rules, requirements, and restrictions that were exhausting to keep track of. Consider the Sabbath when Jesus' disciples were picking grain to eat as they walked through a field. Since the Pharisees considered picking grain to be work, they told Jesus that His disciples were violating the Sabbath. Jesus replied, *"The Sabbath was made for man, not man for the Sabbath"* (Mark 2:27).

In this verse, Jesus made it clear that, for Israel, the Sabbath was not about earning God's favor by doing or not doing something; it was about enjoying God's blessing of rest. Immediately after making this statement, Jesus—who is also referred to as the Son of Man—told the Pharisees, *"So the Son of Man is lord even of the Sabbath"* (v. 28). This was a blasphemous statement that further outraged the Pharisees. Jesus was essentially saying that He was master over the Sabbath, one of the most highly regarded traditions and practices in Judaism.

On another occasion—as proof of His authority over the Sabbath—Jesus entered the synagogue on the Sabbath and healed a man with a withered hand. The Pharisees had ruled that healing on the Sabbath was not lawful unless it was necessary to save a life, so they *went out and immediately held counsel with the Herodians against [Jesus], how to destroy him* (Mark 3:6).

JESUS IS THE PROPHETIC FULFILLMENT OF REST

God gave the Sabbath exclusively to the people of Israel—the physical descendants of Abraham, Isaac, and Jacob—and Jesus was one of those descendants. We can be sure that Jesus never violated the Sabbath because we know that He—the pure and perfect Lamb of God—never committed a sin. Jesus, however, did not keep the extrabiblical man-made Sabbath laws of the Pharisees. As He accurately declared, *"I have kept my Father's commandments"* (John 15:10). In another place Jesus said, *"Do not think that I have come to abolish the Law or the Prophets; I have not come to abolish them but to fulfill them"* (Matthew 5:17). In terms of this discussion, Jesus did not come to abolish the Sabbath law but to fulfill it.

To understand how Jesus fulfilled the Sabbath requires knowing what you already know: the meaning and the purpose of the Sabbath is rest. And Jesus implored His followers, *"Come to me, all who labor and are heavy laden, and I will give you rest"* (Matthew 11:28). Here Jesus offers rest from the burdens of life to all those who go to Him. Then Jesus said: *"Take my yoke upon you, and learn from me, for I am gentle and lowly in heart, and you will find rest for your souls"* (v. 29). Here, in addition to the rest that Jesus provides for the mind and body, Jesus offers spiritual rest for the soul. That kind of rest happens when a believer comes under the yoke of Jesus and learns how to cope with the burdens of life by following His way. Jesus offered encouraging words for believers who are yoked to Him: *"My yoke is easy, and my burden is light"* (v. 30).

JESUS USES THE METAPHOR OF A YOKE FOR REST

Unlike the Sabbath that addresses physical rest on the 7th day, the rest that Jesus offers is also emotional, mental, and spiritual. Jesus used the metaphor of a yoke to illustrate what it means to find rest in Him. When Jesus said, "Take my yoke upon you," He was—and still is—offering rest to believers who are heavily laden. The Greek word for *laden* is *phortizo* (Strong's G5412), which means "to load up (properly, as a vessel or animal), i.e. (figuratively) to overburden with ceremony (or spiritual anxiety):—lade, by heavy laden." All burdens are not eliminated when believers take up the yoke that Jesus offers, but the burdens do become—as Jesus promised—easier and lighter, and in the process believers do find rest for their souls. Believers experience ultimate rest and freedom when they are yoked to Jesus and have faith that *all things work together for good* (Romans 8:28).

Before we move on from this discussion of a yoke, consider the way a farmer in Bible times used the apparatus to plow a field (a method still used today in various places around the world). A yoke enables a farmer to guide two beasts of burden at the same time and thereby harness their combined energy to do hard physical labor. The *yoke* is the wooden piece that connects, for instance, two oxen by joining them at their broad shoulders. The *beam* is the wooden piece that connects to the yoke perpendicularly and runs lengthwise between the two oxen. The short part of the beam extends in front of the yoke between the oxen's heads. The long part of the beam extends in back of the yoke and rests on the ground behind the oxen. The iron blade for plowing is attached to the very end of the beam.

When joined together, the yoke and the beam form a wooden cross (Figure 3.8). The yoke and beam design is therefore compelling as both a physical symbol and a spiritual metaphor: Jesus was crucified on a wooden cross (physical symbol), and His death enables believers to find rest from the burdens of life (spiritual metaphor). The crushing weight of sin and its consequences was permanently eliminated when Jesus died on the cross. As a result, Jesus' yoke is easy and His burden is light: the cross represents rest and freedom.

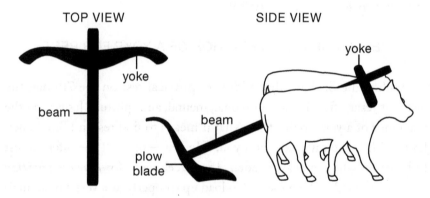

FIGURE 3.8 Yoke and beam form a wooden cross

JESUS OFFERS REST ANY DAY, ANYTIME, ANYPLACE

Again, Jesus said, *"Come to me... and I will give you rest"* (Matthew 11:28). This invitation to rest is open to anyone willing to go to Him. Jesus didn't mention a specific day, time, or place to find rest because the rest that He offers and provides is available any day, anytime, and anyplace. This invitation and its blessings are expressed another way in the New Testament: the call to abide in Christ, which means remaining in continual fellowship with Jesus every moment of every day. Jesus said, *"If you abide in me, and my words abide in you, ask whatever you wish, and it will be done for you"* (John 15:7). Abiding in Jesus does indeed give us rest any day, anytime, and anyplace. Similarly, the Bible encourages believers to regularly gather in community—which is also a source of rest and refreshment—but the Bible does not dictate when, how, or where those gatherings are to happen.

To reiterate, most Christians traditionally attend church on Sunday, but the Bible does not command people to meet on Sunday. The apostle Paul essentially said as much in his letter to believers in Rome: *One person esteems one day as better than another, while another esteems all days alike. Each one should be fully convinced in his own mind. The one who observes the day, observes it in honor of the Lord* (Romans 14:5-6). In another letter, Paul told fellow believers that each individual's personal decision regarding biblical celebrations is to be respected: *Let no one pass judgment on you... with regard to a festival or a new moon or a Sabbath* (Colossians 2:16). Neither of these verses—written to believers—says anything about keeping the Sabbath, but they clearly say no one is to be judged by whether or not they do so.

THE ONE COMMANDMENT NOT EXPRESSLY RESTATED

Have you ever noticed that the Fourth Commandment is the only one of the Ten Commandments that is not expressly restated in the New Testament? The other nine are not only restated, but Jesus expanded their meaning and application for His followers. For example, in the Sermon on the Mount, after Jesus quoted the Sixth Commandment ("You shall not murder"), He said, *"Everyone who is angry with his brother will be liable to judgment"* (Matthew 5:21-22). Similarly, after Jesus quoted the Seventh Commandment ("You shall not commit adultery"), He said, *"Everyone who looks at a woman with lustful intent has already committed adultery with her in his heart"* (vv. 27-28). In essence, Jesus restated nine of the Old Testament's Ten Commandments, applied them to Jew and Gentile alike, and expanded their meaning to include the mind and heart.

Again, nine of the Ten Commandments are restated virtually word for word in the New Testament on multiple occasions; the exception is the Fourth Commandment regarding the Sabbath. Even when the rich young ruler asked Jesus which of the commandments he should keep, Jesus quoted the Fifth, Sixth, Seventh, Eighth, Ninth, and Tenth Commandments in His answer: *"You shall not murder, You shall not commit adultery, You shall not steal, You shall not bear false witness, Honor your father and mother, and, You shall love your neighbor as yourself"* (Matthew 19:18-19). The First, Second, and Third Commandments are also quoted elsewhere in the New Testament. However, the Fourth Commandment to rest on the Sabbath is conspicuously absent. This topic of the Ten Commandments is relevant, but a more detailed analysis will have to wait until chapter 5.

THE SABBATH IS GOD'S COVENANT WITH ISRAEL

For now, it will suffice to know that the New Testament does not repeat the Fourth Commandment to rest on the 7th day of the *shabua*. If it did, the church would most likely meet on Saturday—the 7th day of the week. Furthermore, Jesus did not extend the Fourth Commandment to the Gentile church nor expand its meaning to include mind and heart. But God did say that *"the people of Israel shall keep the Sabbath, observing the Sabbath throughout their generations, as a covenant forever. It is a sign forever between me and the people of Israel"* (Exodus 31:16-17). Since the Bible never revokes the Sabbath law, it must continue to apply to the people of Israel to this day—and faithful Jews do indeed observe the Sabbath. The fact that the Sabbath has been a day of rest for the Jewish people for more than 3,500 years is substantive proof that this covenant between God and the people of Israel continues.

Again, Jesus said that He did not *"come to abolish the Law or the Prophets... but to fulfill them"* (Matthew 5:17). Later, in Matthew 11:28, Jesus said, *"Come to me... and I will give you rest."* To reiterate, rest on the 7th and final day of the *shabua* is neither extended nor expanded to the church: believers are to find total and complete rest in Jesus. But since the Fourth Commandment has never been revoked or abolished for Israel, this command continues for the physical descendants of Abraham, Isaac, and Jacob. Accordingly, since God said the Sabbath is an everlasting covenant between Him and the people of Israel, the Sabbath must continue to apply to the people of Israel at present and in the future.

SABBATH PRECEDENT, PATTERN, AND PROPHECY

As we have seen, the Bible says that in the beginning God rested on the 7th day from His work of Creation (precedent). And God commanded the people of Israel to rest on the 7th day because He rested on the 7th day. God declared that keeping the Sabbath (rest) is an everlasting covenant between Him and the people of Israel, and the Sabbath was to be continually observed throughout all their generations (pattern).

As indicated, precedents and patterns initiated, developed, and expanded in the Old Testament often predict future New Testament events with uncanny accuracy. In regard to this matter of rest, an example of a New Testament fulfillment of an Old Testament prophecy is when Jesus said, *"Come to me... and I will give you rest"* (Matthew 11:28). Jesus is the New Testament fulfillment of the Old Testament precedent and pattern regarding rest (prophecy). Believers can go to Jesus to find rest at any time, on any day, and from any location on planet Earth. The rest that Jesus provides is not limited to Sunday, the Sabbath, or a church building.

Again, the Fourth Commandment—keeping the Sabbath—is never expressly extended to New Testament believers, but it has never been revoked as it applies to the people of Israel. The Israelites were told that the command to rest on the 7th day was to be obeyed as a sign throughout all their generations forever. These explicit instructions cannot be ignored. *Forever* for Israel can only mean... forever. (If the Bible cannot be trusted when such unequivocal language is used, then when can it be trusted?)

GOD'S COMMANDMENT TO THE JEWS

God's Fourth Commandment to rest on the Sabbath was specifically given to the people of Israel, it was to continue forever, and it has not been revoked or canceled. If the Bible is absolutely true, inerrant, and reliable as it claims, the Sabbath must continue to apply to the physical descendants of Abraham, Isaac, and Jacob even after they recognize Jesus as the Messiah. It is noteworthy that Jesus and the disciples—who were in fact Jewish—continued to honor the Sabbath. Furthermore, Jewish Christians (called Messianic

Jews) observe the Sabbath to this very day by resting on Saturday, the 7th and final day of every *shabua*. There are four reasons Gentile believers are not required to keep the Sabbath:

> It was a covenant exclusively given to Israel.
>
> It was never extended to the Gentile church.
>
> Believers are not judged by the day they choose to worship.
>
> Every day with Jesus is a day of rest for believers.

CONCLUDING SUMMARY

In chapter 1 we defined a biblical *shabua* as "a complete time period of seven." In chapter 2 we examined the inaugural *shabua* that was specified as an interval of seven days: this *shabua*-days is the six days of Creation followed by a 7th and final day of rest (precedent). Here in chapter 3 we examined the *shabua*-days of a biblical wedding (pattern). We also saw *shabua*-days applied to the practice of gathering manna in the wilderness following the exodus (pattern). Twenty-one days after the first appearance of that manna, God spoke to Moses and gave the people of Israel the Ten Commandments, including the Fourth Commandment to cease work and rest on the 7th and final day of every *shabua*, the day known as the Sabbath (pattern). Forty days later God chiseled those words on stone tablets and gave them to Moses, and thousands of years later the nation of Israel still observes the Sabbath.

The remaining chapters of this book will build on the foundation established in these first three chapters. We will see that the biblical use of *shabua*-days is always consistent, predictable, and reliable, and it is therefore able to confirm the biblical timeline of actual historical events. These chapters will also continue to show the important role that *shabua*-days has in biblical precedent, pattern, and prophecy. In the next chapter we'll look at precedent, pattern, and prophecy regarding the *shabua*-days of the Feast of Passover (also called the Feast of Unleavened Bread). We will see exactly how, in the first century CE, Jesus was the ultimate fulfillment of this prophetic feast.

CHAPTER 4

THE SEVEN-DAY FEAST

Shabua-days—the continuously repeating pattern of six days of work or activity followed by a 7th and final day of rest—is used for short-term timing in the Bible. In fact, it is very difficult to understand biblical timing without understanding *shabua*-days. So in this chapter we will examine the ways in which *shabua*-days is used in both the Old and New Testaments and learn why it is significant in both Judaism and Christianity. Specifically, this chapter will examine the unique role that *shabua*-days precedent, pattern, and prophecy have in events associated with the exodus, in a specific biblical feast, and in regard to Jesus Himself.

Many people are familiar with the Old Testament record of Moses, the slavery of the Israelites, and their exodus from Egypt, and even nonbelievers have heard about Jesus' crucifixion and His resurrection. However, few people are aware of the extent to which these two series of events are inseparably linked, and even fewer people are aware that a biblical feast is the linchpin that holds them together.

THREE PRIMARY BIBLICAL FEASTS

MANY BIBLICAL CORRELATIONS HAVE BEEN LOST

The interrelationship between the Old Testament, the New Testament, and the biblical feasts is astounding. But because the church no longer follows the biblical timing and because religious traditions and practices often supersede the biblical text, this incredible correlation has generally been lost. Learning the many fascinating and obviously intentional parallels between the Old Testament, the New Testament, and the biblical feasts is definitely worth the time and effort. These connections are preserved for us in the pages of Scripture.

While elements of this subject matter and timing may be foreign to us who live in the twenty-first century, these elements were aspects of everyday life for a farmer or shepherd living in Bible times. This chapter will take us back to the time when the agricultural seasons—and farming cycle— determined years; the moon determined months; *shabua*-days determined weeks; and the sun determined days. This mind-set will result in a much greater appreciation and understanding of the Bible in general and of *shabua*-days in particular. We will begin with a brief overview of the three primary Old Testament feasts.

EACH FEAST IS ASSOCIATED WITH A CROP

The three primary Old Testament feasts were pilgrimage feasts: every able-bodied Jewish male, twelve years and older, was expected to travel to Jerusalem to participate. Each of the feasts had a dedicated purpose and function; each was celebrated at a different time of the year; each was associated with a particular crop; and each had multiple titles. Figure 4.1 identifies the various Old Testament titles used for each feast, the crop harvested, the Hebrew month of the given harvest, the corresponding English months, and the season of the year.

TITLE OF THE FEAST	CROP	HEBREW MONTH	ENGLISH MONTHS	SEASON
Feast of Passover (Unleavened Bread)	Barley	Nisan (Abib)	March/April	Spring
Feast of *Shabua* (Weeks/Sevens/Harvest/*Shavuot*)	Wheat	Sivan	May/June	Spring
Feast of Ingathering (Tabernacles/Booths/*Sukkot*)	Grape	Tishri (Ethanim)	September/ October	Fall

FIGURE 4.1 The three primary biblical feasts

FIRSTFRUITS OF BARLEY AND WHEAT

The Bible refers to the first portion of a crop that is harvested for a special ceremony as firstfruits. In this ceremony, the people presented to God the firstfruits of the crop before beginning the actual work of harvesting the fields. This giving to God the first portion of the crop—symbolic of giving Him the entire harvest—was an act of thanksgiving, a demonstration of faith in God's continuing provision, and a sacrificial offering. (The prophetic significance of the term *firstfruits* will be addressed later in this chapter.)

As indicated in Figure 4.1, each feast is associated with a particular crop. Both barley and wheat are spring crops, and their respective firstfruits ceremonies are celebrated exactly 7 *shabua*-days apart, which is 7 × 7 days = 49 days (more on this in chapter 5). The symbolic firstfruits of both barley and wheat are presented before the general harvest begins.

THE FRUIT OF THE VINE

The grape crop is one of the last crops of the year to be harvested in the Middle East. This final harvest takes place in the fall and has its own special ceremony. Unlike the barley and wheat firstfruits ceremonies in the spring, no firstfruits of the grape crop are presented before the general harvest begins. Instead, the final harvest of the mature grape crop—the fruit of the vine—is presented in a special ceremony at the conclusion of this final harvest season of the year. After that ceremony, the fields are plowed under in preparation for the winter rainy season.

Before we move on, know that the Bible refers to pure fresh grape juice as the fruit of the vine. At the Last Supper, Jesus referred to the contents of the cup as *the fruit of the vine*" (Matthew 26:29, Mark 14:25, Luke 22:18). This beverage had to be pure, fresh grape juice (Strong's H8492) and not the fermented alcoholic beverage (Strong's H3196), although both are referred to as wine. The alcoholic beverage requires the introduction of yeast (leaven) as a fermenting agent. (The Bible uses leaven as a metaphor for sin.) The Lord's Last Supper took place on a holy day—the first day of Unleavened Bread—when leaven in any form was strictly forbidden. Jesus was sinless and never violated a single command of His Father. Therefore, the cup with the fruit of the vine had to be pure, fresh grape juice.

SYMBOLISM IN THE THREE FEASTS

In the New Testament, the harvest of crops is a prophetic metaphor for believers in Jesus being gathered into the family of God. The Bible refers to these Christ followers—and their good deeds—as "fruit." Each Old Testament feast has its unique prophetic aspects.

Feast of Passover: Celebrated at the time of the spring barley harvest, the barley sheaf firstfruits ceremony and the subsequent harvest symbolize the resurrection of Jesus from the dead to gather all those who believe that He suffered and died for their sins (remembered at Easter). The barley crop itself symbolizes fresh new growth. The prophetic aspect of this feast was ultimately fulfilled in the earthly ministry of Jesus who "*came to seek and to save the lost*" (Luke 19:10). Since new believers continue to put their faith and trust in Jesus, this prophesied harvest is ongoing.

Feast of *Shabua*: Celebrated at the time of the spring wheat harvest, the wheat loaves firstfruits ceremony and the subsequent harvest symbolize the Holy Spirit coming to gather all who believe in Jesus into the Christian community called the church (remembered at Pentecost). Like the barley crop, the wheat crop also symbolizes fresh new growth. The prophetic aspect of this feast was ultimately fulfilled when believers in Jesus received the Holy Spirit at Pentecost. Since the work of the Holy Spirit continues in the church at the present time, this prophesied harvest is also ongoing.

Feast of Ingathering: Celebrated at the end of the fall grape harvest, the ceremony marks the very last fruit to be brought into the storehouse before the fields are plowed under. As the final harvest of the year, the grape harvest symbolizes the final gathering of all those who believe in Jesus before the climactic end of the age. The prophetic aspect of the grape harvest has not yet been fulfilled. It will be fulfilled when the last believer is brought into the family of God (final harvest). Following that, nonbelievers will be judged and punished for their sins (the fields will be plowed under).

FEASTS IN PRECEDENT, PATTERN, AND PROPHECY

Each of the three primary biblical feasts commemorates a landmark event at the time of the exodus when the people of Israel escaped from slavery in Egypt (precedent). The people of Israel are commanded to celebrate all three feasts annually (pattern). Each original event and its corresponding annual commemorative feast points to a future event (prophecy). Many prophesied events involving Jesus, Israel, and the church have already happened (fulfilled). However, there are many prophesied events involving Jesus, Israel, and the church that have not yet happened (unfulfilled).

Orthodox Jews generally have an incredible appreciation for Old Testament precedent, pattern, and prophecy, but few understand their New Testament fulfillments in Jesus and the church. Christians generally have an incredible appreciation for New Testament fulfillments in Jesus and the church, but few understand their origin in Old Testament precedent, pattern, and prophecy. Figure 4.2 is a summary of the past, present, and future relevance of the biblical feasts.

Precedent	A landmark event in the year of the exodus from Egypt
Pattern	Annual commemorative feast celebrating the landmark event
Prophecy	A future event foreshadowed by the precedent and pattern Fulfilled: An event that has already happened Unfulfilled: An event that has not yet happened
Timing	The precedent, pattern, and prophecy have identical timing

FIGURE 4.2 Feasts in precedent, pattern, and prophecy

THE EDICT OF MILAN IN 313 CE

As mentioned earlier, knowledge of the incredible correlation between the Old Testament, the New Testament, and the biblical feasts has generally been lost. Consequently, also lost is an understanding of the biblical timing of these feasts. The Bible is very specific about when the feasts are to be observed, and for approximately three centuries after Jesus walked the earth, the early church celebrated the feasts according to the Bible's timeline. These celebrations continued even though the pagan Roman Empire—that ruled the known world at that time—brutally persecuted, tortured, and killed Christians for their religious beliefs and practices.

The harsh treatment ended in 313 CE when the Roman emperor Constantine issued a proclamation called the Edict of Milan. This act marked a complete change in the empire's policy toward religion in general and toward Christianity in particular. The Edict of Milan "granted all persons freedom to worship whatever deity they pleased, assured Christians of legal rights (including the right to organize churches), and directed the prompt return to Christians of confiscated property."[1] This change in policy by the government created an opportunity for Christianity to flourish in an otherwise pagan environment. The church (religion) and the state (government) began to merge.

The positive influences of the church—its morals, ethics, and values like generosity and humility—were certainly beneficial to the state. And the end of persecution was truly a blessing to the Christian church. But the state's support of the church would prove to have a downside. The negative influences of the state—its carnality, corruption, and such guiding principles as selfishness and pride—began to creep into the church. As the church adopted some of the state's ideas about leadership, religious leaders began to assume more and more power in decision-making, and the church's complete reliance on the Bible for guidance began a slow and steady decline.

THE MEETING OF THE COUNCIL OF NICAEA IN 325 CE

A notable example of the church changing the timing of a biblical celebration to be more culturally relevant occurred only twelve years after the Edict of Milan when; "The Council of Nicaea in 325 decreed that Easter should be observed on the first Sunday following the first full moon after the spring equinox (March 21). Easter, therefore, can fall on any Sunday between March 22 and April 25."[2] Following this decree, the resurrection (Easter) would be celebrated the first Sunday after the first full moon following the spring (or vernal) equinox; the day to remember the crucifixion (Good Friday) would be the Friday two days before Easter Sunday; and the day to commemorate the birth of the church (Pentecost) would be the seventh Sunday after Easter. This is not the timing specified in the Bible.

Prior to the decree, the timing of the two New Testament spring feasts (Easter and Pentecost) generally matched the timing of the corresponding two Old Testament primary spring feasts (the Feast of Passover and the Feast of *Shabua*). In other words, before the decree, the two corresponding Old Testament and New Testament spring feasts were generally celebrated—at the same time—according to their specified biblical timing. After the Council of Nicaea, the solar equinox determined the timing.

The spring solar equinox occurs on March 20 or 21. On this unique day of the year, the sun shines equally on the northern and southern hemispheres. *Equinox* means the length of the day equals (*aequus*) the length of the night (*nox*). Since the phases of the moon are not correlated with this equinox, the first full moon after March 20 or 21 can vary significantly. As a result, the first Sunday after the full moon can also vary significantly, which is why the celebration of the resurrection on Easter Sunday can vary significantly. For example, in the last two centuries the earliest date for Easter Sunday was March 22, 1818, and the latest date was April 25, 1943. The range between these two dates for Easter Sunday—March 22 and April 25—is 34 days.

FEASTS ARE A SHADOW OF THINGS TO COME

Although the Council of Nicaea made determining when the feasts are celebrated simpler, it inadvertently undermined their significance. These man-made changes deviated from the Old Testament model as well as from the way the feasts were celebrated by Jesus, His disciples, the apostles, and the early church. The decree also clouded the correlation between the Old Testament and the New Testament, creating an unintended separation between Judaism and Christianity. This separation was a factor in shaping the opinion that the Gentile church had replaced Israel in Bible prophecy, an idea that has anti-Semitic undertones. If—as some people believe—the feasts that are an integral part of the Old Testament are no longer relevant, then the Old Testament must no longer be relevant, and the Jews who observe the feasts must no longer be relevant. Not a single part of that statement is true.

In fact, as you will see, even though their relevance is often greatly misunderstood, if not missed entirely, biblical feasts are as important today as when they were established. But very few believers understand the importance of the feasts and the significance of the timing of those feasts. An individual who takes the time to diligently study the Old Testament feasts will be rewarded with a much greater understanding and appreciation of their New Testament prophetic fulfillment evident in Jesus' life and the birth of the church. Referring specifically to Old Testament feasts, festivals, and holy days, Colossians 2:17 says, *These are a shadow of the things to come, but the substance belongs to Christ.*

This chapter will examine the first spring Old Testament feast the way it is presented in the Bible—the way Jesus celebrated it with His disciples; the way the first Christians celebrated it in the early church; and the way it has been and continues to be celebrated in the practice of Judaism today. This approach clearly reveals the correlation between the foreshadowing ("a shadow of the things to come") and the foreshadowed event ("the substance belongs to Christ"). Let's begin by looking at when this feast is celebrated, which requires both understanding how the Bible reckons time and knowing why it was done that way.

MARKING TIME IN THE BIBLE

BEFORE CALENDARS, CELL PHONES, CLOCKS, COMPUTERS...

As indicated earlier, the Bible uses the sun to mark days, *shabua*-days to mark weeks, the moon to mark months, and the agricultural seasons and farming cycle to mark years. To better understand how and why time was reckoned this way, consider what life was like several thousand years ago. Imagine a world without—among many other aspects of twenty-first century life—calendars, cell phones, clocks, computers, tablets, watches, the Internet, books, newspapers, magazines, electricity, running water, toilets, toilet paper, TV, grocery stores, radios, or cars.

Now imagine a world of tents, mud bricks, oil lamps, tunics, sandals, donkeys, horses, camels, sheep, goats, rams, bulls, seed, crops, farmland, vineyards, and orchards. In this very different world, people still had a precise way to keep track of days, weeks, months, and years that was universally understood. Life today is extremely complicated, highly stressful, and mentally challenging. Life in the past was comparatively simple, but it required long hours of hard physical labor that typically revolved around maintaining a family farm. Among the necessary farming activities were plowing fields, planting seeds, harvesting crops, and caring for livestock.

FARMING CYCLE AND AGRICULTURAL SEASONS

Today, crops are grown all over the world to continuously keep grocery store shelves stocked with an incredible variety of fresh produce all year long, but that was not always the case. Before food could be preserved and transported long distances, only certain crops were produced only in certain regions and only at certain times of the year. Farming provided food for the immediate family, and some of the crops and livestock were exchanged for other goods and services. The farming cycle—plowing, planting, and harvesting—was naturally determined by the agricultural seasons. The farming cycle was used to mark years in Bible times because it was predictable and universally understood.

Since everybody requires food for survival, everyone—including individuals not directly involved in farming—would have been intimately familiar with the region's agricultural seasons. These agricultural seasons determined the farming cycle and were therefore natural points of reference for marking time. For example, an individual leaving on a journey might tell a relative, "I'll be back in time for the barley harvest." A biblical year, then, included all of the region's agricultural seasons. And the farming cycle involved plowing, planting, and harvesting all of the region's seasonal crops.

THE BIBLICAL YEAR AND THE TRADITIONAL YEAR

Before the exodus, the biblical year and the traditional/civil year both began in the month of Tishri. At the time of the exodus, God officially changed the beginning of the biblical year to the month of Nisan: *"This month [Nisan] shall be for you the beginning of months. It shall be the first month of the year for you"* (Exodus 12:2). Tishri remained—and remains—the beginning of the traditional year for civil purposes and important celebrations such as *Rosh Hashanah* (beginning of the year). The significance, relevance, and history of the biblical year and civil year are explained in *Shabua Years*, the sequel to this book.

HEBREW MONTH	ENGLISH MONTHS	HARVEST ACTIVITY
1 - Nisan (Abib)	Mar/Apr	Barley
2 - Iyar (Zif)	Apr/May	Peas/Lentils
3 - Sivan	May/Jun	Wheat/Emmer
4 - Tammuz	Jun/Jul	Grapes
5 - Av	Jul/Aug	Figs/Pomegranates
6 - Elul	Aug/Sep	Olives/Dates
7 - Tishri (Ethanim)	Sep/Oct	Final fall harvests
8 - Cheshvan (Bul)	Oct/Nov	(plowing/planting)
9 - Kislev (Chisleu)	Nov/Dec	(winter rains)
10 - Tevet	Dec/Jan	(winter rains)
11 - Shevat	Jan/Feb	(winter rains)
12 - Adar	Feb/Mar	Flax

FIGURE 4.3 Agricultural seasons and harvest activity

Figure 4.3 displays the primary agricultural seasons and harvest activity in the Middle East for each biblical month. The table begins with the first month of the biblical year (Nisan), not the first month of the traditional/civil year (Tishri). As indicated in the table, the highly symbolic grape harvest begins in the month of Tammuz. However, not indicated in Figure 4.3, the grape harvest continues until the conclusion of all fall harvests in the month of Tishri.

THE BIBLE CITES SPECIFIC DATES

To reiterate, before the calendar, the agricultural seasons were used to determine each biblical year because they were predictable and universally understood. Julius Caesar invented the first official calendar in 45 BCE, but it would be centuries before it was widely used. (This Julian calendar—with numbered years—did not happen soon enough to be used by the writers of the New Testament.) As the calendar became more widespread, it gradually became the international standard for marking time. Pope Gregory XIII modified that Julian calendar in 1582 CE, and the Gregorian calendar continues to be used throughout the world today. The Bible does not use a calendar, and it does not assign numbers to specific years (as in 2019 CE).

In addition to noting the annual agricultural seasons, the people needed a precise way to keep track of months and days that was predictable and universally understood. This fact is relevant because the Bible cites the specific dates—such as the fifteenth day of the first month—on which feasts, festivals, and holy days are to be celebrated, and people were required to know exactly when that was. However, cited biblical dates are meaningless without a uniform method to dictate precisely when months begin and end. In other words, the start of each month is just as important as the cited date itself. For instance, determining Nisan 15 is contingent upon knowing exactly when the month of Adar ends and the month of Nisan begins: it is necessary to establish Nisan 1 in order to determine Nisan 15.

THE MOON MARKS MONTHS AND SEASONS

So in order to know exactly when to celebrate biblical feasts, festivals, and holy days, people needed a precise way to determine when each month began and ended. The lunar cycle (phases of the moon) is the method that was employed because it was predictable and universally understood, and the Bible says God designed the moon for that particular purpose. For example, in Genesis 1:14, God said He created the sun and the moon on the fourth day *to separate the day from the night. And... for signs and for seasons, and for days and years.* Psalm 104:19 clarifies the moon's role: *[God] made the moon to mark the seasons.* The Hebrew word for seasons is *mow'ed* (Strong's H4150), which means "properly an appointment, i.e. a fixed time or season; specifically a festival."

The Bible is precise about when God's people are to celebrate religious feasts for several reasons. First, each feast is a commemoration of a landmark event that took place during the exodus from Egypt (precedent). Second, each feast incorporates in its celebration the harvest of a particular seasonal crop (pattern). Third, each feast foreshadows a future event that has occurred—or will occur—at the exact same time of the year (prophecy). These prophecies are validated by their unmistakable and uncanny completion in a New Testament event (fulfilled). Some events are still future (unfulfilled).

THE FIRST SIGHTING OF THE NEW MOON AT SUNSET

For each feast, the Bible either assigns a specific date or gives detailed instructions that enable an individual to make that determination. Even so, those specific dates and detailed instructions require a uniform method that dictates precisely when months begin and end. (As mentioned earlier, the starting point for each month is just as important as the cited date itself.) This method for determining the beginning and end of each month also needs to be absolutely reliable and consistent. Finally, this method needs to be simple enough to be understood by a farmer 3,500 years ago, yet accurate enough to stand up to the scrutiny of today's professional astronomers using computers to do complex mathematical calculations.

Since the 24-hour period for each biblical day begins at sunset, the first 24-hour period for each biblical month must likewise begin at sunset. Indeed, the first day of each biblical month commenced when the initial sliver of the new moon was visible in the evening sky at sunset. Absolute confirmation of the new moon was essential to determining the precisely appointed times for celebrating all biblical feasts, festivals, and holy days, including both mandatory spring feasts and the one mandatory fall feast.

ROSH CHODESH IS THE NEW MOON FESTIVAL

The Hebrew word used to describe the appearance of the initial sliver of the new moon is *chodesh* (Strong's H2320), which means "the new moon; by implication month." (It is noteworthy that the English words *month* and *moon* are both derived from the same root and have similar meanings.) The meaning of *chodesh* (or *hodesh*) is confirmed by the Theological Wordbook of the Old Testament (TWOT 613b): "this word properly means 'new moon,'... the month began when the thin crescent of the new moon was first visible at sunset."[3] In 1 Samuel 20:5, for example, *David said to Jonathan, "Behold, tomorrow is the new moon."*

New moon confirmation was so important that two independent corroborating eyewitnesses were required to testify before the Sanhedrin (the highest religious court of the day) about the sighting.[4] These eyewitnesses were questioned regarding such details as the crescent's brightness, its location in the sky, and its position. If the two descriptions of the new moon matched, the Sanhedrin would dispatch messengers throughout the land of Israel to announce *Rosh Chodesh* (the first or the head of the month). The day of the new moon is a designated holy day of convocation, and the *shofar* (ram's horn) was blown to signal the start of the new moon festival each month.

THE PHASES OF THE MOON

Upon the initial observation of the new moon in the evening sky, an individual would mark each day of the month by counting 29 or 30 consecutive evenings. (Counting was also done to mark time when the moon could not be seen because of cloud coverage.) Either the 14th or the 15th would mark the middle of the month when the moon appears to be full and completely illuminated. At this point in the cycle, the moon is the brightest, reflecting the maximum possible light from the sun. Then, 14 or 15 evenings after that, the moon seems to vanish as it enters its dark phase.

This lunar cycle, however, has not been used to reckon days and months since the advent of the calendar. In addition, the terminology for the phases of the moon that astronomers use today is different from what the Bible used. Also, according to the Bible, the new moon begins when the first hint of its light is visible. In modern astronomy, the new moon begins when no light from the moon is visible. In other words, the biblical month begins with light; the astronomical month begins with darkness. If we are to understand the Bible's timeline, we need to know the difference. Figure 4.4 illustrates the phases of the moon according to the Bible.

FIGURE 4.4 Phases of the moon according to the Bible

29-DAY AND 30-DAY BIBLICAL MONTHS

Months were not assigned a predetermined number of days until the fourth century CE. Prior to that time, the beginning of each biblical month was entirely dependent on the first sighting of the new moon immediately following the moon's dark phase. One complete cycle from new moon to new moon is called a lunar month (or a synodic month). It averages 29.53059 days—or 29 days, 12 hours, 44 minutes, 2.8 seconds.[5] Since there are no partial days, biblical months generally alternated between 29 and 30 days. However, because months were based entirely on human observation, occasionally two consecutive months had the same number of days, either 29 or 30. Figure 4.5 describes the phases of the moon's cycle during a typical 29-day month as well as a 30-day month.

29-DAY AND 30-DAY BIBLICAL MONTH	
Day 1	The initial sliver of the new moon is visible as the month begins (new)
Day 14/15	The moon is completely illuminated during the middle of the month (full)
Day 28	The last tiny sliver of the moon is visible as the month is ending
Day 29/30	The moon is completely dark on the last day of the month (conjunction)

FIGURE 4.5 A typical 29-day and 30-day biblical month

SYNCHRONIZING THE LUNAR AND SOLAR YEARS

In addition to the fact that the number of days in each month is not uniform, the lunar year[6] and the solar year[7] are not in sync. This variance occurs because a lunar year (354 days) is eleven days less than one solar year (365 days). The problem is, biblical timing requires the two cycles to work in concert with one another. To resolve this problem, a periodic adjustment was necessary to link biblical months (the lunar cycle) to their respective agricultural seasons (the solar cycle). If an adjustment was required, one lunar month was added to the current year to synchronize the biblical months to the agricultural seasons.

Toward the end of each year and prior to the twelfth Hebrew month of Adar, the Sanhedrin would add an additional month if they saw that crops were not maturing as expected. When this happened, the original month of Adar became Adar II and the additional month was Adar I.[8] The additional month enabled the respective seasonal agriculture and farming activity to occur in a particular biblical month.

Figure 4.6 summarizes how the lunar year is synchronized with the solar year. (Keep in mind that one lunar month is one complete orbit of the moon around the earth, and one solar year is one complete orbit of the earth around the sun.) Understanding the relationship between them is key because the three primary biblical feasts are each associated with the harvest of a particular crop—barley, wheat, or grape—at a particular time of the year.

DESCRIPTION	ANALYSIS	CALCULATION
1 lunar month	averages 29.5 days	29.53059 days
12 lunar months	1 lunar year	354.36708 days
1 lunar year	averages 354 days	12 x 29.5 = 354 days
1 solar year	averages 365 days	365.2422 days
1-year variance	365 days vs. 354 days	365 − 354 = 11 days
3-year variance	33 days in 3 years	11 x 3 = 33 days
33 days	about 1 month	33 − 3 = 30 days
1 month added	about every 3 years	Adar I is added

FIGURE 4.6 Synchronizing the lunar and solar years

RABBI HILLEL INTRODUCED A FIXED CALENDAR

The method of reckoning each biblical month by observation alone is no longer practiced in Israel. In 359 CE, Rabbi Hillel (Hillel the Nasi or Hillel II) "introduced a fixed and continuous calendar"[9] that is determined by observation, assignment, and formula. The first day of the first month of the Hebrew year (Nisan 1) was observed as usual. Then a predetermined fixed number of days was assigned to each month. Then, to synchronize this standardized lunar year to the agricultural seasons, Hillel developed a nineteen-year cyclical formula in which an additional month of Adar is added in the 3rd, 6th, 8th, 11th, 14th, 17th, and 19th years. This is the method used today by Orthodox Jews, but it is not the method found in the Bible.

Again, Rabbi Hillel's calendar assigns a fixed number of days to each month and uses a formula for synchronization. This is similar to the Gregorian calendar, which also assigns a predetermined fixed number of days to each month (for example, February has been assigned 28 days). Because a solar year is slightly more than 365 days, the Gregorian calendar adds an extra day to February approximately every four years for synchronization (February has 29 days in a leap year).

SCIENTIFIC DATING AND ASTRONOMICAL EVENTS

Astronomers today are able to calculate the past, present, and future dates and times of the phases of the moon—as well as the rising and the setting of the sun—for any location on planet Earth. These determinations are possible today because modern computers can perform complex algorithms. These algorithms are able to pinpoint the exact dates and times of astronomical events that occurred over 2,000 years ago in Jerusalem. But what in the world do these abilities of today's astronomers have to do with biblical feasts?

As has been mentioned, the Bible is very precise when it specifies the dates and times of events associated with the exodus (precedent) as well as with the annual commemorative biblical feasts (pattern). Those dates and times are inseparably linked to the phases of the moon. Today, we have data on the phases of the moon in Jerusalem dating back to before Jesus was born, which means we are able to determine the exact dates and times of important biblical feasts that Jesus participated in (prophecy). God has given our generation of believers a precious gift: we have the ability to scientifically confirm the accuracy of the Bible.

As King David said, *The heavens declare the glory of God, and the sky above proclaims his handiwork* (Psalm 19:1). God's glory is evident in the sun and the moon, and how they are used to mark time is evidence of His handiwork. When the timing of a biblical event is proven accurate, it adds a degree of credibility to the verse, passage, book, and Bible. That's why, in this book as well as in future books in this series, astronomical events like the phases of the moon and anomalies like solar and lunar eclipses are used to confirm the dates of biblical events and to link the historical record to the Bible. Before we take a closer look at the first primary spring feast, let's review the following principles:

The feasts commemorate events that took place during the exodus.

The feasts feature a particular crop in their harvest ceremonies.

The feasts are used in Bible precedent, pattern, and prophecy.

The Bible specifies the exact date and time to celebrate each feast.

The sunset defines the end and the beginning of each biblical day.

Shabua-days define each biblical week.

The phases of the moon define each biblical month.

The agricultural seasons and farming cycle define each biblical year.

THE SEVEN-DAY FEAST

BARLEY IS HARVESTED DURING NISAN

The Hebrew name for the first month of the biblical year illustrates how closely the feasts are associated with the harvest of a particular seasonal crop. The original Hebrew name for that month is *Abib*. (The name Abib was changed to Nisan during Israel's Babylonian captivity.) According to the Theological Wordbook of the Old Testament, *Abib* "refers to barley that is already ripe, but still soft... in that month it came to ear" (TWOT 1b).[10] The barley crop in the Middle East always becomes ripe and is always harvested during the appropriately named month of Abib. The harvest began after a ritual in which the barley firstfruits sheaf was ceremonially waved in the air. The timing for this annual ceremony is determined by the first day of Passover on Abib (Nisan) 14. In other words, the barley sheaf firstfruits ceremony is not assigned a specific date, but as you will learn, it is linked to Nisan 14.

It is noteworthy that the Bible links the destruction of the barley crop in Egypt to the seventh plague of hail that occurred shortly before the exodus. Exodus 9:31 says that, as a result of the hail, *the flax and barley were struck down, for the barley was in the ear and the flax was in bud.* This statement accurately reflects the growth stage of barley and flax. At that time of the year these crops would have already come up in the fields and begun to ripen, but they would not have been quite ready for harvest. The timing of the hail is also consistent with crops that would not have come up in the fields yet: *the wheat and the emmer were not struck down, for they are late in coming up* (v. 32). Today in the Middle East, the barley crop comes up in the fields and is ready to be harvested approximately seven weeks prior to the wheat and emmer crops.

FEAST OF PASSOVER = FEAST OF UNLEAVENED BREAD

The timing of the barley sheaf firstfruits ceremony and subsequent barley harvest is linked to the Feast of Passover/Feast of Unleavened Bread. This seven-day celebration is called the Feast of Passover because it begins on the first day of Passover (Nisan 14), the day that the Passover lambs were sacrificed before the exodus from Egypt (precedent); the day of the annual sacrifice of the Passover lambs in Jerusalem (pattern); and the day that the Passover Lamb (Jesus) was crucified, died, and buried in Jerusalem. The Feast of Passover ends—seven days after it begins—on Nisan 20 with a holy assembly.

This seven-day celebration is also called the Feast of Unleavened Bread because bread that contained leaven (yeast) was forbidden all seven days of the feast (Nisan 14 through Nisan 20). Even the presence of leaven was forbidden because leaven metaphorically represents sin, and all seven days of the feast are considered sacred. The Bible commands the people of Israel to eat unleavened bread—*matstsah* (Strong's H4682)—from the first day through the seventh day. In addition, the home was required to be free of leaven—*se'or* (Strong's H7603)—all seven days. As you will see, the Feast of Passover/Feast of Unleavened Bread ceremonial meal—also called the Passover Seder—is eaten on the second day (Nisan 15) of this seven-day celebration.

The following verses (Figure 4.7) link the seven days, the Feast of Passover, and the Feast of Unleavened Bread. Since these two descriptive titles are associated with the same seven-day feast, for the purpose of this text, it will hereafter be referred to as the Seven-Day Feast.

Exodus 12:15	*"Seven days you shall eat unleavened bread. On the first day you shall remove leaven out of your houses... from the first day until the seventh day."*
Exodus 12:16	*"On the first day you shall hold a holy assembly, and on the seventh day a holy assembly."*
Exodus 12:19	*"For seven days no leaven is to be found in your houses."*
Leviticus 23:6	*"For seven days you shall eat unleavened bread."*
Numbers 28:16	*"Seven days shall unleavened bread be eaten."*
Ezra 6:22	*They kept the Feast of Unleavened Bread seven days with joy.*
Ezekiel 45:21	*"You shall celebrate the Feast of the Passover, and for seven days unleavened bread shall be eaten."*
Mark 14:1	*It was now two days before the Passover and the Feast of Unleavened Bread.*
Luke 22:1	*Now the Feast of Unleavened Bread drew near, which is called the Passover.*

FIGURE 4.7 The Feast of Passover/Unleavened Bread

NISAN 14: THE FIRST DATE OF THE SEVEN-DAY FEAST

Exodus 12:18 has two parts. The first part specifies exactly when the seven days of the Seven-Day Feast are to begin: *"In the first month, from the fourteenth day of the month at evening, you shall eat unleavened bread."* Nisan 14 is the first day of the Seven-Day Feast, the first day unleavened bread was required to be eaten, and also the day that the Passover lambs were required to be sacrificed. As Figure 4.8 indicates, Nisan 14 has different titles, including the Lord's Passover, Passover, Feast of the Passover, first day of Unleavened Bread, and day of Unleavened Bread. Nisan 14 is also called the day of Preparation. This date plays a significant role in Bible precedent, pattern, and prophecy (details to follow).

Exodus 12:5-6	*"You shall keep [your lamb] until the fourteenth day of this month, when [all] Israel shall kill their lambs at twilight."*
Exodus 12:18	*"In the first month, from the fourteenth day of the month at evening, you shall eat unleavened bread."*

Leviticus 23:5	"In the first month, on the fourteenth day of the month at twilight, is the LORD'S Passover."
Numbers 9:2-3	"Let the people of Israel keep the Passover at its appointed time. On the fourteenth day of this month, at twilight."
Numbers 9:5	They kept the Passover in the first month, on the fourteenth day of the month, at twilight, in the wilderness of Sinai.
Numbers 28:16	On the fourteenth day of the first month is the LORD'S Passover.
2 Chronicles 35:1	Josiah kept a Passover to the LORD in Jerusalem. And they slaughtered the Passover lamb on the fourteenth day of the first month.
Ezra 6:19	On the fourteenth day of the first month, the returned exiles kept the Passover.
Ezekiel 45:21	"In the first month, on the fourteenth day of the month, you shall celebrate the Feast of the Passover."
Matthew 26:17	Now on the first day of Unleavened Bread the disciples came to Jesus, saying, "Where will you have us prepare for you to eat the Passover?"
Mark 14:12	On the first day of Unleavened Bread, when they sacrificed the Passover lamb, [the disciples asked Jesus,] "Where will you have us go and prepare for you to eat the Passover?"
Luke 22:7	Then came the day of Unleavened Bread, on which the Passover lamb had to be sacrificed.

FIGURE 4.8 Nisan 14 is the first date of the Seven-Day Feast

NISAN 20: THE LAST DATE OF THE SEVEN-DAY FEAST

Now let's look at the second part of Exodus 12:18 that specifies exactly when the seven days of the Seven-Day Feast are to end: *"You shall eat unleavened bread until the twenty-first day of the month at evening."* "Until the twenty-first day... at evening" does not mean the 21st is included as one of the seven days. A better rendering is "until the evening of the 21st day." When evening begins on the 21st—after sunset on the 20th—a new 24-hour biblical day begins, but "until" means the seven days of unleavened bread end before that happens.

In Exodus 18:13, similar terminology is used when a single 24-hour biblical day ends at evening and marks the start of a new day: *The next day Moses sat to judge the people, and the people stood around Moses from morning till evening.* "Morning till evening" means Moses judged the people during the daylight hours—from sunrise (morning) until sunset (evening)—but not after sunset when a new day began. In the same way, "until the twenty-first day… at evening" does not include the evening of the 21st day. If the 21st day of the month were included, the Seven-Day Feast would be eight days when seven days are clearly—and repeatedly—specified. Since we know the feast begins on Nisan 14 and lasts seven days, it must end on Nisan 20. Accordingly, the seven days for the Seven-Day Feast are Nisan 14, 15, 16, 17, 18, 19, and 20.

NISAN 14 AND NISAN 20 ARE HOLY DAYS OF ASSEMBLY

The first day (Nisan 14) and the seventh day (Nisan 20) are not only bookends of the feast. Both are also holy days of assembly: *"On the first day you shall hold a holy assembly, and on the seventh day a holy assembly. No work shall be done on those days. But what everyone needs to eat, that alone may be prepared by you"* (Exodus 12:16). Notice that both Nisan 14 and Nisan 20 are designated days of holy assembly, not days of solemn rest. In other words, ordinary work—such as farming—was prohibited because both days were indeed holy, but as you will see, the work required to sacrifice the lamb, mark the doorframe in blood, and prepare the meal was allowed because God had commanded that this preparation work be done.

In addition to the general references to the seven dates of the Seven-Day Feast, the Bible specifies certain activities for each particular day. The various titles and activities designated for each of the seven dates are listed in Figure 4.9. Notice that, as the Lord had commanded, anything with leaven (yeast)—including leavened bread—was strictly forbidden all seven days. In addition, notice that a food offering was presented to the Lord on all seven days.

NISAN 14: THE DATE THE PASSOVER LAMBS WERE KILLED

What the apostle Paul told fellow believers in Colossians 2:17 bears repeating: biblical feasts, festivals, and holy days *are a shadow of the things to come, but the substance belongs to Christ.* Again, there is uncanny and precise

DAY 1: NISAN 14	
1st Day of Unleavened Bread	All leaven was forbidden; only unleavened bread was allowed
1st Day of Food Offering	A food offering was presented to the Lord
Holy Day of Assembly	People gathered on this holy day of convocation
Ordinary Work Prohibited	Only the specified work of preparation was permitted
Day of Preparation	Preparation work Home: House was rid of leaven Unleavened bread: Bread was baked without leaven Lamb: The Passover lamb was sacrificed at the temple Meal: Food and lamb were prepared for Passover Seder Door: The doorframe was marked with the lamb's blood
DAY 2: NISAN 15	
2nd Day of Unleavened Bread	All leaven was forbidden; only unleavened bread was allowed
2nd Day of Food Offering	A food offering was presented to the Lord
Sabbath High Day	A special holy day of solemn rest (not the regular Sabbath)
Passover Seder	During the meal, the sacrificed Passover lamb was eaten
DAY 3: NISAN 16	
3rd Day of Unleavened Bread	All leaven was forbidden; only unleavened bread was allowed
3rd Day of Food Offering	A food offering was presented to the Lord
DAY 4: NISAN 17	
4th Day of Unleavened Bread	All leaven was forbidden; only unleavened bread was allowed
4th Day of Food Offering	A food offering was presented to the Lord
DAY 5: NISAN 18	
5th Day of Unleavened Bread	All leaven was forbidden; only unleavened bread was allowed
5th Day of Food Offering	A food offering was presented to the Lord
DAY 6: NISAN 19	
6th Day of Unleavened Bread	All leaven was forbidden; only unleavened bread was allowed
6th Day of Food Offering	A food offering was presented to the Lord
DAY 7: NISAN 20	
7th Day of Unleavened Bread	All leaven was forbidden; only unleavened bread was allowed
7th Day of Food Offering	A food offering was presented to the Lord
Holy Day of Assembly	People gathered on this holy day of convocation
Ordinary Work Prohibited	The general barley harvest could not begin on this day

FIGURE 4.9 The seven days of the Seven-Day Feast

symmetry between the precedents and patterns in the Old Testament ("a shadow of the things to come") and the prophetic fulfillments in the New Testament ("the substance belongs to Christ"). Case in point: Jesus (the Lamb of God) precisely fulfills the Old Testament precedent and pattern (the Passover lamb) for Nisan 14, the first day of the Seven-Day Feast. As indicated, one of the biblical names for this day is the day of Preparation.

In the year of the exodus, Nisan 14 was the day before the Hebrew families left Egypt and the day that the first-ever Passover lambs were sacrificed (precedent). Nisan 14 was also the first day of the Seven-Day Feast, the day on which the Passover lambs were sacrificed every year in Jerusalem (pattern). Nisan 14 was also the very day that Jesus the Lamb of God was crucified on a cross in Jerusalem (prophecy). According to John 19:14-15, the crucifixion happened on the day of Preparation, which is Nisan 14: *Now it was the day of Preparation of the Passover... [The Jews] cried out, "Away with [Jesus], away with him, crucify him!"*

Proof that Jesus was crucified on the day of Preparation (Nisan 14) is also found in the gospels of Matthew, Mark, and Luke. As noted previously in Figure 4.8, both Matthew 26:17 and Mark 14:12 called the day of Preparation the *first day of Unleavened Bread,* and Mark immediately clarified that the first day of Unleavened Bread is *when they sacrificed the Passover lamb.* Although Luke 22:7 simply calls it the *day of Unleavened Bread,* it is clear that the author is referring to the first day of the Seven-Day Feast because later in the verse Luke said that this was the day *on which the Passover lamb had to be sacrificed.* In essence, Matthew, Mark, Luke, and John all link the first day of the Seven-Day Feast to the day of Preparation (Nisan 14), the exact day on which Passover lambs had to be sacrificed. The exact day on which Jesus was crucified.

JESUS WAS BURIED ON THE DAY OF PREPARATION

John 19:31 indicates that Jesus was not only crucified but that He also died on the day of Preparation: *Since it was the day of Preparation, and so that the bodies would not remain on the cross... the Jews asked Pilate that their legs might be broken and that they might be taken away.* The executioners would break the lower legs of crucified individuals to hasten their death. Crucifixion was a particularly gruesome way to die, and the process could last for days. When the legs of the condemned were broken with an iron rod, the dying were not able to push themselves up to fill their lungs with air. Deprived of oxygen, these individuals quickly died of asphyxiation.

The legs of the two criminals crucified with Jesus were broken to hasten their deaths so that their bodies could be taken away and buried before sunset on the day of Preparation (Nisan 14). It was unlawful for bodies to be left hanging on the cross after sunset—when the Sabbath High Day (Nisan 15) began—because it was one of the holiest days of the Jewish year. However, *when the [soldiers] came to Jesus and saw that he was already dead, they did not break his legs* (John 19:33). (When the soldiers did not break Jesus' legs, they fulfilled the prophecy that said *"not one of his bones will be broken"* [v. 36].) Jesus was crucified, died, removed from the cross, and buried in a nearby tomb—all on the day of Preparation (Nisan 14).

SEQUENCE OF EVENTS ON THE DAY OF PREPARATION

Figure 4.10 shows the sequence of events that occurred on the day of Preparation (Nisan 14) in the year Jesus was crucified. This 24-hour day is broken down into three categories: *halves* for when it was dark (evening/night) and when it was light (morning/day); *quarters* for the four watches when it was dark and the four watches when it was light; and *twelfths* for the twelve hours when it was dark and the twelve hours when it was light. The descriptions of the events that took place on this day are taken from the gospels of Matthew, Mark, Luke, and John. Since the Gospels do not specify exactly when each event took place, all of the times are approximate except for the events mentioned in Mark 15.

Remember, each 24-hour biblical day ends at sunset, and each new 24-hour day begins immediately after sunset. The Hebrew month of Nisan occurs during the months of March and April on the Gregorian calendar. The average time of sunset in Jerusalem was 5:47 p.m. for March 2018 and 6:08 p.m. for April 2018 (after an adjustment was made for daylight savings time).[11] The average time of sunset when these two months are

EVENING/NIGHT OF NISAN 14		
First Watch of the Night	6:01-7:00 p.m. (1st hour)	Jesus said, *"[Tell a man] my time is at hand. I will keep the Passover at your house"* (Matthew 26:18).
		Two of the disciples went and followed a man carrying a jar of water to a house with an upper room.
	7:01-8:00 p.m. (2nd hour)	The upper room was furnished and ready—cleansed of leaven—for the first day of the Seven-Day Feast.
	8:01-9:00 p.m. (3rd hour)	Jesus and all twelve disciples began the Last Supper meal with unleavened bread—and no lamb.
		Jesus rose from the meal, set aside His garments, and humbly washed the feet of His disciples.
Second Watch of the Night	9:01-10:00 p.m. (4th hour)	Jesus said, *"He who has dipped his hand in the dish with me will betray me"* (Matthew 26:23).
		Judas left the Last Supper meal in order to plot with the chief priests about betraying Jesus.
	10:01-11:00 p.m. (5th hour)	The Lord's Last Supper meal continued with the eleven remaining disciples after Judas departed.
	11:01-12:00 p.m. (6th hour)	Jesus shared an important final message with the eleven remaining disciples (John 13:31 – 17:26).
		Jesus went to the garden of Gethsemane when it was night to pray with the eleven disciples.
Third Watch of the Night	12:01-1:00 a.m. (7th hour)	The disciples were not able to stay awake to pray with Jesus and fell asleep (1st time).
		The disciples were not able to stay awake to pray with Jesus and fell asleep (2nd time).
	1:01-2:00 a.m. (8th hour)	The disciples were not able to stay awake to pray with Jesus and fell asleep (3rd time).
	2:01-3:00 a.m. (9th hour)	Judas led a great crowd of people armed with swords and clubs to Gethsemane to arrest Jesus.
		Jesus was arrested and taken to Annas, the former high priest and the father-in-law of Caiaphas.
Fourth Watch of the Night	3:01-4:00 a.m. (10th hour)	The entire Sanhedrin was assembled at the house of Caiaphas, the reigning temple high priest.
		Annas bound Jesus and sent Him to the house of Caiaphas to be tried by the whole Sanhedrin.
	4:01-5:00 a.m. (11th hour)	False witnesses testified at the trial, Caiaphas questioned Jesus, and Jesus remained silent.
	5:01-6:00 a.m. (12th hour)	Caiaphas accused Jesus of blasphemy and condemned Him to death; Jesus was mocked and beaten.
		Outside the house of Caiaphas, Peter denied knowing Jesus three times before the rooster crowed.

MORNING/DAY OF NISAN 14		
First Watch of the Day	6:01-7:00 a.m. (1st hour)	Caiaphas delivered Jesus to Governor Pilate who was in Jerusalem to keep order during the feast.
		Pilate found no fault in Jesus and sent Him to King Herod who was also in Jerusalem to keep order.
	7:01-8:00 a.m. (2nd hour)	Herod found no fault in Jesus and sent Him back to Pilate who had Jesus beaten and scourged.
	8:01-9:00 a.m. (3rd hour)	Pilate presented Jesus to the crowd saying, "Behold the Man," but they demanded He be crucified.
		It was the third hour when they crucified him (Mark 15:25).
Second Watch of the Day	9:01-10:00 a.m. (4th hour)	Jesus hung on the cross at Golgatha.
	10:01-11:00 a.m. (5th hour)	
	11:01-12:00 p.m. (6th hour)	
Third Watch of the Day	12:01-1:00 p.m. (7th hour)	*When the sixth hour had come, there was darkness over the whole land until the ninth hour* (Mark 15:33).
	1:01-2:00 p.m. (8th hour)	
	2:01-3:00 p.m. (9th hour)	
		At the ninth hour... Jesus uttered a loud cry and breathed his last (Mark 15:34, 37).
Fourth Watch of the Day	3:01-4:00 p.m. (10th hour)	A Roman soldier pierced the lifeless body of Jesus with a spear, and blood and water came out.
		Joseph of Arimathea went to Governor Pilate to ask permission to take away the body of Jesus.
	4:01-5:00 p.m. (11th hour)	Using linen cloths and spices, Joseph and Nicodemus prepared the body of Jesus for burial.
	5:01-6:00 p.m. (12th hour)	The body of Jesus was placed in a nearby rock-hewn tomb owned by Joseph of Arimathea.
		The day of Preparation (Nisan 14) ended at sunset just before the Sabbath High Day (Nisan 15) began.

FIGURE 4.10 The day of Preparation in the year Jesus was crucified

combined is 5:58 p.m. We rounded up the time of sunset from 5:58 p.m. to 6:00 p.m. for Figure 4.10. Again, all times in Figure 4.10 are approximate except for the Mark 15 events. For the purposes of this text, each biblical day ends at 6:00 p.m. (sunset), and each new biblical day begins at 6:01 p.m. (after sunset).

LAMBS WERE SACRIFICED AT 9:00 A.M. AND 3:00 P.M.

According to Mark 15:25, *it was the third hour [9:00 a.m.] when they crucified him [Jesus]*, when He was nailed to the cross at Golgotha. Mark 15:34, 37 says that *at the ninth hour [3:00 p.m.] Jesus uttered a loud cry and breathed his last*. Both 9:00 a.m. and 3:00 p.m. are specific times of the day that originated as a precedent, continued as a pattern, and have prophetic significance.

When God established the sacrificial system for the people of Israel in the year of the exodus (precedent), He said: *"Now this is what you shall offer on the altar: two lambs a year old day by day regularly. One lamb you shall offer in the morning, and the other lamb you shall offer at twilight"* (Exodus 29:38-39). And, each day on the altar in the courtyard of the temple (for over one thousand years) a blemish–free male lamb was sacrificed in the morning, and a blemish-free male lamb was sacrificed in the afternoon (pattern). God gave very specific instructions regarding the timing of the sacrifices: *"you shall be careful to offer [each lamb] to me at its appointed time"* (Numbers 28:2-4). Based on the prophetic fulfillment in Mark 15, a case can be made that 9:00 a.m. was the appointed time for the morning sacrifice, and 3:00 p.m. was the appointed time for the afternoon sacrifice. Jesus (the sinless Lamb of God) was nailed to the cross (the biblical altar) at 9:00 a.m., and He died on the cross at 3:00 p.m. (prophecy).

NISAN 15: THE DATE THE PASSOVER LAMBS WERE EATEN

The date of the ceremonial meal (Nisan 15) immediately follows the day of Preparation (Nisan 14). Nisan 15 was a landmark day at the time of the exodus: it was the actual date that God brought the people of Israel out of

Egypt (precedent). It was—and is—celebrated with an elaborate ceremonial meal, subsequently called the Passover Seder (pattern). The titles "Feast of Unleavened Bread" and "Feast of Passover" are used both generally to refer to the seven days of the Seven-Day Feast and specifically to refer to the day of the ceremonial meal. The Passover lambs that were sacrificed and prepared on Nisan 14 were eaten during the ceremonial meal on Nisan 15, the second day of the Seven-Day Feast (Figure 4.11).

Exodus 12:11	*"In this manner you shall eat it: with your belt fastened, your sandals on your feet, and your staff in your hand. And you shall eat it in haste. It is the Lord's Passover."*
Exodus 12:14	*"This day shall be for you a memorial day, and you shall keep it as a feast to the Lord; throughout your generations, as a statute forever, you shall keep it as a feast."*
Exodus 12:17	*"You shall observe the Feast of Unleavened Bread, for on this very day I brought your hosts out of the land of Egypt."*
Leviticus 23:6	*"On the fifteenth day of the same month is the Feast of Unleavened Bread to the Lord."*
Numbers 28:16-17	*"On the fourteenth day of the first month is the Lord's Passover, and on the fifteenth day of this month is a feast."*
Numbers 33:3	*They set out from Rameses [Egypt] in the first month, on the fifteenth day of the first month. On the day after the Passover, the people of Israel went out triumphantly in the sight of all the Egyptians.*

FIGURE 4.11 Nisan 15 is the date the Passover lambs were eaten

THE PASSOVER SEDER INCLUDES FIFTEEN RITUALS

On Nisan 15, during the ceremonial meal called the Passover Seder, Passover lambs were eaten as a reminder of the Passover lambs the Israelites ate hastily on that same date before leaving Egypt. The Bible designates Nisan 15 as the Sabbath High Day, a solemn day of rest to be observed in addition to the regular Sabbath. The word *seder* means "order" which is appropriate for the evening.[12] According to the *Haggadah* (the book of detailed Hebrew instructions for the Seder), the Passover Seder meal is an arrangement of fifteen rituals in a specific order. Figure 4.12 lists the Hebrew names of those fifteen rituals and provides a brief description of each.[13]

#	RITUAL	DESCRIPTION
1	*Kaddesh*	A blessing is recited over the first cup of wine in honor of the holiday.
2	*Urechatz*	Hands are washed without saying a blessing.
3	*Karpas*	A vegetable (usually parsley) is dipped in salt water, a blessing is said, and the vegetable is eaten.
4	*Yachatz*	One of the three *matzahs* (unleavened bread) on the table is broken, part is returned to the pile, the other part is set aside.
5	*Maggid*	Prompted by The Four Questions, the story of the exodus from Egypt and the first Passover is told. Then a blessing is recited over the second cup of wine, and it is drunk.
6	*Rachtzah*	In preparation for eating the *matzah*, hands are washed a second time, and a blessing is said.
7	*Motzi*	A blessing is recited over the *matzah*. This first blessing of the bread is the same *motzi* blessing recited before any bread meal.
8	*Matzah*	A second blessing is recited over the *matzah*, which is then broken, and a piece is given to everyone to eat. This second blessing was a special blessing regarding the commandment to eat *matzah*, which is recited only at *Pesach* (the Passover Seder).
9	*Maror*	A blessing is recited over a bitter vegetable (usually horseradish), it is dipped in *charoset* (a sweet apple-cinnamon-wine-nut mixture), and then it is eaten.
10	*Korekh*	A bitter vegetable (usually romaine lettuce) and *charoset* (a sweet apple-cinnamon-wine-nut mixture) are eaten together on a piece of *matzah*.
11	*Shulchan Orekh*	A festive meal is eaten at a leisurely pace.
12	*Tzafun*	The piece of *matzah* that was set aside is located and/or ransomed back and eaten as the last part of the meal, a sort of dessert.
13	*Barekh*	Grace is said after the meal, the third cup of wine is poured, and *birkat ha-mazon* (grace after meals) is recited. Then a blessing is said over that third cup, and it is drunk. The fourth cup is poured.
14	*Hallel*	Psalms of praise are recited, a blessing is recited over the fourth cup of wine, and it is drunk.
15	*Nirtzah*	The Seder is pronounced complete and the wish expressed that next year the Seder might be observed in Jerusalem.

FIGURE 4.12 The fifteen parts of the Passover Seder

JESUS USED THE MOTZI BLESSING

The Bible does not indicate that any of the unique rituals listed in Figure 4.12 were performed at the meal Jesus ate with His disciples on the day of Preparation (Nisan 14). Similarily the *motzi* blessing said by Jesus at the Last Supper was not unique. It was said prior to every meal with bread—leavened or unleavened—throughout the entire year. Jesus used the customary *motzi* blessing at the Last Supper when He gave thanks for the bread before breaking it and giving it to His disciples. The blessing on that day was not unique, but the bread was.

The Last Supper took place on the first day of the Seven-Day Feast (Nisan 14) according to the Leviticus 23:6 command that *"for seven days you shall eat unleavened bread."* So the bread Jesus said the *motzi* blessing over at the Last Supper was unleavened. The *motzi* blessing was also said on the second day of the Seven-Day Feast (Nisan 15) during the Passover Seder. However, only during the Seder, the *motzi* blessing was followed by a second special blessing—called *matzah*—before the unleavened bread was broken and distributed. The *motzi* blessing was also said prior to eating unleavened bread on the third, fourth, fifth, sixth, and seventh days of the Seven-Day Feast.

THE LAST SUPPER WAS NOT THE PASSOVER SEDER

The day of Preparation meal that Jesus ate with His twelve disciples on Nisan 14 is typically referred to as the Lord's Supper or the Last Supper. As indicated, this was also the first day of the Seven-Day Feast when the house was rid of leaven, and unleavened bread was prepared and eaten. The only reference to food at the Last Supper is to the bread—no doubt unleavened—that Jesus broke and gave to His disciples saying, *"This is my body, which is given for you"* (Luke 22:19). The Last Supper meal on Nisan 14 could not have been the ceremonial Passover Seder observed on Nisan 15 for the following ten reasons.

Lambs were sacrificed on Nisan 14: Each household was required to sacrifice a lamb on the day of Preparation (Nisan 14). This mass sacrifice of lambs did not take place during the first half of the day (after the sun had set and it was dark outside); it took place during the last half of the day (after the sun had risen and it was light outside). A large number of Levitical priests sacrificed the lambs in the courtyard of the temple. (The Jewish historian Flavius Josephus says at least 256,500 lambs were killed during one Passover.[14]) After the lambs were killed, each household took their lamb home to prepare it, dress it, and roast it over a fire. The Last Supper evening meal that Jesus ate with His disciples took place before the lambs were killed, prepared, dressed, and roasted.

No Passover lamb was eaten: Not one of the Gospels indicates that Jesus or His disciples ate a Passover lamb on the day of the Last Supper. In fact, no lamb is even mentioned, and an indirect reference at the meal suggests they didn't have one (explained in the next paragraph). The absence of a lamb during the Last Supper meal is one of many reasons supporting the argument that it took place on the evening of Nisan 14, not the evening of the Passover Seder on Nisan 15. The reason that Jesus and His disciples did not eat a Passover lamb at the Last Supper is because, although lambs were sacrificed on the day of Preparation—on the first day of the Seven-Day Feast (Nisan 14)—they were not eaten until the Passover Seder on the second day of the Seven-Day Feast (Nisan 15).

Jesus and the disciples were not prepared for the Passover Seder: The Last Supper evening meal on Nisan 14 took place at a house that Mark 14:15 says had *a large upper room furnished and ready.* "Furnished" implies the room had been physically set up for a communal meal. (It was most likely set up for the Passover Seder the following evening on Nisan 15.) "Ready" implies the house had been cleansed of leaven and unleavened bread was available; both are required on the first day of the Seven-Day Feast. The day of the Last Supper meal—with unleavened bread—was also the day to prepare for the Passover Seder feast. When Judas left during the Last Supper, *some [of the disciples] thought that, because Judas had the moneybag, Jesus was telling him, "Buy what we need for the feast"* (John 13:29). This verse indicates the disciples did not have on Nisan 14 what they needed—a lamb, for instance—for the Passover Seder on Nisan 15.

Jesus only said one blessing over the bread: According to the Gospels, at the Last Supper *Jesus took bread, and after blessing it broke it and gave it to the disciples* (Matthew 26:26); *[Jesus] took bread, and after blessing it* *broke it and gave it to them* (Mark 14:22); *[Jesus] took bread, and when he had given thanks, he broke it and gave it to them* (Luke 22:19). Each Gospel account indicates Jesus broke bread and gave it to His disciples after a single blessing; none of the Gospel accounts mention a second blessing. This is significant because two blessings are said over the bread during the Passover Seder: "The first blessing is the same *motzi* blessing recited over bread before every bread meal. This is followed by a special [second] blessing regarding the commandment to eat *matzah,* which is recited only at *Pesach.*"[15] (*Pesach* means "Passover."[16]) The absence of a second blessing over the bread is further evidence that the Last Supper on Nisan 14 was not the Passover Seder that would be observed on Nisan 15.

Jesus could not eat this Passover: In Luke 22:15 Jesus said, *"I have earnestly desired to eat this Passover with you before I suffer."* The word *earnestly* in Greek is *epithymia* (Strong's G1939), which means "a longing (especially for what is forbidden)." And the word *desired* in Greek is *epithymeo* (Strong's G1937), which means "to set the heart upon, i.e. long for (rightfully or otherwise)." This verse does not say anything about Jesus eating a Passover lamb during the Last Supper meal: a lamb would have been eaten if the meal had been the Passover Seder. This verse simply says Jesus *wanted* to eat the Passover. Jesus knew that the Passover lamb was killed on Nisan 14 but not eaten until the Passover Seder on Nisan 15. In addition, Jesus knew that He—the Lamb of God—would be killed at 3:00 p.m. on Nisan 14. Therefore, Jesus knew it was not possible for Him to eat the Passover lamb unless He disobeyed God and refused to go to the cross, which is why Jesus could only long to share in that meal.

Jesus said He would not eat this Passover: In the verse immediately after Jesus told His disciples, *"I have earnestly desired to eat this Passover"* (Luke 22:15), Jesus plainly said He was not going to eat it—the Passover lamb at the Seder—until the kingdom of God comes: *"I tell you I will not eat it until it is fulfilled in the kingdom of God"* (v. 16). This statement makes it quite clear that Jesus did not eat the Passover lamb at the Last Supper, and there is no reason to believe the disciples ate it at that time either.

Jesus was killed before the Passover Seder: Mark 14:1-2 says that *two days before the Passover and the Feast of Unleavened Bread... the chief priests* *and the scribes were seeking how to arrest [Jesus] by stealth and kill him, for they said, "Not during the feast, lest there be an uproar from the people."* This meeting took place on Nisan 12, which was two days before Nisan 14—the first day of the Seven-Day Feast. At this meeting the religious leaders plotted to arrest and kill Jesus but decided "not during the feast"—the Passover Seder on Nisan 15—to avoid causing an uproar. Furthermore, Jewish law forbids killing on the Sabbath, and Nisan 15 was a Sabbath High Day. Since killing was not forbidden on Nisan 14, Jesus and the two criminals were crucified on Nisan 14 to avoid violating the Sabbath High Day.

The Last Supper preceded the Passover Seder: The following three verses from the gospel of John (Figure 4.13) all indicate that the Last Supper of Jesus and His disciples (Nisan 14) preceded the ceremonial Passover Seder (Nisan 15).

John 13:1-2	*Now before the Feast of the Passover... Jesus knew that his hour had come to depart out of this world... During supper... the devil had already put it into the heart of Judas... to betray him.*
John 13:29	*[During the Last Supper] some thought that, because Judas had the moneybag, Jesus was telling him, "Buy what we need for the feast."*
John 18:28	*[The religious leaders] led Jesus... to the governor's headquarters. It was early morning. They themselves did not enter the governor's headquarters, so that they would not be defiled, but could eat the Passover.*

FIGURE 4.13 The Last Supper preceded the Passover Seder

There is a 24-hour difference in timing: Jesus and His disciples ate the Last Supper meal when evening began on Nisan 14. Nisan 14 was the day of Preparation when Passover lambs were killed, prepared, dressed, and roasted before sunset. The people of Israel ate their Passover lambs when evening began on Nisan 15 (after sunset on Nisan 14). Nisan 15 was the specially designated Sabbath High Day for the ceremonial Passover Seder. The Last Supper meal the evening of Nisan 14 occurred 24 hours before the ceremonial Passover Seder the evening of Nisan 15.

Jesus fulfilled the precedent, pattern, and prophecy for Nisan 14: Jesus and His disciples did not sacrifice a Passover lamb on the day of the Last

Supper (Nisan 14) because Jesus Himself was—on that very day—the Passover Lamb who was sacrificed: *Christ, our Passover lamb, has been sacrificed* (1 Corinthians 5:7). The initial sacrifice of lambs in Egypt (precedent), the ritual sacrifice of lambs on the first day of the Seven-Day Feast (pattern), and the sacrifice of Jesus—the Lamb of God—on a cross in Jerusalem (prophecy) all occurred on the exact same date: Nisan 14. Once again, Old Testament feasts, festivals, and holy days *are a shadow of the things to come, but the substance belongs to Christ* (Colossians 2:17).

SEVEN DAYS IN EVERY SHABUA

Nisan 14 offers a clear example of the way the Bible uses specific dates in precedent, pattern, and prophecy. Similarly, in addition to using specific dates like Nisan 14 to communicate timing, the Bible also uses specific days of a *shabua*. Figure 4.14 pairs the English names for the seven days of the week with the Hebrew names for the seven days of the *shabua*. For the purpose of this text, the English names for the days of the week are used except for Saturday. Hereafter, Saturday will be referred to as the *regular Sabbath*.

DAY	DAY OF THE WEEK	DAY OF THE SHABUA	THIS BOOK
1	Sunday	*Yom Reshon*	Sunday
2	Monday	*Yom Shaynee*	Monday
3	Tuesday	*Yom Shleeshee*	Tuesday
4	Wednesday	*Yom Revi'i*	Wednesday
5	Thursday	*Yom Khameeshee*	Thursday
6	Friday	*Yom Sheeshee*	Friday
7	Saturday	*Shabbath*	Regular Sabbath

FIGURE 4.14 Days of the week and days of the *shabua*

We will refer to it as the regular Sabbath in order to distinguish it from other days during the Hebrew year that the Bible designates as holy days of solemn rest when no work or activity is allowed. These days are also called the Sabbath even though they may not be the 7th and final day of the *shabua*.

For example, the day of the ceremonial Passover Seder that always falls on Nisan 15 is called a *Sabbath High Day* (to be discussed in the section titled "That Sabbath Was a High Day").

THE DISTINCTION BETWEEN A DAY AND A DATE

It is important to understand that the Bible uses DAYS as well as DATES to specify exactly when biblical feasts, festivals, and holy days are to be celebrated, and this can be confusing. For the purposes of this discussion, DAY will be used when referring to a specific day of the *shabua* (Sunday, Monday, Tuesday, Wednesday, Thursday, Friday, regular Sabbath), and DATE will be used when referring to a specific date of the month (Nisan 1, 2, 3, 4...). Figure 4.15 is a synopsis of the important DAYS and DATES in the month of Nisan. It is difficult to understand the relationship between the precedent, pattern, and prophecy without knowing the way the Bible uses DAYS and DATES. As you begin your review, here are several things to keep in mind:

> The DAY of the regular Sabbath is always the 7th and final DAY of the *shabua*-days (without regard to the DATE).
>
> The DAY of the regular Sabbath can be the DATE of the Sabbath High Day, but only when the regular Sabbath falls on Nisan 15.
>
> The DAY after every regular Sabbath is always Sunday; the first DAY of a new *shabua*-days (without regard to the DATE).
>
> The DAY after the regular Sabbath during the Seven-Day Feast is always Sunday, the DAY of the barley sheaf firstfruits ceremony.

NISAN 15 IS ALWAYS THE SABBATH HIGH DAY

As indicated, Nisan 14 is always the DATE of the day of Preparation regardless of the DAY of the *shabua* (Sunday, Monday, etc.). In the same way, Nisan 15 is always the DATE of the Sabbath High Day regardless of the DAY of the *shabua*. The Sabbath High Day on Nisan 15 has always been and continues to be the DATE of the ceremonial Passover Seder. That evening, the Passover lamb was eaten along with unleavened bread and herbs as the story of the exodus was retold. Even today, many symbolic rituals are performed during the Passover Seder.

In order to participate in the Passover Seder and eat the Passover lamb on the Sabbath High Day (Nisan 15), a Jew had to be ritually clean. This means that prior to the DATE of the feast, Jews could not enter a Gentile's home, business, or establishment. For this reason, the Jewish religious leaders did not enter the headquarters of the Roman Governor Pontius Pilate with Jesus shortly before He was crucified on the day of Preparation (Nisan 14): *They themselves did not enter the governor's headquarters, so that they would not be defiled, but could eat the Passover* (John 18:28).

THAT SABBATH WAS A HIGH DAY

The apostle John called specific attention to the day following the day of Preparation in the year Jesus was crucified. He called it the Sabbath High Day: *Since it was the day of Preparation, and so that the bodies would not remain on the cross on the Sabbath (for that Sabbath was a high day), the Jews asked Pilate that their legs might be broken and that they might be taken away* (John 19:31—the parenthetical insert is in the original Bible text).

The parenthetical insert "for that Sabbath was a high day" is not necessary. Everyone would have known that the day after the day of Preparation was the Sabbath High Day because Nisan 15 always follows Nisan 14. It would be like telling someone that the day after the last day of the year is New Year's Day. Everyone already knows January 1 always follows December 31. Since it is not necessary to establish the day after the day of Preparation as the Sabbath High Day, there must be a reason John made this a point of emphasis. One very important reason is to distinguish this DATE of the Sabbath High Day from the DAY of the regular Sabbath.

The Sabbath High Day during the Seven-Day Feast (annual) and the regular Sabbath specified by the Fourth Commandment (weekly) are both called the Sabbath. Since Nisan 15 can fall on any DAY of the *shabua* (Sunday, Monday, etc.), Nisan 15 can therefore fall on the DAY of the regular Sabbath (the 7th and final day of the *shabua*). John's point was that this particular Sabbath High Day on Nisan 15 did not fall on the DAY of the regular Sabbath

NISAN 10: ALWAYS THE DATE OF SELECTION (REGARDLESS OF THE DAY OF THE SHABUA)	
Precedent	One male lamb—completely free of defects—was selected by each Israel household in Egypt.
Pattern	One male lamb—completely free of defects—was selected for the nation by the priests in Jerusalem.
Prophecy	Jesus, the sinless Lamb of God, was selected as king of the Jews and highly exalted in Jerusalem.
Timing	Since Nisan 10 is a DATE, it can fall on any DAY of the *shabua* (Sunday, Monday, etc.). Nisan 10 was a Sunday in the year Jesus was selected, and it is referred to as Palm Sunday.

NISAN 10, 11, 12, 13: FOUR CONSECUTIVE DATES OF LAMB INSPECTION AND TESTING BEFORE THE DATE OF THE SACRIFICE	
Precedent	Each household in Egypt carefully inspected and tested its lamb to make sure it was free of defects.
Pattern	The lamb for the nation was kept at the temple where it was inspected and tested to make sure it was free of defects.
Prophecy	Jesus taught openly at the temple where every word and deed was evaluated and scrutinized (inspected and tested).

NISAN 14: ALWAYS THE DATE OF THE SACRIFICE (REGARDLESS OF THE DAY OF THE SHABUA)	
Precedent	The Passover lamb for each household in Egypt was killed at 3:00 p.m. and then roasted before sunset.
Pattern	The Passover lamb for the nation of Israel was killed at 3:00 p.m. and then roasted before sunset. This was the special Passover lamb for the nation that was selected on Nisan 10, and then kept at the temple where it was inspected and tested for four consecutive days.
Prophecy	Jesus, the Lamb of God, died on the cross at 3:00 p.m. and was laid in the tomb before sunset.
Timing	Since Nisan 14 is a DATE, it can fall on any DAY of the *shabua* (Sunday, Monday, Tuesday, etc.). Nisan 14 was a Thursday in the year Jesus was crucified; however, the day to remember the crucifixion was changed to the Friday before Easter—called Good Friday—after the Council of Nicaea (discussed earlier in the section titled "The meeting of the Council of Nicaea in 325 CE").

NISAN 15: ALWAYS THE DATE OF THE SABBATH HIGH DAY OF SOLEMN REST (REGARDLESS OF THE DAY OF THE SHABUA)	
Precedent	The Passover lamb was eaten during the evening on this DATE in Egypt shortly before the exodus.
Pattern	The Passover Seder meal was/is eaten during the evening on the DATE of the Sabbath High Day.
Prophecy	The body of Jesus remained in the tomb on the DATE of the Sabbath High Day.

THE DAY OF THE REGULAR SABBATH THAT OCCURS DURING THE SEVEN-DAY FEAST (NO DATE ASSIGNED)	
Precedent	During the exodus God designated the 7th and final DAY of the *shabua* a DAY of solemn rest.
Pattern	The 7th and final DAY of the *shabua* during the Seven-Day Feast is always a DAY of solemn rest.
Prophecy	The body of Jesus remained in the tomb on the DAY of the regular Sabbath of solemn rest.
Timing	The DATE of the regular Sabbath during the Seven-Day Feast varies. In the year of the crucifixion, the DATE of this regular Sabbath was Nisan 16.

THE DAY AFTER THE REGULAR SABBATH THAT OCCURS DURING THE SEVEN-DAY FEAST (NO DATE ASSIGNED)	
Precedent	At Mount Sinai, God gave Moses instructions for the barley sheaf firstfruits ceremony and harvest.
Pattern	The barley firstfruits sheaf was ceremonially waved in the air in Jerusalem before the harvest began.
Prophecy	Jesus was resurrected (firstfruits) and appeared to many in Jerusalem as He began to harvest souls.
Timing	The DATE of the Sunday barley sheaf firstfruits ceremony varies. In the year of the crucifixion, the DATE of this Sunday was Nisan 17. Jesus was resurrected on Sunday, and this DAY is referred to as Easter Sunday.

FIGURE 4.15 DAYS and DATES in the month of Nisan

specified by the Fourth Commandment. The significance of this fact will become clear when the unique purpose and function of this important regular Sabbath during the Seven-Day Feast is explained next.

THE REGULAR SABBATH DURING THE SEVEN-DAY FEAST

One of the seven DATES of the Seven-Day Feast (Nisan 14, 15, 16, 17, 18, 19, 20) is the DAY of the regular Sabbath, the 7th and final DAY of the *shabua*-days. This regular Sabbath is of course the weekly holy DAY of solemn rest on which no work could be done. It was necessary to identify this particular Sabbath—the regular Sabbath that occurs during the Seven-Day Feast—each and every year. The Bible does not specify the DATE for this regular Sabbath; it only specifies the DAY (the Sabbath).

Since the context and timeframe is the Seven-Day Feast, the regular Sabbath is limited to one of those seven possible DATES within that finite range. Determining the regular Sabbath within the Seven-Day Feast is critical. Once identified, it was used as the point of reference to determine when each distinct spring harvest ceremony took place: one for barley and one for wheat. Following each ceremony, the respective general harvest of the barley crop and the wheat crop began.

Most Old Testament scholars mistakenly believe the starting point for determining when to celebrate both spring harvest ceremonies is the DATE of the Sabbath High Day on Nisan 15. This view, however, does not take into account *shabua*-days, something that everyone would have been extremely familiar with when the Bible was written. In chapter 5 we will demonstrate beyond a reasonable doubt that the starting point for determining the harvest ceremonies can only be the DAY of the regular Sabbath. (As will be addressed in chapter 5, the proof is found in the fifty-day Counting of the Omer ritual that precedes the Feast of *Shabua*.)

THE REGULAR SABBATH VS. THE SABBATH HIGH DAY

To reiterate, although the regular Sabbath and the Sabbath High Day are both called the Sabbath—and both are holy days of solemn rest—they are not one and the same. The Sabbath High Day is a fixed DATE (Nisan 15) during the Seven-Day Feast; the DATE that the Passover lamb, unleavened bread, and herbs were eaten during the Passover Seder meal. The Sabbath High Day can fall on any DAY of the *shabua*-days (Sunday, Monday, Tuesday, Wednesday, Thursday, Friday, regular Sabbath).

At the same time, since the regular Sabbath is a fixed DAY (regular Sabbath) within the *shabua*-days, it can fall on any DATE of the Seven-Day Feast (Nisan 14, 15, 16, 17, 18, 19, 20). As a result—when the DAY and the DATE overlap—the DATE of the Sabbath High Day (Nisan 15) will occasionally fall on the DAY of the regular Sabbath.

THE REGULAR SABBATH IN THE YEAR OF THE CRUCIFIXION

In the year that Jesus was crucified, the Sabbath High Day (Nisan 15) was immediately followed by the DAY of the regular Sabbath (which that year fell on the DATE of Nisan 16). After Joseph of Arimathea took Jesus down from the cross, he wrapped His body in linen and placed Him in a tomb. According to Luke 23:54, Joseph did this on *the day of Preparation, and the Sabbath was beginning.* The Sabbath that was beginning—at sunset—was the designated Sabbath High Day. To reiterate, the day of Preparation (Nisan 14) is always immediately followed by the Sabbath High Day (Nisan 15), the DATE of the Passover Seder.

Two verses after mentioning the day of Preparation (Nisan 14) and the Sabbath High Day (Nisan 15), Luke indicated that Jesus' friends rested on the DAY of the regular Sabbath: *On the Sabbath [Joseph and the women who had gone from Galilee to Jerusalem with Jesus] rested according to the commandment* (Luke 23:56). The Sabbath in this verse is specifically identified with "the commandment": the Fourth Commandment instructs the people of Israel to rest on the 7th and final day of every *shabua*-days. Verse 56 establishes this particular DAY as the regular Sabbath and distinguishes it from the DATE of the Sabbath High Day in verse 54. Therefore, according to Luke, in the year that Jesus was crucified, the regular Sabbath followed the Sabbath High Day.

So far, we have looked at three significant days during the month of Nisan in the year that Jesus was crucified (Figure 4.16). In the sections that follow, numerous Bible verses will confirm this alignment of DAYS and DATES, and they will also establish the DAY and DATE of Jesus' resurrection as Sunday, Nisan 17.

DAY AND DATE	TITLE	DESCRIPTION
Thursday, Nisan 14	Day of Preparation	Jesus' Last Supper, arrest, trials, crucifixion, death, and burial
Friday, Nisan 15	Sabbath High Day	The Passover Seder is celebrated on this holy day of solemn rest
Regular Sabbath, Nisan 16	Regular Sabbath	The 7th and final day of every shabua-days (Fourth Commandment)

FIGURE 4.16 Nisan 14, 15, and 16 in the year of the crucifixion

DESIGNATED DAY WITHIN A FINITE RANGE OF DATES

It is not unusual for the Bible to use the regular Sabbath during the Seven-Day Feast as a point of reference for determining other feasts, festivals, and holy days. Designating a particular DAY instead of a DATE to celebrate holy days is still quite common today: we always celebrate Palm Sunday, Good Friday, and Easter Sunday on those designated DAYS of the week within a finite range of DATES. Several other American holidays always occur on a designated DAY of the week within a finite range of DATES. Examples include the Monday holidays for Martin Luther King Day, Presidents' Day, Memorial Day, Labor Day, and Columbus Day. Other examples include Thanksgiving Day (which is always celebrated on a Thursday) and Election Day (which always takes place on a Tuesday).

So there is a finite range of seven possible DATES for the regular Sabbath that occurs during the Seven-Day Feast. Each year, the first DAY of the Seven-Day Feast (Nisan 14) determines the DATE that the regular Sabbath falls on. The first column in Figure 4.17 lists each of the seven possible DAYS of the shabua that could be Nisan 14 during the Seven-Day Feast. The second column lists the number of days from Nisan 14 to the regular Sabbath. The third column lists the seven possible DATES of the regular Sabbath that occurs during the Seven-Day Feast. These DATES are derived by adding the number of days in the second column to Nisan 14.

DAY OF THE SHABUA	PLUS	DATE OF THE REGULAR SABBATH
Sunday, Nisan 14	6 days	Nisan 20: Sabbath
Monday, Nisan 14	5 days	Nisan 19: Sabbath
Tuesday, Nisan 14	4 days	Nisan 18: Sabbath
Wednesday, Nisan 14	3 days	Nisan 17: Sabbath
Thursday, Nisan 14	2 days	Nisan 16: Sabbath
Friday, Nisan 14	1 day	Nisan 15: Sabbath
Sabbath, Nisan 14	0 days	Nisan 14: Sabbath

FIGURE 4.17 DATES for the regular Sabbath during the Seven-Day Feast

Thursday, Nisan 14: When the DATE Nisan 14 falls on a Thursday, there are two Sabbaths in a row. Friday, Nisan 15 (not listed in Figure 4.17), is the designated DATE of the Sabbath High Day for the Passover Seder. Sabbath, Nisan 16, is the DAY of the regular Sabbath during the Seven-Day Feast, the 7th and final DAY of the *shabua*-days. This particular scenario represents the actual alignment of DAYS and DATES during the month of Nisan in the year that Jesus was crucified.

Friday, Nisan 14: When the DATE Nisan 14 falls on a Friday, the Sabbath on Nisan 15 is both the DAY of the regular Sabbath during the Seven-Day Feast and also the DATE of the designated Sabbath High Day. In other words, when Nisan 14 falls on a Friday, the next day is both the regular Sabbath and the Sabbath High Day. The Passover Seder meal was—and is—always eaten during the evening on Nisan 15.

Sabbath, Nisan 14: When the DATE Nisan 14 falls on the DAY of the regular Sabbath, there appears to be a conflict. No work is permitted on the regular Sabbath, yet work is required on Nisan 14 because it is also the day of Preparation, the day to kill and roast the lamb, to rid the house of leaven, to put blood on the doorframe, to bake unleavened bread, and to prepare the Passover Seder meal that is to be eaten on Nisan 15. God specifically addressed this scenario in Leviticus 23:7: *"On the first day [Nisan 14]... you shall not do any ordinary work."* On this day, ordinary work (such as fishing, harvesting, shepherding, etc.) was strictly prohibited;

however, the once-a-year day of Preparation work was allowed since it was not considered ordinary work.

THE DAY AFTER THE SABBATH

THE BARLEY AND THE WHEAT HARVEST CEREMONIES

Again, identifying the regular Sabbath during the Seven-Day Feast was absolutely necessary for determining the time of both the barley harvest and the wheat harvest ceremonies in the spring. In fact, the original events (precedent), the annual commemorative feasts (pattern), and the future fulfillments (prophecy) are all linked to this particular regular Sabbath. As will be discussed in chapter 5, the timing of the two Old Testament spring feasts (pattern) is identical to the timing of the two New Testament spring feasts (prophecy). Each spring feast is determined by counting a specific number of days, beginning with the day after the regular Sabbath that occurs during the Seven-Day Feast.

Each of these two spring feasts took place at the time of year when a particular crop was harvested, and each involved a symbolic harvest ceremony. The first spring ceremony was associated with the barley harvest. At Mount Sinai, God commanded Moses to establish this particular day: "*Speak to the people of Israel and say to them, When you come into the land that I give you and reap its harvest, you shall bring the sheaf of the firstfruits of your harvest to the priest, and he shall wave the sheaf before the LORD, so that you may be accepted. On the day after the Sabbath the priest shall wave it*" (Leviticus 23:9-11).

DATES FOR THE BARLEY SHEAF FIRSTFRUITS CEREMONY

The barley sheaf firstfruits ceremony "on the day after the Sabbath" was the day that the priest waved the "sheaf of the firstfruits." As indicated, the Sabbath referred to in this passage is the DAY of the regular Sabbath—the 7th and final day of the *shabua*-days that occurs during the Seven-Day Feast— not the DATE of the Sabbath High Day. The DAY after the regular Sabbath is always a Sunday, the first DAY of a new *shabua*-days. Sunday is the first DAY that work (such as harvesting) is permitted after the regular Sabbath of solemn rest. The symbolic barley sheaf firstfruits ceremony took place on this Sunday. The general harvest of the barley crop began immediately after the ceremony unless this Sunday fell on Nisan 15 (the Sabbath High Day) or Nisan 20 (the DATE designated as a holy day in Exodus 12:16). Figure 4.18 shows the seven possible DATES of the Sunday barley sheaf firstfruits ceremony.

DATE OF THE REGULAR SABBATH	PLUS	DATE OF THE CEREMONY
Nisan 14: Sabbath	1 day	Nisan 15: Sunday
Nisan 15: Sabbath	1 day	Nisan 16: Sunday
Nisan 16: Sabbath	1 day	Nisan 17: Sunday
Nisan 17: Sabbath	1 day	Nisan 18: Sunday
Nisan 18: Sabbath	1 day	Nisan 19: Sunday
Nisan 19: Sabbath	1 day	Nisan 20: Sunday
Nisan 20: Sabbath	1 day	Nisan 21: Sunday

FIGURE 4.18 DATES for the Sunday barley sheaf firstfruits ceremony

Sunday, Nisan 15: Nisan 15 is always the designated DATE of the Sabbath High Day, the holy day of solemn rest for the Passover Seder. If the DATE after the regular Sabbath was Sunday, Nisan 15—the DATE ordinary work was prohibited—then the general harvest could not begin until Monday, Nisan 16.

Sunday, Nisan 20: The last possible DATE of the Seven-Day Feast is Nisan 20, a specially designated holy day of convocation (Exodus 12:16). If the DATE after the regular Sabbath is Sunday, Nisan 20—when work is prohibited—then the general harvest could not begin until Monday, Nisan 21.

SYMBOLISM IN THE BARLEY SHEAF FIRSTFRUITS CEREMONY

After the winter rainy season in the Middle East, the barley crop begins to ripen in the fields. It is ready to be harvested by the middle of the month of Nisan at the time of the Seven-Day Feast. However, as indicated, harvesting was not permitted until after a special Sunday ceremony. During the ceremony—in the courtyard of the temple—the Jewish high priest lifted the barley firstfruits sheaf above his head and waved it in the air as a tangible sign that God had provided food. The general harvest followed the ceremony. Sunday was a regular day of work and not a holy day of solemn rest unless it fell on Nisan 15, the designated DATE of the Sabbath High Day, or Nisan 20, the designated DATE of holy assembly. The symbolism behind the crop, the ceremony, the waving, and the harvest is described in Figure 4.19.

SYMBOL	DESCRIPTION
Crop	The barley crop that comes up in the fields after the dead of winter symbolizes people who are dead because of their sin and in need of a Savior.
Ceremony	The barley sheaf firstfruits ceremony symbolizes the resurrection of the Firstfruits (Jesus), the Savior who *"came to seek and save the lost"* (Luke 19:10).
Waving	The high priest waving the barley firstfruits sheaf in the air symbolizes God's promise to provide a resurrected Savior who would be seen by many.
Harvest	The general barley harvest following the ceremony symbolizes the Savior (Jesus) gathering believers into the family of God.

FIGURE 4.19 Symbolism in the barley sheaf firstfruits ceremony

It is noteworthy that the Bible does not assign a specific name or title to the day of the barley sheaf firstfruits ceremony. Although many often refer to this day as the feast of firstfruits, there is a problem with using that label. The problem is that it can be confused with the wheat loaves firstfruits ceremony that occurs exactly 7 *shabua*-days (7 × 7 days = 49 days) after the barley sheaf firstfruits ceremony (more on this in chapter 5). One harvest ceremony presents barley, the other presents wheat, and both of these symbolic portions are called firstfruits.

THE RESURRECTION AND THE BARLEY FIRSTFRUITS SHEAF

The barley sheaf firstfruits ceremony (pattern) has a corresponding fulfillment in the resurrection of Jesus after He was crucified (prophecy). If

Jesus did not come back from the dead as He had repeatedly said He would, then nothing He said can be trusted. According to 1 Corinthians 15:20-23, the resurrection of Jesus is the foundation of a believer's faith: *In fact Christ has been raised from the dead, the firstfruits of those who have fallen asleep. For as by a man came death, by a man has come also the resurrection of the dead. For as in Adam all die, so also in Christ shall all be made alive. But each in his own order: Christ the firstfruits, then at his coming those who belong to Christ.*

In this passage Jesus is twice called the "firstfruits." This term links the resurrection of Jesus to the barley sheaf firstfruits ceremony. Both are associated with the Seven-Day Feast. Risen Jesus is represented by the highly symbolic barley firstfruits sheaf that is brought up from the fields before the general harvest. Glorified Jesus—who appeared to many people after the resurrection—is represented by the high priest waving the barley firstfruits sheaf in the air as a sign for all to see that God had indeed provided—a Savior—as He promised. The harvest of believers after Jesus was resurrected is represented by the general barley harvest, which immediately followed the barley sheaf firstfruits ceremony.

THE SIGNIFICANCE OF THE RESURRECTION

The significance of the resurrection of Jesus cannot be overstated. It is because of this resurrection that a believer has confidence that Jesus is the Son of God: *[Jesus] was declared to be the Son of God in power according to the Spirit of holiness by his resurrection from the dead* (Romans 1:4). In addition, the resurrection of Jesus gives believers confidence that their sins are forgiven and that there is life after death: *If the dead are not raised, not even Christ has been raised. And if Christ has not been raised, your faith is futile and you are still in your sins. Then those also who have fallen asleep in Christ have perished. If in Christ we have hope in this life only, we are of all people most to be pitied* (1 Corinthians 15:16-19).

Through the ages many false prophets have claimed to be the Messiah or Christ. Some have even attracted followers by performing miraculous signs and wonders. However, no one ever claimed he would die and then come back to life, and then did it. No one, that is, except Jesus. In effect, the resurrection not only proves that Jesus was the long-awaited Messiah, but it also validates everything He said, including His promise of the future resurrection of believers.

JESUS WAS RESURRECTED ON SUNDAY

As indicated, the barley sheaf firstfruits ceremony always takes place the DAY after the regular Sabbath that occurs during the Seven-Day Feast. (The day after every regular Sabbath is always Sunday, the first DAY of a new *shabua*-days.) On this particular Sunday—the first day of the week—Jesus was resurrected from the dead. Figure 4.20 lists four verses from the gospels of Matthew, Mark, Luke, and John that unequivocally link the resurrection of Jesus to this Sunday, the day of the barley sheaf firstfruits ceremony. Notice the terms used to describe the time of day on this particular Sunday: *toward the dawn, very early in the morning, at the rising of the sun, early dawn, early,* and *while it was still dark.*

Matthew 28:1	*Now after the Sabbath, toward the dawn of the first day of the week, Mary Magdalene and the other Mary went to see the tomb.*
Mark 16:1-2 (KJV)	*And when the sabbath was past... very early in the morning the first day of the week, they came unto the sepulcher at the rising of the sun.*
Luke 24:1	*But on the first day of the week, at early dawn, they went to the tomb, taking the spices they had prepared.*
John 20:1	*Now on the first day of the week Mary Magdalene came to the tomb early, while it was still dark, and saw that the stone had been taken away from the tomb.*

FIGURE 4.20 The resurrection took place on Sunday

THE FIRST HALF OF SUNDAY, THE THIRD DAY

The verses in Figure 4.20 all indicate that people began to arrive at the empty tomb early on Sunday morning. By the time Mary Magdalene and the other Mary arrived at the tomb, Jesus had already risen. Although the Bible does not specify exactly when it happened, it does indicate that Jesus was resurrected sometime during the first half of Sunday. The first half of Sunday (the first 12-hour period) began after sunset (approximately 6:00 p.m.) and ended at sunrise (approximately 6:00 a.m.). Jesus was resurrected sometime during that finite period of time. This is consistent with the verses in Figure 4.21, all of which indicate Jesus would rise from the dead on that third day.

Matthew 16:21	*[Jesus must] suffer many things from the elders and chief priests and scribes, and be killed, and on the third day be raised.*
Matthew 17:23	*"They will kill him [the Son of Man], and he will be raised on the third day."*
Matthew 20:19	*"[The Son on Man will] be mocked and flogged and crucified, and he will be raised on the third day."*
Luke 9:22	*"The Son of Man must suffer many things… and be killed, and on the third day be raised."*
Luke 18:33	*"After flogging [the Son of Man], they will kill him, and on the third day he will rise."*
Luke 24:7	*"The Son of Man must be delivered into the hands of sinful men and be crucified and on the third day rise."*
Luke 24:46	*"Thus it is written, that the Christ should suffer and on the third day rise from the dead."*

FIGURE 4.21 The resurrection took place on the third day

THREE DAYS AND THREE NIGHTS IN THE TOMB

Again, nowhere does the Bible specify the actual time on Sunday that Jesus was resurrected. The only certainty is that Jesus was no longer in the tomb at the time of the morning *while it was still dark* (John 20:1). The Sunday resurrection—on the third day—is consistent with what Jesus (referring to Himself as "the Son of Man") had said concerning the sign of His death and resurrection: *"For just as Jonah was three days and three nights in the belly of the great fish, so will the Son of Man be three days and three nights in the heart of the earth"* (Matthew 12:40).

In this verse, Jesus predicted that He would be in the tomb for "three days and three nights." At first glance, there does not appear to be anything unusual about what Jesus said. However, because Jesus specified days before nights, this chronology would have been odd to a Jewish audience that reckons each 24-hour day beginning with evening (night before day). Jesus intentionally deviated from the customary biblical reckoning to prophesy that His time in the tomb would begin during the "day" and end at "night," in that particular order. And, in fact, Jesus precisely fulfilled this prophecy when His body was in the tomb Thursday *day* through Sunday *night*.

THE DAY AND DATE OF THE CRUCIFIXION AND RESURRECTION

The Bible verses covered so far indicate the following about the crucifixion and the resurrection:

Jesus was killed on the day of Preparation (Nisan 14), the DATE that the Passover lambs were killed.

Jesus was dead, and His body remained in the tomb for three days and three nights, in that particular order.

Jesus was resurrected on the third day (Sunday), the DAY of the barley sheaf firstfruits ceremony.

The Bible does not specify either the DAY of the crucifixion or the DATE of the resurrection, but we know that:

Nisan 14 is the biblical DATE of the crucifixion (the day of Preparation).

Sunday is the biblical DAY of the resurrection (the day of the barley sheaf firstfruits ceremony).

There are three days and three nights between the crucifixion and the resurrection.

Three DATES after Nisan 14 is Nisan 17 (14 + 3 = 17).

Three DAYS before Sunday is Thursday (Thursday *day*, Friday, Sabbath, Sunday *night*).

Based on what we know, Figure 4.22 shows the timing of the events from the crucifixion through the resurrection. (Refer to Figure 4.10 for a detailed chronology of the sequence of events that took place on Thursday, Nisan 14.)

DAY AND DATE	TIME OF DAY	DESCRIPTION	DAYS/NIGHTS
Thursday, Nisan 14	Evening/Night	Last Supper and Gethsemane	
	Morning/Day	Crucifixion, death, and burial	1st day
Friday, Nisan 15	Evening/Night	Passover Seder	1st night
	Morning/Day		2nd day
Sabbath, Nisan 16	Evening/Night	Regular Sabbath	2nd night
	Morning/Day		3rd day
Sunday, Nisan 17	Evening/Night	Resurrection	3rd night
	Morning/Day	Empty Tomb	

FIGURE 4.22 Three days and three nights

EIGHT LANDMARK DAYS AND DATES INVOLVING JESUS

Now, putting it all together, Figure 4.23 offers a chronology of the events involving Jesus during the month of Nisan in the year of His crucifixion and resurrection. The DAY of the *shabua*; the corresponding Nisan DATE; the description of the key events involving Jesus; and the traditional church titles for three landmark days are provided.

DAY AND DATE	JESUS WAS...	CHURCH TITLE
Sunday, Nisan 10	Exalted as king and went to the temple	Palm Sunday
Monday, Nisan 11	Questioned as He taught at the temple	
Tuesday, Nisan 12	Questioned as He taught at the temple	
Wednesday, Nisan 13	Questioned as He taught at the temple	
Thursday, Nisan 14	Crucified/died/buried on the day of Preparation	Good Friday
Friday, Nisan 15	In the tomb on the DATE of the Sabbath High Day	
Sabbath, Nisan 16	In the tomb on the DAY of the regular Sabbath	
Sunday, Nisan 17	Resurrected on the DAY after the regular Sabbath	Easter Sunday

FIGURE 4.23 Eight landmark DAYS and DATES involving Jesus

SHABUA-DAYS IN PRECEDENT, PATTERN, AND PROPHECY

This chapter examined the correlation of the *shabua*-days of the exodus (precedent), the *shabua*-days of the Seven-Day Feast (pattern), and the *shabua*-days of Jesus in the first century CE (prophecy). The next chapter will examine the incredible correlation of the *shabua*-days of the exodus (precedent), the *shabua*-days of the Feast of *Shabua* (pattern), and the *shabua*-days of the church in the first century CE (prophecy).

CHAPTER 5

THE FEAST OF SHABUA

In the previous chapter we carefully examined the first primary biblical feast celebrated in the spring. The Bible refers to it as both the Feast of Passover and the Feast of Unleavened Bread; we called it the Seven-Day Feast. The regular Sabbath that occurs on one of the seven days of the feast determines when the barley sheaf firstfruits ceremony takes place. The Seven-Day Feast is indicative of the link between the Old and New Testaments, Judaism and Christianity, and Jews and Gentiles. The consistent and repeated use of Bible precedent, pattern, and prophecy makes a compelling case that the symmetry is by design and not merely a coincidence. This chapter will examine the Feast of *Shabua* (also called Feast of Weeks and Feast of Sevens), the second primary biblical feast celebrated in the spring.

Like the Seven-Day Feast, the Feast of *Shabua* commemorates an original landmark event in the year of the exodus of the people of Israel from slavery in Egypt (precedent). Also like the Seven-Day Feast, the people of Israel were commanded to celebrate the Feast of *Shabua* in Jerusalem at the same time each year. The Feast of *Shabua* is associated with the harvest of a particular crop (wheat), a special ceremony takes place before the general wheat harvest, the symbolic portion of wheat is called firstfruits, and the same regular Sabbath that occurs on one of the seven days of the Seven-Day Feast determines when the wheat loaves firstfruits ceremony takes place (pattern). Finally, there is an unmistakable correlation between the Old Testament Feast of *Shabua* and the New Testament day called Pentecost (prophecy).

A COMMEMORATION AND A FORESHADOWING

As we have seen again and again, precedents and patterns initiated in the Old Testament are often associated with prophecy, and many of these prophecies have already been fulfilled in the New Testament. The appointed times the Bible calls feasts are a pattern that acts like a hinge pin, linking the precedent to the prophecy. In referring to the Old Testament biblical feasts, God said, *"These are the appointed feasts of the LORD, the holy convocations, which you shall proclaim at the time appointed for them"* (Leviticus 23:4). In referring to these feasts in the New Testament, the apostle Paul said, *These are a shadow of the things to come, but the substance belongs to Christ* (Colossians 2:17).

The Feast of *Shabua* (pattern) is a hinge pin that both commemorated a past Old Testament landmark event and foreshadowed a future New Testament event. As a commemoration, it looked back to the day the nation of Israel was born: God gave His people the Ten Commandments at Mount Sinai (precedent). As a foreshadowing, the Feast of *Shabua* looked forward to the day the church would be born: God would give His people the Holy Spirit in Jerusalem (prophecy). This foreshadowing was completed on the day called Pentecost (fulfillment).

THE FEAST OF SHABUA IS ON THE DAY OF PENTECOST

The Bible never refers to this fulfillment as the "feast of Pentecost." It is simply called Pentecost or the day of Pentecost. Strong's Concordance indicates that *Pentecost* (G4005) is "feminine of the ordinal of [pentekonta]; fiftieth ([hemera] being implied) from Passover, i.e. the festival of 'Pentecost':- Pentecost." As you will soon see, *Pentecost* literally means "the fiftieth day," and it refers to the identical fiftieth day as the Feast of *Shabua*. The church generally does not celebrate the Feast of *Shabua* on the biblical day of Pentecost, but that does not mean the Feast of *Shabua* has no significance for believers.

The Feast of *Shabua* commemorated the spiritual birth of Israel and also pointed to the spiritual birth of the church. When believers received the Holy Spirit on the day of Pentecost, the Feast of *Shabua* became a commemoration for the church as well. Now the Feast of *Shabua*—observed on the day of Pentecost—looks back not only to the day God established the nation of Israel and gave them the Ten Commandments, but also to the day God established the church of believers and gave them the Holy Spirit. Believers in the church now stand side by side with the people of Israel as firstfruits to the Lord, as the wheat loaves firstfruits ceremony illustrates.

ISRAEL AND BELIEVERS ARE AS FIRSTFRUITS TO THE LORD

On the day the Feast of *Shabua* was celebrated, two symbolic firstfruits wheat loaves were presented in a special ceremony. According to Leviticus 23:17, "*You shall bring from your dwelling places two loaves of bread to be waved... baked with leaven, as firstfruits to the LORD.*" Then, in the courtyard of the temple, the high priest waved these two loaves of bread (the firstfruits of the wheat harvest) in the air. The two wheat loaves used in the Feast of *Shabua* firstfruits ceremony symbolize the two stone tablets that were engraved with God's laws against sin. God etched His Ten Commandments in stone at Mount Sinai in the year of the exodus.

These two wheat loaves also represent two groups of people: the nation of Israel and the followers of Jesus. In the Bible, leaven (yeast) is used as a metaphor for sin. The fact that leaven was baked into the two loaves represents the presence of sin in people who are prone to violating God's laws against sin. One leavened loaf represents the presence of sin in the nation of Israel, and one leavened loaf represents the presence of sin in followers of Jesus. Notwithstanding the presence of sin, both groups of people are referred to "*as firstfruits to the LORD*" (v. 17).

God said the Feast of *Shabua* "*is a statute forever in all your dwelling places throughout your generations*" (v. 21). In order for the people of Israel to honor this holy day of convocation—forever—requires knowing exactly when the Bible says it is to be celebrated. That timing is discussed next.

FEAST OF SHABUA TIMING

THE DAY TO CELEBRATE THE FEAST OF SHABUA

As discussed in chapter 4, the timing of the first springtime feast—according to the Bible—changed following the meeting of the Council of Nicaea in 325 CE. Since the first and second feasts are linked, this change also affected the timing of the second springtime feast. As a result, the intended correlations were lost between the landmark event at Mount Sinai (precedent), the annual commemorative Feast of *Shabua* (pattern), and the foreshadowed event on the day of Pentecost (prophecy). This chapter will examine the symmetry that existed between the precedent, pattern, and prophecy of the second springtime biblical feast prior to the meeting of the Council of Nicaea.

The unusual emphasis the Bible places on the timing of the Feast of *Shabua* is evident in the feast's name: most modern English Bibles translate Feast of *Shabua* as either Feast of Weeks or Feast of Sevens. Other biblical titles for the Feast of *Shabua* include *Shavuot* and Pentecost. As you will soon see, the words *Shabua*, Weeks, Sevens, *Shavuot*, and Pentecost have nothing to do with Bible precedent, pattern, and prophecy. Instead, all these words are associated with timing, and it is very difficult to understand the timing unless you understand *shabua*-days. Figure 5.1 introduces the four key Bible verses that specify when the Feast of *Shabua* is to be celebrated. Despite the different wording, all four verses refer to the same day for the Feast of *Shabua*. The terms will become clear as you read on.

LEVITICUS 23:15 (PART 1)
"You shall count seven full weeks from the day after the Sabbath."
Seven full weeks is 7 *shabua*-days (7 × 7 days = 49 days).
Shabua-days always begin on Sunday and end on the day of the regular Sabbath.
The seven full weeks begin the day after the regular Sabbath during the Seven-Day Feast.
The Feast of *Shabua* is the day after 7 *shabua*-days (49 days + 1 day = 50 days).
The Feast of *Shabua* is 50 days after the regular Sabbath during the Seven-Day Feast.

LEVITICUS 23:15 (PART 2)

"You shall count seven full weeks... from the day that you brought the sheaf of the wave offering."

"The sheaf of the wave offering" is the barley sheaf firstfruits ceremony.
The barley sheaf firstfruits ceremony is on Sunday, the day after the regular Sabbath.
Seven full weeks is 7 *shabua*-days (7 × 7 days = 49 days).
The Feast of *Shabua* is 7 *shabua*-days after the barley sheaf firstfruits ceremony.
The Feast of *Shabua* is 49 days after the Sunday barley sheaf firstfruits ceremony.

LEVITICUS 23:16

"You shall count fifty days to the day after the seventh Sabbath. Then
you shall present a grain offering of new grain to the LORD."

The last day of every *shabua*-days is the day of the regular Sabbath.
The day after every regular Sabbath is Sunday.
The count begins the day after the regular Sabbath during the Seven-Day Feast.
The 50 days are calculated: (7 × 7 days = 49 days) and (49 days + 1 day = 50 days).
"A grain offering of new grain" refers to the Feast of *Shabua* wheat loaves
    firstfruits ceremony.
The Feast of *Shabua* is celebrated on Sunday, the day after the seventh regular Sabbath.

NUMBERS 28:26

"On the day of the firstfruits, when you offer a grain offering of new grain to the LORD at
your Feast of Weeks, you shall have a holy convocation. You shall not do any ordinary work."

"A grain offering of new grain" refers to the Feast of *Shabua* wheat loaves
    firstfruits ceremony.
The wheat loaves firstfruits ceremony takes place "at your Feast of Weeks."
The Feast of *Shabua* is often translated as Feast of Weeks or Feast of Sevens.
The Feast of *Shabua* "on the day of the firstfruits" is a day of holy convocation.
The Feast of *Shabua* is celebrated on Sunday, the day after the seventh regular Sabbath.
Ordinary work is allowed on Sunday, the day after the regular Sabbath.
The Feast of *Shabua* is on Sunday, but God commands, "You shall not do any
    ordinary work."
To prohibit work on Sunday, the command "You shall not do any ordinary work"
    is needed.

DEUTERONOMY 16:9
"You shall count seven weeks. Begin to count the seven weeks from the time the sickle is first put to the standing grain."
Seven weeks is 7 *shabua*-days (7 × 7 days = 49 days). "The time the sickle is first put to the standing grain" is the barley sheaf firstfruits ceremony. The barley sheaf firstfruits ceremony is the day after the regular Sabbath during the Seven-Day Feast. The day after every regular Sabbath is always Sunday. The barley sheaf firstfruits ceremony always occurs on Sunday. The Feast of *Shabua* occurs 7 *shabua*-days after the barley sheaf firstfruits ceremony. The Feast of *Shabua* occurs 49 days after the Sunday barley sheaf firstfruits ceremony. The Feast of *Shabua* and the barley sheaf firstfruits ceremony are on Sundays seven weeks apart.

FIGURE 5.1 Timing of the Feast of *Shabua*

THE REGULAR SABBATH DURING THE SEVEN-DAY FEAST

As indicated in chapter 4, the day after the regular Sabbath that occurs during the Seven-Day Feast is always Sunday. On that particular Sunday, the barley sheaf firstfruits ceremony—called *"the sheaf of the wave offering"* (Leviticus 23:15)—was held. This was *the time the sickle is first put to the standing grain* (Deuteronomy 16:9). The general barley harvest began immediately following this ceremony. According to the Leviticus passages, the regular Sabbath that occurs during the Seven-Day Feast also determines the timing of the Feast of *Shabua*. This second springtime biblical feast occurs the day after the seventh regular Sabbath, which is also always Sunday. On this particular Sunday, the wheat loaves firstfruits ceremony—called *"a grain offering of new grain"* (Leviticus 23:16)—was held.

The timing of the aptly titled Feast of *Shabua* is—not surprisingly—determined by *shabua*-days. It bears repeating that *shabua*-days govern short-term timing in the Bible. It is a complete time period of seven days that includes six days of work or activity followed by a 7th and final day of rest. *Shabua*-days begin on Sunday and end on the regular Sabbath. The day after every regular Sabbath is always Sunday, the first day of the new *shabua*-days. The Feast of *Shabua* is celebrated on the particular Sunday that is exactly fifty days after the regular Sabbath that occurs during the Seven-Day Feast.

Stated another way, there are seven full weeks between the Sunday barley sheaf firstfruits ceremony and the Sunday wheat loaves firstfruits ceremony.

SEVEN WEEKS AND 7 SHABUA-DAYS

In Deuteronomy 16:9 God commanded, *"You shall count seven weeks."* The Hebrew word translated as *weeks* in this verse is *shabua* (Strong's H7620). Although the *shabua* time period interval is not directly specified, we can— based on the context—determine that, here, *shabua* refers to a complete time period of seven days, not seven years. Therefore, a literal rendering of this verse is "You shall count seven *shabua*-days," which is forty-nine days (7 × 7 days = 49 days). Although 7 *shabua*-days and seven weeks are similar, they are not synonymous.

In this instance, the English word *week* and the Hebrew word *shabua* cover the same period of time: seven 24-hour days. The first day of every week and the first day of every *shabua* is also the same: Sunday. What is significant, however, is the treatment of the seventh day. For the people of Israel, the 7th and final day of every *shabua*-days is the regular Sabbath. The regular Sabbath is more than just a day off from work; it is an integral part of Jewish heritage, culture, and religion. The regular Sabbath and Saturday are both the seventh and final day of every week. Only the Jewish people, however, generally regard Saturday as a holy day of solemn rest on which no work is to be done.

In the practice of Judaism, the Feast of *Shabua* is often referred to as *Shavuot*, a Hebrew word that means "weeks." However, the word *Shavuot* is not used in the Bible, and it has not been assigned a number by Strong's. Nevertheless, in the same way as the other titles for the feast, *Shavuot* also refers to timing.

THE DAY AFTER 7 SHABUA-DAYS

Since one *shabua*-days is a complete time period of seven days that begins on Sunday (the first day) and ends on the regular Sabbath (the 7th day), it follows that 7 *shabua*-days are 7 consecutive complete time periods of seven days, each of which begins on Sunday (the first day) and ends on the regular Sabbath (the 7th day). Since one *shabua*-days is 7 days (1 × 7 days = 7 days), it follows that 7 *shabua*-days are 49 days (7 × 7 days = 49 days). Again, each of the 7 distinct *shabua*-days—including the 7th and final *shabua*-days—begins on Sunday and ends on the regular Sabbath.

Now, it is important to understand how the Bible links these 7 *shabua*-days together because the Feast of *Shabua* is to be celebrated the day after the seventh regular Sabbath. The seventh regular Sabbath is the last day— the forty-ninth day—of 7 consecutive *shabua*-days. Naturally, the day after this seventh regular Sabbath is Sunday, the fiftieth day (49 days + 1 day = 50 days). God commanded the Feast of *Shabua* to be celebrated each year on this particular Sunday, exactly 50 days after the regular Sabbath that occurs during the Seven-Day Feast. As indicated, that same day is also called Pentecost, which means "fiftieth."

THE FEAST OF SHABUA ALWAYS OCCURS ON SUNDAY

The Bible states that the Feast of *Shabua* is to be celebrated on a particular DAY, not a particular DATE. That DAY is Sunday; technically speaking, the day after the seventh regular Sabbath. If the Feast of *Shabua* were improperly linked to a DATE (such as Sivan 6), the DAY would incorrectly vary from year to year, and it would often incorrectly fall on one of the six DAYS of the *shabua*-days other than Sunday (namely, Monday, Tuesday, Wednesday, Thursday, Friday, or the regular Sabbath). Since the Bible requires the Feast of *Shabua* to always be celebrated on a particular DAY—Sunday—the DATE of that Sunday will naturally vary within a finite range of DATES (Sivan 4-5-6-7-8-9-10-11).

Like the Feast of *Shabua*, Thanksgiving in America is always celebrated on a particular DAY. That DAY is Thursday; technically speaking, the fourth Thursday in the month of November. If Thanksgiving were improperly linked to a DATE (such as November 25), the DAY would incorrectly vary from year to year, and it would often incorrectly fall on one of the six DAYS of the week other than Thursday (namely, Sunday, Monday, Tuesday, Wednesday, Friday, or Saturday). Since the American tradition is for Thanksgiving to always be celebrated on a particular DAY—Thursday—the DATE of that Thursday will naturally vary within a finite range of DATES (November 22-23-24-25-26-27-28).

NO ORDINARY WORK ON DAY OF HOLY CONVOCATION

Every *shabua*-days includes six days of work or activity followed by the 7th and final day of rest. Work was allowed every day except for the regular Sabbath. Because the Feast of *Shabua* is always celebrated on Sunday, and because Sunday is always a day to do ordinary work (such as farming, building, cleaning...), God told Moses: *"You shall make a proclamation on the same day. You shall hold a holy convocation. You shall not do any ordinary work. It is a statute forever in all your dwelling places throughout your generations"* (Leviticus 23:21).

This command was necessary to prevent ordinary work on the day of the Feast of *Shabua*, a specially designated day of holy convocation. Other than the harvest of wheat for the two firstfruits loaves, no ordinary work was allowed on this particular Sunday. The general wheat harvest was therefore prohibited until the day after the Feast of *Shabua*. (In contrast, ordinary work—the general barley harvest—was not prohibited on the day of the barley sheaf firstfruits ceremony, which is also always on Sunday.) Since the Feast of *Shabua* is always on Sunday, the general wheat harvest always began on Monday.

DATES FOR THE FEAST OF SHABUA

The seven DATES for the Feast of *Shabua* are listed in Figure 5.2 (the calculations are based on 30-day months for both Nisan and Iyar, which is explained in the upcoming section titled "The Counting of the Omer"). The first column lists the seven DATES for the regular Sabbath that falls on one of the seven days of the Seven-Day Feast from Figure 4.18. The second column is 7 *shabua*-days (7 × 7 days = 49 days). The third column lists the seven DATES for the seventh regular Sabbath. The fourth column is one additional day needed to arrive at Sunday, the DAY after the seventh regular Sabbath.

The fifth column lists the seven DATES for the Sunday Feast of *Shabua*: the 50th day after the regular Sabbath that occurs during the Seven-Day Feast.

DATE OF THE SABBATH		DATE OF THE 7TH SABBATH		DATE OF THE FEAST OF SHABUA
Nisan 14: Sabbath		Sivan 3: Sabbath		Sivan 4: Sunday-50th day
Nisan 15: Sabbath	7 *shabua*-days	Sivan 4: Sabbath	The day after	Sivan 5: Sunday-50th day
Nisan 16: Sabbath		Sivan 5: Sabbath		Sivan 6: Sunday-50th day
Nisan 17: Sabbath		Sivan 6: Sabbath		Sivan 7: Sunday-50th day
Nisan 18: Sabbath	+ 49 days =	Sivan 7: Sabbath	+ 1 day =	Sivan 8: Sunday-50th day
Nisan 19: Sabbath		Sivan 8: Sabbath		Sivan 9: Sunday-50th day
Nisan 20: Sabbath		Sivan 9: Sabbath		Sivan 10: Sunday-50th day

FIGURE 5.2 DATES for the Sunday Feast of *Shabua*

TWO SUNDAYS 7 SHABUA-DAYS APART

In summary, the Seven-Day Feast's barley sheaf firstfruits ceremony and the Feast of *Shabua*'s wheat loaves firstfruits ceremony are both celebrated on Sundays in the spring. Although the Bible does not assign either ceremony a specific DATE, it does indicate the DAY they are to be celebrated. The regular Sabbath that occurs during the Seven-Day Feast is the point of reference for determining when each ceremony takes place. The first ceremony is celebrated the day after that regular Sabbath (Sunday). The second ceremony is celebrated 50 days after that same regular Sabbath (Sunday). The two Sunday ceremonies occur exactly 7 *shabua*-days apart (7×7 days = 49 days).

To reiterate, the regular Sabbath that occurs during the Seven-Day Feast determines the timing of the Feast of *Shabua*. Specifying that this feast takes place "the day after the seventh Sabbath" means that seven regular Sabbaths must pass. The point of reference for the Feast of *Shabua* cannot be Nisan 15—the DATE of the designated Sabbath High Day—unless Nisan 15 falls on the DAY of the regular Sabbath. The DATE, Nisan 15, can fall on Sunday, Monday, Tuesday, Wednesday, Thursday, or Friday as well as on the regular Sabbath.

The Feast of *Shabua* requires seven complete weeks; each begins on Sunday and ends on the day of the regular Sabbath. These 7 *shabua*-days begin the day after the regular Sabbath that occurs during the Seven-Day Feast. It is impossible to count either seven complete weeks or 50 days if any DAY other than Sunday is used as the starting point because the first week would be partial. In other words, starting on Monday, Tuesday, Wednesday, Thursday, Friday, or the Sabbath cannot achieve seven complete weeks (or 50 days).

THE COUNTING OF THE OMER

The timing of the Feast of *Shabua* is so important that God commanded the people to literally count the days: *"You shall count fifty days to the day after the seventh Sabbath"* (Leviticus 23:16). The fifty days were ritually counted out loud beginning with the day after the regular Sabbath that occurs during the Seven-Day Feast. This tradition is called the Counting of the Omer. Each day for fifty days—in the courtyard of the temple—the high priest presented an omer (approximately 2 liters) of highly sifted and ritually purified barley as an offering to God. This ritual was performed as spiritual preparation for the Feast of *Shabua* on the 50th day.

When the Bible was written, months were determined by observing the phases of the moon; months were not assigned a fixed number of days until 359 CE when Rabbi Hillel proposed his way of marking time (discussed in chapter 4). In *Shabua Seventy*, we will demonstrate that the Hebrew months of Nisan and Iyar both had 30 days in the year of the crucifixion (back-to-back 30-day months). Due to the consistent, predictable, and reliable use of timing in Bible precedent, pattern, and prophecy, it is reasonable to assume that Nisan and Iyar both had 30 days in the year of the exodus as well.

Based on this, the DATE of the 50th day after the regular Sabbath was Sivan 6 in both the year of the crucifixion and the year of the exodus (Figure 5.3). "The regular Sabbath in the year of the crucifixion" and Figure 4.16 in chapter 4 establish Nisan 16 as the DATE of the regular Sabbath that occurred during the Seven-Day Feast in the year of the crucifixion. And that means Nisan 16 is the DATE of the regular Sabbath in the year of the exodus as well.

COUNT	DATES	DESCRIPTION
0 days	Nisan 16	The DATE of the regular Sabbath
14 days	Nisan 17-30	14 days to complete the month of Nisan (30 - 16 = 14)
30 days	Iyar 1-30	30 days for the entire month of Iyar
6 days	Sivan 1-6	6 days to begin the month of Sivan
50 days	Nisan 17-Sivan 6	Sunday, Sivan 6 was the 50th day after the regular Sabbath

FIGURE 5.3 Counting 50 days in the years of the crucifixion and exodus

OVERVIEW OF THE FEAST OF SHABUA

The landmark event at Mount Sinai in the year of the exodus (precedent) is the origin of the annual commemorative Feast of *Shabua* (pattern). The day that the landmark event took place is identical to the day that the feast is celebrated. The landmark event and the commemorative feast foreshadow an event in the future (prophecy). The precedent, pattern, and prophecy are completed in an event that occurred on the same day in the year of Jesus' crucifixion (fulfillment). Figure 5.4 offers an overview of the Feast of *Shabua* in precedent, pattern, and prophecy. The feast begins with the same regular Sabbath that falls on one of the seven days of the Seven-Day Feast (from Figure 4.18). Here are several things to keep in mind that may be helpful:

THE DAY OF THE REGULAR SABBATH THAT OCCURS DURING THE SEVEN-DAY FEAST (NO DATE ASSIGNED)	
Precedent	During the exodus God designated the 7th and final DAY of the *shabua* a DAY of solemn rest.
Pattern	The 7th and final DAY of the *shabua* during the Seven-Day Feast is always a DAY of solemn rest.
Prophecy	The body of Jesus remained in the tomb on the DAY of the regular Sabbath of solemn rest.
Timing	The DATE of the regular Sabbath during the Seven-Day Feast varies. In the year of the crucifixion, the DATE of this regular Sabbath was Nisan 16.

THE DAY AFTER 7 SHABUA-DAYS AFTER THE REGULAR SABBATH IS THE FEAST OF SHABUA (NO DATE ASSIGNED)	
Precedent	Spiritual Israel was born when God came down in fire on Mount Sinai and the people heard Him speak.
Pattern	Two firstfruits wheat loaves were ceremonially waved in the air in Jerusalem on the Feast of *Shabua*.
Prophecy	The church was born when God came down as fire on the apostles, and the people from afar heard the apostles speak their native languages.
Timing	The DATE of the Sunday Feast of *Shabua* varies. In the year of the crucifixion, the DATE of this Sunday was Sivan 6. The church was born on Sunday; this DAY is referred to as Pentecost Sunday.

FIGURE 5.4 Outline of the Feast of *Shabua*

CREATING A BIBLE CALENDAR

MANNA IN THE MORNING ON IYAR 15

The Bible specifies DATES for several important events at the time of the exodus (Nisan 14, 15…), but it does not specify the DAY of the *shabua*-days (Sunday, Monday…). Fortunately, the Bible does provide all the information needed to make that determination. Revisiting the first *shabua*-days of manna (discussed in chapter 3), we find the key verse for establishing a direct link between a DAY and a DATE in the year of the exodus. Exodus 16:1 says, *All the congregation of the people of Israel came to the wilderness of Sin… on the fifteenth day of the second month after they had departed from the land of Egypt.*

The fifteenth day of the second month on the Hebrew calendar is Iyar 15. This was exactly thirty days after the people of Israel left Egypt with a seven-day supply of bread, and they were very hungry. That evening—biblical days begin in the evening—God provided quail for meat, and in the morning of that same day He provided manna for bread: *In the evening quail came up and covered the camp, and in the morning dew lay around the camp. And when the dew had gone up, there was on the face of the wilderness a fine, flake-like thing, fine as frost on the ground* (Exodus 16:13-14). The fine, flake-like thing on the ground was called manna. Moses told the people, *"It is the bread that the LORD has given you to eat"* (v. 15).

After this, Exodus 16:21-22 says, *Morning by morning they gathered [manna], each as much as he could eat; but when the sun grew hot, it melted. On the sixth day they gathered twice as much bread.* Exodus 16:23 records what Moses said to the leaders on the sixth day of the *shabua*-days: *This is what the LORD has commanded: "Tomorrow is a day of solemn rest, a holy Sabbath to the LORD; bake what you will bake and boil what you will boil, and all that is left over lay aside to be kept till the morning"* (v. 23). On the 7th and final day of the *shabua*-days, Exodus 16:24-26 reports, the manna *did not stink, and there were no worms in it.* Moses said, *"Eat it today, for today is a Sabbath to the LORD; today you will not find it in the field. Six days you shall gather it, but on the seventh day, which is a Sabbath, there will be none."*

DATING THE FIRST SHABUA-DAYS OF MANNA

So, according to Exodus 16, manna appeared for the first time on the morning of Iyar 15 (Day 1). Then for five consecutive mornings—Iyar 15-16-17-18-19 (Day 1-2-3-4-5)—the people of Israel gathered a one-day supply of manna. But on the morning of Iyar 20 (Day 6), the people gathered a two-day supply of manna. And on the morning of Iyar 21 (Day 7), manna did not appear and therefore could not be gathered. Iyar 21 was the 7th and final day of the *shabua*-days called the Sabbath, the holy day of solemn rest on which work was prohibited. On this DAY and DATE the people ate the remaining supply of the double portion of manna they had gathered on Iyar 20 (Day 6).

Six days of work were followed by a 7th and final day of rest, making this seven-day cycle for manna one biblical *shabua* (a complete time period of seven). Manna appeared and was gathered for the very first time on the morning of Iyar 15. This was the first DATE that manna appeared; it was also the first DAY of the *shabua*-days. Since the first DAY of every *shabua*-days is always Sunday, Iyar 15 was a Sunday. By linking a biblical DATE (Iyar 15) to a biblical DAY (Sunday), we are able to DATE the entire *shabua*-days for the first appearance of manna in the year of the exodus (Figure 5.5).

SHABUA	DATE	DAY
Day 1	Iyar 15	Sunday
Day 2	Iyar 16	Monday
Day 3	Iyar 17	Tuesday
Day 4	Iyar 18	Wednesday
Day 5	Iyar 19	Thursday
Day 6	Iyar 20	Friday
Day 7	Iyar 21	Regular Sabbath

FIGURE 5.5 DATES of the first *shabua*-days of manna

THREE MONTHS IN THE YEAR OF THE EXODUS

At the time of the exodus, God changed the start of the biblical year to the month of Nisan (Abib). Exodus 12:2 records what God told Moses and Aaron: "*This month [Nisan] shall be for you the beginning of months. It shall be the first month of the year for you.*" Prior to this change, Tishri (Ethanim) was the beginning of both the biblical year and the traditional/civil year. After this change, Tishri remained the beginning—the first month—of the *traditional/civil* year (*Rosh Hashanah*), but Nisan was designated the new beginning—the first month—of the *biblical* year (as reflected in Figure 4.3). This reckoning remains in effect today.

Because the Bible provides both a DAY and a DATE for the first *shabua*-days of manna, we can determine those seven days began on Sunday, Iyar 15, and ended on Sabbath, Iyar 21. Using these seven firmly established biblical DAYS and DATES from Figure 5.5 as a benchmark, we are able to create the following calendar (Figure 5.6) for the Hebrew months of Nisan, Iyar, and Sivan in the year of the exodus. This alignment of DAYS and DATES is identical in the year of the crucifixion. (See Figure 5.3 for an illustration of the back-to-back 30-day months of Nisan and Iyar during the year of the crucifixion and the year of the exodus.)

NISAN						
SUN	MON	TUE	WED	THU	FRI	SABBATH
					1	2
3	4	5	6	7	8	9
10	11	12	13	14	15	16
17	18	19	20	21	22	23
24	25	26	27	28	29	30

IYAR						
SUN	MON	TUE	WED	THU	FRI	SABBATH
1	2	3	4	5	6	7
8	9	10	11	12	13	14
15	16	17	18	19	20	21
22	23	24	25	26	27	28
29	30					

SIVAN						
SUN	MON	TUE	WED	THU	FRI	SABBATH
		1	2	3	4	5
6	7	8	9	10	11	12
13	14	15	16	17	18	19
20	21	22	23	24	25	26
27	28	29				

DATES		DESCRIPTION OF EVENTS
Nisan	1	First new moon of the inaugural Nisan biblical year
	10	Passover lambs were selected by each family
	10-13	Passover lambs were inspected and tested for four days
	14	Passover lambs were killed on the day of Preparation
	15	Passover lambs were eaten in haste
		Tenth plague of death of the firstborn
		Exodus of the Israelites from Egypt
	16	7th and final day of the *shabua*-days (regular Sabbath)
	17	Day after the 7th and final day of the *shabua*-days (Sunday)
Iyar	1	Second new moon of the inaugural Nisan biblical year
	15	First day that God supplied manna in the morning
	15-21	First *shabua*-days of manna in the wilderness
	20	Double portion of manna was gathered on the sixth day
	21	First official regular Sabbath day of solemn rest
Sivan	1	Third new moon of the inaugural Nisan biblical year
		Arrived at Mount Sinai on the day of the third new moon
	5	Seventh regular Sabbath after the Sabbath of Nisan 16
		Last day of 7 *shabua*-days after the exodus
		49 days after Sabbath, Nisan 16
	6	Day after the seventh Sabbath after Sabbath, Nisan 16
		Day after 7 *shabua*-days after Sabbath, Nisan 16
		50 days after Sabbath, Nisan 16
		God came down in fire on Mount Sinai and spoke

FIGURE 5.6 Nisan, Iyar, and Sivan in the year of the exodus

OBSERVATIONS BASED ON FIGURE 5.6

Nisan 16: In the year of the exodus, God established the regular Sabbath for Israel, the 7th and final day of every *shabua*-days. The first regular Sabbath for Israel occurred at the time of the first *shabua*-days of manna (Iyar 15 through Iyar 21). The Bible does not provide a DATE for the regular Sabbath during the month of Nisan in the year of the exodus, but that DATE can be determined by working backward from the DATES of the first *shabua*-days of manna. Working backward reveals that the DATE of that regular Sabbath in the year of the exodus was Nisan 16 (precedent). As indicated in chapter 4, we know that the DATE of that regular Sabbath—during the Seven-Day Feast—in the year of the crucifixion was also Nisan 16 (prophecy).

Nisan 17: In the year of the exodus, God established the barley sheaf firstfruits ceremony and commanded Israel to celebrate it on the day after the regular Sabbath that occurs during the Seven-Day Feast. This command was not in effect until after the people of Israel entered Canaan and began to farm the land. The day after the regular Sabbath is always Sunday. The Bible does not provide a DATE for that Sunday during the month of Nisan in the year of the exodus, but that DATE can be determined by working backward from the DATES of the first *shabua*-days of manna. Working backward reveals that the DATE of that Sunday in the year of the exodus was Nisan 17 (precedent). As indicated in chapter 4, we know that the DATE of that Sunday—the day after the regular Sabbath—in the year of the crucifixion was also Nisan 17 (prophecy).

Sivan 6: In the year of the exodus, God established the Feast of *Shabua*'s wheat loaves firstfruits ceremony and commanded Israel to celebrate it on the day after 7 *shabua*-days after the regular Sabbath that occurs during the Seven-Day Feast: 7×7 days = 49 days and 49 days + 1 day = 50 days. This command was not in effect until after the people of Israel entered Canaan and began to farm the land. The day after the seventh regular Sabbath is always Sunday. The Bible does not provide a DATE for that Sunday during the month of Sivan in the year of the exodus, but that DATE can be determined by working forward from the DATES of the first *shabua*-days of manna. Working forward reveals that the DATE of that Sunday in the year of the exodus was

Sivan 6 (precedent). Since the 50 days in the year of the crucifixion begin the day after the same regular Sabbath during the Seven-Day Feast, we know that the DATE of that Sunday in the year the Holy Spirit arrived—the day of Pentecost—was also Sivan 6 (prophecy).

THE EXODUS AND THE CRUCIFIXION ARE LINKED

The exodus and the crucifixion are linked through precedent, pattern, and prophecy. The symmetry between these two events is so detailed, specific, and comprehensive that coincidence can virtually be ruled out. In both the year of the exodus and the corresponding year of the crucifixion over 1,500 years later, the DAYS of the *shabua*-days as well as the DATES of the Hebrew months are identical (Figure 5.7). These DAYS and DATES were determined using only information from the Bible. In our future book *Shabua Seventy*, we use science, history, mathematics, and astronomy to confirm the precise Gregorian calendar day, month, and year of all significant first-century CE biblical events in Jesus' life. That study requires a thorough understanding of *shabua*, and that begins here in *Shabua Days*.

DAY AND DATE	IN THE YEAR OF THE EXODUS	IN THE YEAR OF THE CRUCIFIXION
Thursday, Nisan 14	Passover lamb was killed.	Lamb of God (Jesus) was killed.
Friday, Nisan 15	Exodus from Egypt.	Designated Sabbath High Day.
Sabbath, Nisan 16	The regular Sabbath (see note).	The regular Sabbath.
Sunday, Nisan 17	The day after the regular Sabbath.	The day after the regular Sabbath. Jesus was resurrected (Easter).
Sunday, Sivan 6	50 days after the regular Sabbath. Spiritual Israel was born.	50 days after the regular Sabbath. The church was born (Pentecost).

FIGURE 5.7 The exodus and the crucifixion are linked

Note: Technically speaking, the regular Sabbath—the 7th and final day of the *shabua*-days—was not declared a holy day of solemn rest until thirty days after the exodus from Egypt (discussed in chapter 3). Working backward from the first *shabua*-days of manna reveals that the DATE of the regular Sabbath in the year of the exodus was Nisan 16. Once Sabbath, Nisan 16, was established, it was possible to determine both Sunday, Nisan 17 (the day after), and Sunday, Sivan 6 (50 days after).

SIX DAYS AT MOUNT SINAI

ON THE DAY OF THE THIRD NEW MOON

According to the Bible, after the first *shabua*-days of manna in the wilderness of Sin—from Iyar 15 through Iyar 21—the people of Israel departed for Rephidim. There, Moses struck the rock at Horeb and water came out. (Rephidim is also the place where Joshua and his men prevailed against the attacking Amalekites.) After leaving Rephidim, Exodus 19:1 says, *on the third new moon after the people of Israel had gone out of the land of Egypt, on that day they came into the wilderness of Sinai.*

Every biblical month begins with the first visible sighting of the new moon immediately after sunset, an event referred to as *Rosh Chodesh* (the first or head of the month). In the year of the exodus, the Bible teaches, God established a new beginning for the people of Israel that began on Nisan 1. Therefore, Nisan 1 is the first new moon, Iyar 1 is the second new moon, and Sivan 1 is the third new moon. The Israelites came into the wilderness of Sinai "on the third new moon... on that day," which was Sivan 1.

SIVAN 1 THROUGH SIVAN 6

The first DATE of Sivan is Sivan 1. The sixth DATE of Sivan is Sivan 6. We know that Sivan 6 was Sunday because the 50th day after the regular Sabbath is always a Sunday. Since we know that Sivan 6 was a Sunday, we can determine that Sivan 1 was a Tuesday by working backwards. This reckoning is consistent with the calendar for the months of Nisan, Iyar, and Sivan in the year of the exodus (Figure 5.6). Based on this, we can assign a DAY to each DATE from Sivan 1 through Sivan 6 (Figure 5.8). The significance of the 1st day, 2nd day, and 3rd day on Sivan 4, 5, and 6 will be discussed in the sections that follow.

DATE	DAY	DESCRIPTION	VERSE
Sivan 1	Tuesday	Day of the third new moon	Exodus 19:1
Sivan 2	Wednesday		
Sivan 3	Thursday		
Sivan 4	Friday	1st day ("today")	Exodus 19:10
Sivan 5	Regular Sabbath	2nd day ("tomorrow")	Exodus 19:10
Sivan 6	Sunday	3rd day ("the third day")	Exodus 19:11

FIGURE 5.8 Sivan 1-6 in the year of the exodus

THE CHRONOLOGY OF THE FIRST SIX DAYS OF SIVAN

Exodus 19 provides a detailed chronology of the first six days of the Hebrew month of Sivan in the year of the exodus. Very few scenarios can accommodate all of the events within the timeframe of Tuesday, Sivan 1, through Sunday, Sivan 6. We believe the following analysis of each of those days is the most natural, logical, and reasonable way to accommodate the entire sequence. Each day is subdivided by its two natural time periods: when it was dark (evening/night) and when it was light (morning/day).

The terrain at Mount Sinai is relevant. There is a gain in elevation of approximately 700 meters (2,300 feet) from the valley floor to the most likely summit. The most likely path covers a distance of approximately 3.5 kilometers (2.17 miles). A healthy adult could make this ascent in 1 to 2 hours. Since Moses was 80 years old, it could have taken him 3 to 4 hours or more. However, even 6 hours (one quarter of a day) is plenty of time for Moses to ascend Mount Sinai.

The number of people present at Mount Sinai is also relevant. The Bible says that at the time of the exodus, the people of Israel numbered *about six hundred thousand men on foot, besides women and children* (Exodus 12:37). This figure is associated with men who were at least twenty years old. If each of these men had a wife and three children, the multitude would have numbered 3 million ($600,000 \times 5 = 3,000,000$). Three children per father and mother is a conservative estimate given the fact that, at the time they left Canaan, the average number of children for Jacob and his twelve sons is greater than five.

And it is reasonable to assume they had more children after they arrived in Egypt. (In addition to the Israelites, verse 38 says *a mixed multitude also went up with them.*)

TUESDAY, SIVAN 1

Evening/Night—The people encamped en route from Rephidim: Each day begins in the evening after sunset, and each month begins in the evening when the initial sliver of the new moon appears. Sivan 1 began when the initial sliver of the third new moon of the year appeared after sunset. (No part of the moon would have been visible the previous evening on the last day of the Hebrew month of Iyar.) It is reasonable to assume that during their multiday trek from Rephidim to the wilderness of Sinai, the people of Israel—with their children and livestock—encamped during the evening/night while it was dark. (The sky is particularly dark at the beginning of each month because moonlight is scant.)

Morning/Day—The people arrived in the wilderness of Sinai: According to Exodus 19:1, the people of Israel *on the third new moon... on that day they came into the wilderness of Sinai.* The 24-hour biblical day (*yom*) always begins in the evening after sunset, but the Bible often uses the terms *evening, night, morning,* and *day* to break each 24-hour period into four quarters. It is noteworthy that the root of the Hebrew word *yom*—transliterated as *yowm*—(Strong's H3117) means "to be hot." In other words, *day* can refer to both a full 24-hour period as well as to the specific period of time when the sun is shining. It is reasonable to assume that the multitude hiked during the morning/day while there was natural sunlight so people could see where they were going. And *on that day they came into the wilderness of Sinai* (v. 1).

WEDNESDAY, SIVAN 2

Evening/Night—Israel encamped; Moses ascended Mount Sinai; God spoke to Moses: Sivan 2 began this evening after sunset. After settling at Mount Sinai, *they encamped in the wilderness. There Israel encamped* *before the mountain, while Moses went up to God* (Exodus 19:2-3). We are told that two things happened: Israel encamped, and Moses went up to God. After Moses ascended Mount Sinai, *the LORD called to him out of the mountain, saying, "Thus you shall say to the house of Jacob, and tell the people of Israel"* (v. 3). While the people of Israel slept, Moses received instructions from the Lord. As the Lord finished speaking to Moses on the mountain, He said, *"These are the words that you shall speak to the people of Israel"* (v. 6).

Morning/Day—Moses descended Mount Sinai; Moses spoke to the elders; the word went out: In order to obey the Lord, Moses had to descend Mount Sinai: *So Moses came and called the elders of the people and set before them all these words that the LORD had commanded him* (Exodus 19:7). After coming down from the mountain, Moses gathered the elders and told them what the Lord had said. It is reasonable to assume that the elders then spread the Lord's message throughout the camp, and it would have taken some time to reach a multitude of more than 3 million people.

THURSDAY, SIVAN 3

Evening/Night—Moses, the elders, and the people slept: Sivan 3 began this evening after sunset. After the words of the Lord had gone out to all of the people, it is reasonable to assume that Moses, the elders, and the people would have gone to sleep when it was dark.

Morning/Day—All the people answered; Moses ascended Mount Sinai: Apparently Moses and the elders successfully communicated the words of the Lord to the entire multitude because Exodus 19:8 says, *All the people answered together and said, "All that the LORD has spoken we will do."* Hearing their words, *Moses reported the words of the people to the LORD* (v. 8). This statement implies that Moses ascended Mount Sinai to speak to the Lord for a second time. In the next section, this inference is confirmed by verse 14 that says—after speaking to the Lord—*Moses went down from the mountain to the people.* In other words, Moses had to ascend Mount Sinai for the second time before he could come down from the mountain for the second time.

FRIDAY, SIVAN 4 ("TODAY")

Evening/Night—Moses spoke to God; God gave Moses instructions; Moses descended Mount Sinai: Sivan 4 began this evening after sunset. In the previous section, we find Moses ascending Mount Sinai for the second time. On this occasion, the Lord gave Moses a series of instructions for the next three days. In Exodus 19:10-11, *the LORD said to Moses, "Go to the people and consecrate them today and tomorrow, and let them wash their garments and be ready for the third day. For on the third day the LORD will come down on Mount Sinai in the sight of all the people."* After receiving some additional instructions, *Moses went down from the mountain to the people* (v. 14). This was the second time Moses descended Mount Sinai.

Morning/Day—The first day of consecration: Now present with the people, Moses *consecrated the people; and they washed their garments* (v. 14). Before Moses went down from the mountain earlier on Sivan 4 (during the evening/night), the Lord instructed Moses to go to the people and consecrate them "today" (Figure 5.8). After Moses came down from the mountain later on Sivan 4 (during the morning/day), he consecrated the people and had them wash their garments "today." It is reasonable to assume that these events took place during the morning/day while there was sunlight so people could see.

REGULAR SABBATH, SIVAN 5 ("TOMORROW")

Evening/Night—Moses, the elders, and the people slept: Sivan 5 began this evening after sunset. It is reasonable to assume that Moses, the elders, and the people would have gone to sleep when it was dark.

Morning/Day—The second day of consecration: On the preceding day, the Lord had instructed Moses to consecrate the people for two days ("today" and "tomorrow" [Figure 5.8]). If Friday, Sivan 4, was "today" (the first day of consecration), then the regular Sabbath, Sivan 5, was "tomorrow" (the second day of consecration). This was the second day that Moses consecrated the people. It is reasonable to assume that this event took place during the morning/day while there was sunlight so people could see.

SUNDAY, SIVAN 6 ("THE THIRD DAY")

Evening/Night—Moses, the elders, and the people slept: Sivan 6 began this evening after sunset. It is reasonable to assume that Moses, the elders, and the people would have gone to sleep when it was dark.

Morning/Day—God appeared in the sight of all the people and spoke: This is "the third day" (Figure 5.8) referred to in Exodus 19:11: *Be ready for the third day. For on the third day the LORD will come down on Mount Sinai in the sight of all the people.* And we know that this happened in the morning because verses 16-18 say: *On the morning of the third day there were thunders and lightnings... [and] Mount Sinai was wrapped in smoke because the LORD had descended on it in fire.* On the morning of this landmark day the Lord came down in fire on Mount Sinai, and the people of Israel heard Him speak.

MIRACLES DURING THE EXODUS FROM EGYPT

What took place on Sunday, Sivan 6—the third day—in the year of the exodus was a turning point for the Jewish people, and that day has left an indelible mark in history. Consider what had happened during the days leading up to Sivan 6. Before the exodus, the people of Israel were witnesses to God's power over nature. During the exodus, they saw God perform many miraculous signs and wonders. After the exodus, the people continued to experience God's presence. The following is a list of some of the major miracles God did and the people of Israel witnessed:

The ten plagues only afflicted the Egyptians and not the Israelites.

The firstborn children of Israel were passed over by death.

The Israelite oppression and slavery in Egypt came to an end.

The Egyptian people gave the Israelites gifts of gold, silver, etc.

A pillar of fire guided the Israelites when they traveled by night.

A pillar of cloud guided the Israelites when they traveled by day.

The Red Sea parted and the Israelites crossed on dry land.

The entire Egyptian army drowned as the Red Sea returned.

Bitter water was made sweet at Marah in the wilderness of Shur.

Quail was provided for meat in the wilderness of Sin.

Manna was provided for bread in the wilderness of Sin.

A one-day supply of manna was provided each day for five days.

A double portion of manna was provided on the sixth day only.

The extra manna on the sixth day was preserved for the 7th day.

Water came from the rock of Horeb at Massah (called Meribah).

Israel's fledgling army prevailed over the Amalekites at Rephidim.

THUNDER, LIGHTNING, FIRE, SMOKE, AND TREMBLING

As impressive as each miracle was, they do not compare to what happened on Sunday, Sivan 6. On that day the people of Israel saw God descend in fire on Mount Sinai and heard Him speak. This event is described in Exodus 19:16-19:

On the morning of the third day there were thunders and lightnings and a thick cloud on the mountain and a very loud trumpet blast, so that all the people in the camp trembled. Then Moses brought the people out of the camp to meet God, and they took their stand at the foot of the mountain. Now Mount Sinai was wrapped in smoke because the LORD had descended on it in fire. The smoke of it went up like the smoke of a kiln, and the whole mountain trembled greatly. And as the sound of the trumpet grew louder and louder, Moses spoke, and God answered him in thunder.

Prior to this day, the people of Israel had never heard God speak. God had communicated exclusively with Moses, who then told the people what God said. But on Sunday, Sivan 6, after Moses brought the people out of the camp to the foot of Mount Sinai, Moses spoke to God, and God answered him in thunder. On this occasion, all the people heard God speak; all the people saw God descend in fire on Mount Sinai; all the people saw the mountain wrapped in smoke; and all the people felt God's presence when the whole mountain trembled greatly.

THE TEN COMMANDMENTS

GOD GAVE ISRAEL THE TEN COMMANDMENTS

What happened at Mount Sinai is widely viewed as the spiritual birth of the nation of Israel. The memory of this event continues to shape the religion, culture, and community of the Jewish people to this very day. The account has been passed down from generation to generation for almost 3,500 years. While the people stood at the foot of Mount Sinai, *God spoke all these words, saying, "I am the LORD your God, who brought you out of the land of Egypt, out of the house of slavery"* (Exodus 20:1-2).

While enslaved in Egypt, the people of Israel were exposed to a myriad of Egyptian gods and religious practices, including the worship of idols and nature. In Egypt, God demonstrated His ultimate power and authority over all the Egyptian gods, idols, and even nature itself when He sent the ten plagues to pressure Pharaoh to let the people of Israel go. At Mount Sinai, God told the Israelites that He performed the miracles that set the people free. As the Lord continued to speak from Mount Sinai, He audibly gave the people of Israel the Ten Commandments.

THREE OBLIGATIONS IN THE TEN COMMANDMENTS

The Ten Commandments are found in Exodus 20:3-17. These laws define our duties and responsibilities as human beings created by God and over whom He continues to maintain sovereign authority. The commandments naturally fall into three distinct categories (Figure 5.9). The first three commandments are obligations to God; the fourth is a unique obligation for the people of Israel; and the last six commandments are obligations we human beings have to other human beings.

OBLIGATIONS	COMMANDMENT	DESCRIPTION
	First	Do not have other gods
To God	Second	Do not create images or idols
	Third	Do not take God's name in vain
For Israel	Fourth	Keep the Sabbath (rest)
	Fifth	Honor your father and mother
	Sixth	Do not murder
	Seventh	Do not commit adultery
To Others	Eighth	Do not steal
	Ninth	Do not bear false witness (lie)
	Tenth	Do not covet

FIGURE 5.9 Three obligations in the Ten Commandments

TWO TABLETS OF STONE WRITTEN BY GOD

After God audibly gave the people of Israel the Ten Commandments, the people *said to Moses, "You speak to us, and we will listen; but do not let God speak to us, lest we die"* (Exodus 20:19). So God called Moses to go back up the mountain. That is when he received the Ten Commandments on stone tablets. Moses said this in Deuteronomy 9:9-10:

> *When I went up the mountain to receive the tablets of stone, the tablets of the covenant that the LORD made with you, I remained on the mountain forty days and forty nights. I neither ate bread nor drank water. And the LORD gave me the two tablets of stone written with the finger of God, and on them were all the words that the LORD had spoken with you on the mountain out of the midst of the fire on the day of the assembly.*

According to Exodus 32:15, the two tablets of stone that God gave Moses *were written on both sides; on the front and on the back they were written*. Moses spent forty days and forty nights with the Lord on the mountain. When Moses came back down with the tablets, *as soon as he came near the camp and saw the calf and the dancing, Moses' anger burned hot, and he threw the tablets out of his hands and broke them at the foot of the mountain* (v. 19). Moses broke this original set of tablets when he saw the people worshipping a golden calf. Before Moses went back up the mountain to receive a replacement set, God told Moses, *"Cut for yourself two tablets of stone like the first, and I will write on the tablets the words that were on the first tablets, which you broke"* (Exodus 34:1).

The replacement set of the two stone tablets was kept in a sacred gold chest called the Ark of the Covenant. This Ark was guarded and specially cared for: the Israelites took the Ark everywhere they went and housed it in a special tent called the tabernacle when they encamped in the wilderness. When King Solomon built the First Temple in Jerusalem, the Ark containing the two tablets engraved with the Ten Commandments was set on the foundation stone within the temple's Most Holy Place (also called the Holy of Holies).

JESUS DID NOT ABOLISH THE TEN COMMANDMENTS

God defined His relationship with the people of Israel when He gave them this message through Moses: *"Now therefore, if you will indeed obey my voice and keep my covenant, you shall be my treasured possession among all peoples, for all the earth is mine; and you shall be to me a kingdom of priests and a holy nation. These are the words that you shall speak to the people of Israel"* (Exodus 19:5-6). In essence, God's relationship and great plans for the people of Israel were dependent on their obeying God's voice and keeping His covenant, specifically the Ten Commandments. In both doctrine and practice, the Ten Commandments have been—and continue to be—a major component of Judaism.

Followers of Mohammad do not accept the Old Testament (including the Ten Commandments) as authoritative because they believe it has been corrupted by the Jews. Nevertheless, one section of the Qur'an contains many of the same basic prohibitions. Not surprisingly, there is no mention in the Qur'an of the command to rest and not work on the Sabbath: that command was given exclusively to the people of Israel in the Fourth Commandment.

Followers of Jesus generally accept the Old Testament (including the Ten Commandments) as authoritative. This is clear from what Jesus said in Matthew 5:17, "*Do not think that I have come to abolish the Law or the Prophets; I have not come to abolish them but to fulfill them.*" In chapter 3 we indicated that nine of the Ten Commandments are restated virtually word for word in the New Testament on multiple occasions. In fact, not only are these nine commandments restated at least four times, but each one is also expanded and applied to believers in the church (Figure 5.10). The one exception is the Fourth Commandment regarding rest on the Sabbath: this commandment is not restated in the New Testament, nor is it applied to the church.

#	BRIEF DESCRIPTION	OLD TESTAMENT	NEW TESTAMENT			
1	No other gods	Exodus 20:3	Matthew 4:10	Matthew 22:37	Luke 4:8	1 Cor 8:4-6
2	No idolatry	Exodus 20:4-6	Acts 15:20	1 Cor 10:14	Colossians 3:5	1 John 5:21
3	No abusing God's name	Exodus 20:7	Matthew 12:31-32	Romans 2:23-24	1 Timothy 6:1	James 2:6-7
4	Keep the Sabbath	Exodus 20:8-11				
5	Honor your parents	Exodus 20:12	Matthew 19:19	Mark 10:19	Luke 18:20	Ephesians 6:2
6	Do not murder	Exodus 20:13	Matthew 19:18	Mark 10:19	Luke 18:20	Romans 13:9
7	Do not commit adultery	Exodus 20:14	Matthew 19:18	Mark 10:19	Luke 18:20	Romans 13:9
8	Do not steal	Exodus 20:15	Matthew 19:18	Mark 10:19	Luke 18:20	Romans 13:9
9	Do not lie	Exodus 20:16	Matthew 19:18	Mark 10:19	Luke 18:20	Colossians 3:9
10	Do not covet	Exodus 20:17	Romans 7:7	Romans 13:9	Ephesians 5:3-5	Colossians 3:5

FIGURE 5.10 Nine of the Ten Commandments are in the New Testament

THE CHURCH AND THE SABBATH

As Figure 5.10 illustrates, the Fourth Commandment to rest on the Sabbath is the only one of the Ten Commandments that is not expressly restated in the New Testament. This is evidence that the Fourth Commandment is not extended to Gentile believers in the church, and explains why the church does not honor the 7th and final day of every *shabua*-days (except Seventh-day Adventists and Messianic Jews). This understanding—that the Sabbath is not extended to the Gentile church—is confirmed in Colossians 2:16: *let no one pass judgment on you... with regard to... a Sabbath.* In other words, people are no longer to be judged by what they do—or do not do—on the Sabbath

As explained in chapter 3, believers are not commanded to rest on the Sabbath because Jesus is the prophetic fulfillment of rest. Instead of regarding one day above another, Jesus told believers in Matthew 11:28, *"Come to me, all who labor and are heavy laden, and I will give you rest."* Jesus provides rest for the body, soul, and spirit, and that rest is available any day, time, or place. In essence, rest for believers is not limited to physical rest on the Sabbath.

In practice, believers have traditionally gathered on the first day of the week, which is Sunday. However, meeting on Sunday does not comply with the Sabbath rest requirements as described in the Bible and practiced by the Jewish people for millennia. Consider these facts:

The Fourth Commandment was given to the people of Israel as an everlasting covenant.

The Fourth Commandment is not restated in the New Testament.

Colossians 2:16 says nobody is to be judged by whether or not they keep the Sabbath.

The church does not rest on the Sabbath as dictated by the Fourth Commandment.

The church has traditionally gathered on the first day of the week (Sunday), not the Sabbath (Saturday).

Jesus is the prophetic fulfillment of rest—any day, time, or place—for the Gentile church.

Jesus never even mentioned the Fourth Commandment obligation to rest on the Sabbath.

JESUS LEFT OUT THE SABBATH OBLIGATION

The last point bears repeating. As indicated in the section titled "Three obligations in the Ten Commandments" and in Figure 5.9, the Ten Commandments fall into three distinct categories: obligations to God, an obligation for Israel, and obligations we human beings have to other human beings. When the Jewish religious leaders asked Jesus which commandment was the most important, Jesus' response would have shocked the scribes who heard Him: Jesus intentionally left out the Fourth Commandment obligation that Israel was to rest on the Sabbath. In Mark 12:29-31, Jesus explained:

> *"The most important [commandment] is, 'Hear, O Israel: The Lord our God, the Lord is one. And you shall love the Lord your God with all your heart and with all your soul and with all your mind and with all your strength.' The second is this: 'You shall love your neighbor as yourself.' There is no other commandment greater than these."*

In essence, Jesus summarized nine of the Ten Commandments in just two obligations: an obligation to God and an obligation to other human beings. Jesus made no reference whatsoever to the Fourth Commandment obligation for Israel to rest on the Sabbath. As indicated in the previous section, the only reference Jesus made to rest is in Matthew 11:28-29 where He encouraged His followers with these words: *"Come to me, all who labor and are heavy laden, and I will give you rest. Take my yoke upon you, and learn from me, for I am gentle and lowly in heart, and you will find rest for your souls."*

A SABBATH REST REMAINS FOR ISRAEL

The New Testament book of Hebrews was written decades after the resurrection. Its primary purpose was and is to inform Hebrew people—as the title implies—that Jesus was and is the promised Jewish Messiah (Christ).

The book of Hebrews repeatedly demonstrates how Jesus is the ultimate fulfillment of Old Testament precedent, pattern, and prophecy. Hebrews 4:1 says that *the promise of entering his rest still stands* for those who have received the good news and are united by faith. *For we who have believed enter that rest* (v. 3). This means in the same way as Gentile Christians, the people of Israel can find rest today by believing in Jesus.

In addition, a future time period of rest for the people of Israel is mentioned in the book of Hebrews. This future period that God repeatedly calls "my rest" is associated with a time when the enemies of Israel will be vanquished and there will be peace throughout the land. This future time period of rest will fulfill a promise God made to the physical descendants of Abraham, Isaac, and Jacob. Although this topic of rest is incredibly relevant today, it is beyond the scope of this work. This subject will be covered extensively in *Shabua Years*.

PRECEDENTS, PATTERNS, AND PROPHECIES

MOUNT SINAI, THE FEAST OF SHABUA, AND PENTECOST

The original landmark event at Mount Sinai (precedent), the annual commemorative Feast of *Shabua* (pattern), and the landmark event on the day of Pentecost in Jerusalem (prophecy) are inseparably linked. Multiple examples of the uncanny correlation between Bible precedent, pattern, and prophecy are presented on the pages that follow. These correlations repeatedly demonstrate that the relationship between the Old and New Testaments—as well as Judaism and Christianity—was not only intended but is ongoing.

The odds that so many unique and specific associations—spanning thousands of years—happened by chance defies the laws of probability and common sense. The meticulous attention to detail coupled with unparalleled accuracy creates a compelling case that the precedents, patterns, and prophecies are in fact God breathed and true. That being said, there must be a reason they are in the Bible.

ON THE 50TH DAY

Precedent: God came down in fire on Mount Sinai and spoke to the people of Israel on Sunday, Sivan 6. This was the 50th day after the regular Sabbath that occurred in the year of the exodus from Egypt. On this DAY and DATE God spoke from the mountain, and the people heard the Ten Commandments for the first time.

Pattern: The Feast of *Shabua* is always celebrated on a particular DAY (Sunday) in the month of Sivan (the DATE is variable). It occurs on the 50th day after the regular Sabbath that occurs during the Seven-Day Feast. This feast commemorates the Sunday that God (the Lord) came down in fire on Mount Sinai and spoke to the people of Israel. It also commemorates the Sunday that God (the Holy Spirit) would come down on the apostles in tongues as of fire.

Prophecy: The Holy Spirit came down on the apostles in tongues as of fire on Sunday, Sivan 6. This day—called Pentecost—was the 50th day after the regular Sabbath that occurred during the Seven-Day Feast. It occurred on the exact same DAY and DATE as the landmark events at Mount Sinai, and the day of Pentecost commemorates the same DAY (Sunday) as the Feast of *Shabua*.

TWO TABLETS, TWO LOAVES, TWO SIDES OF THE HEART

Precedent: After God audibly gave the people of Israel the Ten Commandments—laws against sin—from Mount Sinai, *the LORD said to Moses, "Come up to me on the mountain and wait there, that I may give you the tablets of stone, with the law and the commandment, which I have written for their instruction"* (Exodus 24:12). When Moses went back up the mountain, God gave him *the two tablets of the testimony, tablets of stone, written with the finger of God* (Exodus 31:18). Exodus 32:15-16 adds that the tablets *were written on both sides; on the front and on the back they were written. The tablets were the work of God, and the writing was the writing of God, engraved on the tablets.* God personally engraved the two stone tablets with His laws against sin.

Pattern: On the day of the Feast of *Shabua*, two loaves of bread were ceremonially waved in the air. The two loaves symbolized the Ten Commandments—laws against sin—spoken by God from Mount Sinai on that same day, and subsequently recorded on the two stone tablets. God specified that these two loaves were to be "*made of two tenths of an ephah. They shall be of fine flour, and they shall be baked with leaven, as firstfruits to the LORD*" (Leviticus 23:17). The two loaves also represent people. In contrast to the symbolic bread—without leaven—at Passover that represents sinless Jesus, the two symbolic loaves of bread—with leaven—at the Feast of *Shabua* represent the people of Israel and the church. (The Bible often uses leaven as a metaphor for sin.) Since both Israel and the church (the two loaves) are prone to sin (the leaven) by breaking God's Law (the Ten Commandments), both require sinless Jesus (the bread of life).

Prophecy: On the day of Pentecost in Jerusalem, the gospel was proclaimed in every language. The good news—then and now—is that people are no longer slaves to sin or condemned by God's laws and commandments. Instead, according to Acts 2:21, *everyone who calls upon the name of the Lord shall be saved.* In 2 Corinthians 3:3, the apostle Paul explained that this message of the gospel is *written not with ink but with the Spirit of the living God, not on tablets of stone but on tablets of human hearts.* The gospel is not etched on two stone tablets or represented in two loaves of bread. The gospel is written on tablets (plural) of the human heart. It is noteworthy that, like the two stone tablets and the two loaves of bread, the human heart has two distinct sides. The heart has a thick wall of muscle—called the septum—that separates the chamber on the right side from the chamber on the left side.

ISRAEL AND THE CHURCH ARE BOTH FIRSTFRUITS

Precedent: The spiritual birth of the nation of Israel—the descendants of Abraham, Isaac, and Jacob—occurred on the day that God descended on Mount Sinai. Spiritual Israel is symbolized by one of the loaves that was waved at the Feast of *Shabua*'s wheat loaves firstfruits ceremony. Since both of the loaves were called *firstfruits to the* LORD (Leviticus 23:17), the people of Israel are firstfruits in God's harvest of people.

Pattern: The day of the wheat loaves firstfruits ceremony is called the Feast of *Shabua*. (The ceremony always preceded the general wheat harvest.) During the ceremony in the courtyard of the temple, the high priest waved two loaves of bread that had been prepared from the firstfruits of the wheat harvest. One of the loaves was commemorative, representing the spiritual birth and harvest of sin-prone Israel. The other loaf was prophetic, representing the spiritual birth and harvest of sin-prone believers. Waving the two loaves together symbolized that the nation of Israel and believers in the church are equal; both are *firstfruits to the* LORD (v. 17) in God's harvest of people.

Prophecy: The spiritual birth of the church—believers in Jesus—occurred on the day that the Holy Spirit descended on the apostles in Jerusalem. The church is symbolized by one of the loaves that was waved at the Feast of *Shabua*'s wheat loaves firstfruits ceremony. Since both of the loaves were called *firstfruits to the* LORD (v. 17), believers in the church are firstfruits in God's harvest of people.

THE ROCK, A MASS OF ROCK, A STONE, A PIECE OF ROCK, LIVING STONES

The paragraphs in this section feature a discussion of a unique precedent and prophecy involving "the Rock." It is important to know what "the Rock" means in order to understand the identical timing that links Old Testament events in the year of the exodus to New Testament events in the year of the crucifixion.

Precedent—Jesus Christ is "the Rock": At various times during the exodus from Egypt and their journey in the dry desert wilderness, the people of Israel were without water. Rephidim was one of the places that God miraculously supplied water from a Rock for the people to drink. The apostle Paul wrote about the people drinking from this Rock: *all drank the same spiritual drink. For they drank from the spiritual Rock that followed them, and the Rock was Christ* (1 Corinthians 10:4). The Greek word translated as *Rock* in this verse is *petra* (Strong's G4073), which means "a (mass of) rock (literally or figuratively)." This verse tells us that Christ (Jesus) was literally the Rock that provided water for the people to drink in the wilderness and enabled them to continue on their trek.

Prophecy (Part 1)—Jesus Christ is "a mass of rock": In Matthew 16:16, the apostle Peter told Jesus, *You are the Christ, the Son of the living God.* To which Jesus replied, *"And I tell you, you are Peter, and on this rock I will build my church"* (v. 18). The Greek word translated as *rock* in this verse is *petra*, the identical word that is used in 1 Corinthians 10:4 that identifies the Rock as Jesus. As already stated, *petra* (Strong's G4073) means "a (mass of) rock (literally or figuratively)." When Jesus told Peter "on this *petra* I will build my church," this *petra* that Jesus is referring to is Jesus Himself. Jesus is the immovable mass of rock (*petra*) upon which the church is built. This metaphor is consistent with numerous Bible verses that refer to Jesus as the foundation stone or chief cornerstone, the most important rock that supports and defines an entire building. Just as structures today are built upon a solid foundation of iron and concrete, the church is built upon the rock-solid foundation of Jesus Christ. In Matthew 7:24-25 Jesus said; *"Everyone then who hears these words of mine and does them will be like a wise man who built his house on the rock. And the rain fell, and the floods came, and the winds blew and beat on that house, but it did not fall, because it had been founded on the rock"* (the Greek word translated twice as *rock* in this passage is *petra*). The church, however, is neither a building nor an institution. The church is believers: people who acknowledge—just as Peter did—that Jesus is the Christ. Jesus is the reason the church exists, and Jesus is the reason the church endures.

Prophecy (Part 2)—*Cephas* is "a stone": Why in Matthew 16:18 did Jesus say, *"And I tell you, you are Peter"* after Peter stated his faith by acknowledging that Jesus was the Christ? The answer to this question requires an understanding of the etymology of Peter's names. According to Matthew 4:18, Peter's original name was Simon: *While walking by the Sea of Galilee, [Jesus] saw two brothers, Simon (who is called Peter).* Simon (Strong's G4613) is a Greek name whose root—*Shim'own* (Strong's H8095)—is of Hebrew origin. *Shama* (Strong's H8085)—the root of *Shim'own*—means "to hear intelligently (often with implication of attention, obedience, etc.; causatively, to tell, etc.)." The name *Simon* appropriately describes Peter when he first met Jesus: Peter listened attentively. When Jesus first met Peter, He called (in the present) him *Simon*, but Jesus told him he was going to be called (in the future) by a different name: *Jesus looked at him and said, "You are Simon the son of John. You shall be called Cephas" (which means Peter)* (John 1:42). In the King James Version, this passage reads: *When Jesus beheld him, he said, Thou art Simon the son of Jona: thou shalt be called Cephas, which is by interpretation, A stone.* Accordingly, the name *Cephas* (Strong's G2786)—an Aramaic name for Peter—means "a stone." In essence, Jesus said, "Right now you are called Simon: you have listened attentively as I have taught the truth. In the future you will be called *Cephas*—a name that means 'a stone'—because you will be part of Me: you will be a piece of the Rock."

Prophecy (Part 3)—Peter is "a piece of rock": Jesus did not say to Simon, "You are Peter" until after the fisherman told Jesus, "You are the Christ." Note Jesus' immediate response to Peter's statement of belief in Him: *Jesus answered him, "Blessed are you, Simon Bar-Jonah! For flesh and blood has not revealed this to you, but my Father who is in heaven. And I tell you, you are Peter, and on this rock I will build my church"* (Matthew 16:17-18). The Greek word translated as *Peter* in this verse is *Petros* (Strong's G4074), which means "a (piece of) rock." What Jesus said when is relevant: Jesus called him by his name Simon before He said, "You are Peter." It was not until after Simon acknowledged that Jesus was the Christ (the Rock) that Jesus called Simon by his new name *Peter* (a piece of rock). In essence, by calling him Peter, Jesus was saying, "You are now part of Me, a piece of the Rock." This appears to be the future event Jesus was referring to when He first told Simon, *"Thou shalt be called Cephas," which is by interpretation, A stone* in John 1:42 (KJV).

Prophecy (Part 4)—Believers are "living stones": Later in 1 Peter 2:5-6, this same Peter told fellow believers, *You yourselves like living stones are being built up as a spiritual house... For it stands in Scripture: "Behold, I am laying in Zion a stone, a cornerstone chosen and precious, and whoever believes in him will not be put to shame."* In essence, the "spiritual house" (the church) is built upon Him who is the "Cornerstone" (Jesus). The "living stones" are all those people who believe in Jesus and are supported and defined by Jesus, the Cornerstone. In other words, Jesus is the mass of Rock (the Cornerstone), and believers are pieces of the Rock (living stones built upon the Cornerstone). This understanding is confirmed by the apostle Paul who wrote that believers are *members of the household of God, built on the foundation of the apostles and prophets, Christ Jesus himself being the cornerstone, in whom the whole structure, being joined together, grows into a holy temple in the Lord* (Ephesians 2:19-21).

THE ROCK WAS STRUCK ONE TIME AND WATER CAME OUT

Precedent: As indicated, there was no water at Rephidim—a remote desert wasteland—and the people believed they were going to die of thirst. After the people sinned by grumbling about the lack of water, the Lord spoke to Moses: *"Pass on before the people, taking with you some of the elders of Israel, and take in your hand the staff with which you struck the Nile, and go. Behold, I will stand before you there on the rock at Horeb, and you shall strike the rock, and water shall come out of it, and the people will drink"* (Exodus 17:5-6). The Rock (Jesus) was struck at Rephidim after the people of Israel sinned by grumbling and quarreling. Water came out of the Rock to symbolize that their sins had been washed away, but it was only temporary. The Rock (Jesus) was struck at Rephidim for the sins of Israel.

Prophecy: Jesus was also struck when He was crucified to take away the sins of the world. Isaiah prophesied concerning the manner in which Jesus would suffer and die over 700 years before it happened: *Surely he has borne our griefs and carried our sorrows; yet we esteemed him stricken, smitten by God, and afflicted. But he was pierced for our transgressions; he was crushed for our iniquities; upon him was the chastisement that brought us peace, and with his wounds we are healed* (Isaiah 53:4-5). Just as water came out of the Rock (Jesus) at Rephidim, water came out of Jesus (the Rock) when His body was pierced as He hung on the cross in Jerusalem. According to John 19:34, *one of the soldiers pierced [Jesus'] side with a spear, and at once there came out blood and water*. Water came out of Jesus to symbolize that the sins of the world had been washed away. The blood that came out of Jesus was the atonement for sin, and this was eternal. Jesus (the Rock) was struck in Jerusalem for the sins of the world.

TALK TO THE ROCK AFTER IT HAD BEEN STRUCK ONE TIME

Precedent: At another remote desert wasteland called Kadesh (less than two years after they left Rephidim), the people of Israel again grumbled and quarreled because there was no water. Numbers 20:2-3 offers this report: *Now there was no water for the congregation. And they assembled themselves together against Moses and against Aaron. And the people quarreled with Moses.* Then the Lord told Moses: *"Take the staff, and assemble the congregation, you and Aaron your brother, and tell the rock before their eyes to yield its water. So you shall bring water out of the rock for them"* (v. 8). On this occasion Moses was specifically instructed to speak to the rock ("tell the rock"), not strike it. *But Moses lifted up his hand and struck the rock with his staff twice, and water came out abundantly, and the congregation drank* (v. 11). Moses disobeyed God by striking the rock instead of speaking to it. As a consequence, Moses was not allowed to enter the Promised Land. Although the penalty of not entering into the Promised Land seems harsh, it demonstrates how important Bible precedent, pattern, and prophecy is to God. The Rock (at Rephidim) was struck once; the Rock (at Kadesh) was not supposed to be struck at all.

Prophecy: Jesus was struck—He suffered and died on the cross—once; Jesus will never suffer and die again. The Lord told Moses to *strike* the Rock (at Rephidim) the first time Israel needed water, but He told Moses to *speak* ("tell") to the Rock (at Kadesh) the second time Israel needed water. Jesus Himself was *struck* on the cross, died, and was resurrected, and now He wants us to *tell* Him that we believe He died to save us from our sins. In Romans 10:9-10 the apostle Paul stated this important truth: *If you confess with your mouth that Jesus is Lord and believe in your heart that God raised him from the dead, you will be saved. For with the heart one believes and is justified, and with the mouth one confesses and is saved.* The apostle John added, *If we confess our sins, he is faithful and just to forgive us our sins and to cleanse us from all unrighteousness* (1 John 1:9).

LIFE-SUSTAINING WATER PROVIDED BY THE ROCK

Precedent: The Rock (Jesus) that the Bible says followed the people of Israel in the wilderness provided life-sustaining water at both Rephidim and Kadesh: *all drank the same spiritual drink. For they drank from the spiritual Rock that followed them, and the Rock was Christ* (1 Corinthians 10:4). Because the Rock (Jesus) followed the people of Israel when they departed from both Rephidim and Kadesh, the water God provided at those locations was temporary. Water no longer flows from the rock at either Rephidim or Kadesh today. The water God provided for the people of Israel in the wilderness was indeed life sustaining, but that water would not continue to flow forever.

Prophecy: In John 6:35 Jesus said, *"Whoever believes in me shall never thirst."* Jesus explained more about the living water that He gives to believers when He said, *"If anyone thirsts, let him come to me and drink. Whoever believes in me, as the Scripture has said, 'Out of his heart will flow rivers of living water'"* (John 7:37-38). Verse 39 explains: *Now this [Jesus] said about the Spirit, whom those who believed in him were to receive.* The living water is the Holy Spirit who permanently enters the heart and soul of every individual who becomes a believer in Jesus Christ. As Jesus said to the woman at the well, *"Everyone who drinks of this water will be thirsty again, but whoever drinks of the water that I will give him will never be thirsty again. The water that I will give him will become in him a spring of water welling up to eternal life"* (John 4:13-14). Jesus (the Rock) provides life-sustaining water for all those who believe in Him, and this water is eternal and continues to flow forever.

THE LAST DAY AND DATE WITH THE ROCK

Precedent: After keeping the first regular Sabbath on Iyar 21 (Figure 5.5), the people of Israel left the wilderness of Sin and camped at Dophkah. Then they left Dophkah and camped at Alush, and they left Alush and camped at Rephidim. There at Rephidim Moses struck the Rock—the first time—and water came out. (Joshua also defeated the army of the Amalekites at Rephidim.) The Bible does not indicate the Israelites' last day at Rephidim, but only one day matches the biblical timeline, and that day has prophetic significance. Based on the timeline that follows (Figure 5.11), the last DAY and DATE the people were with the Rock (Jesus) at Rephidim before departing for the wilderness of Sinai was Thursday, Iyar 26.

DAY AND DATE	DESCRIPTION	VERSE
Sabbath, Iyar 21	First regular Sabbath for the Israelites in the wilderness of Sin.	Exodus 16:30
Sunday, Iyar 22	Left the wilderness of Sin and camped at Dophkah.	Numbers 33:12
Monday, Iyar 23	Left Dophkah and camped at Alush.	Numbers 33:13
Tuesday, Iyar 24	Left Alush and camped at Rephidim; water from the Rock.	Numbers 33:14; Exodus 17:1, 6
Wednesday, Iyar 25	The Israelites defeated the Amalekites in battle at Rephidim.	Exodus 17:8-13
Thursday, Iyar 26	Last day with the Rock at Rephidim before departing for Sinai.	Exodus 19:2

FIGURE 5.11 The last DAY and DATE with the Rock (Jesus)

Prophecy: Jesus appeared to many people during the forty-day period that began on the day of His resurrection and ended on the day of His ascension. According to Acts 1:3, the resurrected Jesus *presented himself alive to them after his suffering by many proofs, appearing to them during forty days.* Then, after Jesus gave His apostles some final instructions, *as they were looking on, he was lifted up, and a cloud took him out of their sight* (v. 9). The forty days began on Sunday, Nisan 17—the DAY and DATE of the resurrection (Figure 4.22 and 4.23)—and ended on Thursday, Iyar 26 (Figure 5.12). The last DAY and DATE the apostles were with Jesus (the Rock) in Jerusalem was Thursday, Iyar 26, which is identical to the last DAY and DATE the Israelites were with the Rock (Jesus) at Rephidim before departing for the wilderness of Sinai.

COUNT	DATES	DESCRIPTION
14 days	Nisan 17-30	14 days for the month of Nisan (includes the 17th).
26 days	Iyar 1-26	26 days for the month of Iyar (includes the 1st).
40 days	Nisan 17-Iyar 26	Thursday, Iyar 26, was the last day with Jesus (the Rock).

FIGURE 5.12 The last DAY and DATE with Jesus (the Rock)

GOD APPEARED TEN DAYS AFTER THURSDAY, IYAR 26

Precedent: The last DAY and DATE with the Rock (Jesus) at Rephidim before the people of Israel departed for the wilderness of Sinai was Thursday, Iyar 26. On Sunday, Sivan 6—exactly ten days later—God (the Lord) manifested His presence to the Israelites from the top of Mount Sinai (Figure 5.13).

DAY	DATE	DESCRIPTION OF EVENTS	DAYS
Thursday	Iyar 26	Last day with the Rock (Jesus) at Rephidim before departing to Sinai.	0
Friday	Iyar 27	En route to the wilderness of Sinai.	1
Regular Sabbath	Iyar 28	Kept the regular Sabbath and did not travel.	2
Sunday	Iyar 29	En route to the wilderness of Sinai.	3
Monday	Iyar 30	En route to the wilderness of Sinai.	4
Tuesday	Sivan 1	Arrived in the wilderness of Sinai on the day of the third new moon.	5
Wednesday	Sivan 2	Moses ascended and descended Mount Sinai the same day.	6
Thursday	Sivan 3	Moses ascended Mount Sinai.	7
Friday	Sivan 4	Moses descended Mount Sinai; the first day of consecration ("today").	8
Regular Sabbath	Sivan 5	Moses was with the people; the second day of consecration ("tomorrow").	9
Sunday	Sivan 6	God was manifest in fire on Mount Sinai on the tenth day ("the third day").	10

FIGURE 5.13 God appeared ten days after Thursday, Iyar 26

Prophecy: After Jesus (the Rock) was resurrected from the dead on Sunday, Nisan 17, He appeared to the people for forty days: *He presented himself alive to them after his suffering by many proofs, appearing to them during forty days and speaking about the kingdom of God* (Acts 1:3). The fortieth day was Thursday, Iyar 26 (Figure 5.12), the day that Jesus (the Rock) ascended to heaven. Ten days after that was Sunday, Sivan 6 (Figure 5.14), the day the Holy Spirit arrived on the day of Pentecost. This was fifty days (40 + 10 = 50) after the regular Sabbath (Figure 5.7).

COUNT	DATES	DESCRIPTION
4 days	Iyar 27-30	4 days for the month of Iyar (includes the 27th).
6 days	Sivan 1-6	6 days for the month of Sivan (includes the 1st).
10 days	Iyar 27-Sivan 6	Sunday, Sivan 6 was the day of Pentecost.

FIGURE 5.14 Ten days after the ascension

TWO HOLY DAYS BEFORE GOD APPEARED ON SUNDAY

Precedent: When all the people were encamped at the foot of Mount Sinai, the Lord told Moses, *"Go to the people and consecrate them today and tomorrow, and let them wash their garments and be ready for the third day"* (Exodus 19:10-11). As previously discussed (Figure 5.8), the first day of consecration ("today") was Friday, and the second day of consecration ("tomorrow") was the regular Sabbath. The Hebrew word for *consecrate* is *qadash* (Strong's H6942), which means "to be (causatively, make, pronounce or observe as) clean (ceremonially or morally)." The notes for *qadash* list these synonyms: "appoint, bid, consecrate, dedicate, defile, hallow, (be, keep) holy(-er, place), keep, prepare, proclaim, purify, sanctify(-ied one, self), wholly." God set aside both Friday, Sivan 4, and the regular Sabbath, Sivan 5 (Figure 5.13)—two consecutive holy days of consecration—prior to appearing to the people on Sunday ("the third day").

Prophecy: Jesus was crucified, died, and buried before sunset on the Thursday, Nisan 14, the day of Preparation (discussed in chapter 4). The next day—Friday, Nisan 15—was the DATE of the designated annual Sabbath

High Day. The Sabbath High Day was (and is) always a designated holy day of solemn rest regardless of the DAY of the *shabua*. And the day after that particular Sabbath High Day was the DAY of the regular Sabbath—the 7th and final day of the *shabua*—which is always a holy day of solemn rest for Israel. So Jesus was in the tomb for both the Sabbath High Day on Friday and the regular Sabbath—two consecutive holy days—before appearing to people on Sunday ("the third day"): *God raised [Jesus] on the third day and made him to appear... [to people] chosen by God as witnesses... after he rose from the dead* (Acts 10:40-41).

GOD CAME DOWN FROM HEAVEN MANIFEST AS FIRE

Precedent: On Sunday, Sivan 6, when the Israelites were all gathered together at the foot of Mount Sinai, the mountain *was wrapped in smoke because the LORD had descended on it in fire. The smoke of it went up like the smoke of a kiln, and the whole mountain trembled greatly* (Exodus 19:18). At Mount Sinai, God—the Lord—came down from Heaven, manifested His presence in fire, and rested on the top of the mountain.

Prophecy: On Sunday, Sivan 6, when the apostles were all gathered together at a house in Jerusalem, *suddenly there came from heaven a sound like a mighty rushing wind, and it filled the entire house where they were sitting. And divided tongues as of fire appeared to them and rested on each one of them* (Acts 2:2-3). In Jerusalem, God—the Holy Spirit—came down from Heaven, manifested His presence as fire, and rested on the apostles.

GOD SPOKE TO THE PEOPLE AND THROUGH THE APOSTLES

Precedent: After all the people had assembled at the foot of Mount Sinai—before Moses went up to receive the Ten Commandments on the two stone tablets—Exodus 20:1 indicates *God spoke all these words*, and the words God spoke from the top of the mountain were the Ten Commandments (vv. 3-17). After God had finished speaking, the people *said to Moses, "You speak to us, and we will listen; but do not let God speak to us, lest we die"* (v. 19). *And the Lord said to Moses, "Thus you shall say to the people of Israel:*

'You have seen for yourselves that I have talked with you from heaven'" (v. 22). When the word of God came down from Heaven at Mount Sinai, the people of Israel heard God speak.

Prophecy: On the day Jesus ascended to Heaven, He told the apostles, *"You will be baptized with the Holy Spirit not many days from now,"* and *"you will receive power when the Holy Spirit has come upon you, and you will be my witnesses in Jerusalem and in all Judea and Samaria, and to the end of the earth"* (Acts 1:5, 8). Ten days later on the day of Pentecost, the apostles *were all filled with the Holy Spirit and began to speak in other tongues as the Spirit gave them utterance… And at this sound the multitude came together, and they were bewildered, because each one was hearing them speak in his own language* (2:4, 6). When the word of God came down from Heaven in Jerusalem, people from every nation—in Jerusalem for the Feast of *Shabua*—heard God speak through the apostles in their own language.

3,000 DIED UNDER THE LAW; 3,000 WERE SAVED BY GRACE

Precedent: On the very day that Moses came back down from Mount Sinai, *as soon as he came near the camp and saw the calf and the dancing, Moses' anger burned hot, and he threw the tablets out of his hands and broke them at the foot of the mountain* (Exodus 32:19). The people broke the Ten Commandments when they made a golden calf, worshipped it, and made sacrifices to it. That same day Moses literally broke the two stone tablets on which God had engraved the Ten Commandments. *And that day about three thousand men of the people fell* (v. 28). On the day that the Ten Commandments were broken at Mount Sinai—spiritually and literally—about 3,000 people died under the law as a consequence of their sin.

Prophecy: On the very day—Pentecost—that Peter preached the good news to the people gathered in Jerusalem, *those who received [Peter's] word were baptized, and there were added that day about three thousand souls* (Acts 2:41). When these new believers accepted Jesus as their Lord and Savior, their sins were forgiven, they were baptized with the Holy Spirit, and they received eternal life. On the day that the apostles preached the gospel in Jerusalem, about 3,000 people were saved by grace from the consequence of their sin.

MOUNT SINAI, THE FEAST OF SHABUA, AND PENTECOST

In conclusion, the landmark Old Testament event at Mount Sinai (precedent), the annual commemorative Old Testament Feast of *Shabua* (pattern), and the foreshadowed New Testament event in Jerusalem on the day of Pentecost (prophecy) are all linked by subject matter as well as by timing. The precedent was set when God came down in fire on Mount Sinai and gave the people of Israel the Ten Commandments. To commemorate this event, two firstfruits wheat loaves were presented to God during the annual Feast of *Shabua*. This pattern—initiated in the Old Testament—was fulfilled in the New Testament event on the day of Pentecost. On that day, the Holy Spirit came down and appeared as tongues of fire resting on the first believers, and the church was born.

The Feast of Passover and the Feast of Unleavened Bread (the Seven-Day Feast) are titles that describe the precedent as well as the pattern, but the titles Feast of *Shabua* and Pentecost do not describe anything about the precedent, pattern, or prophecy. These titles suggest nothing about God coming down in fire on the mountain, God speaking to the people of Israel, the spiritual birth of Israel, the giving of the Law, the Ten Commandments, the two symbolic firstfruits wheat loaves, or the prophetic fulfillment on the day of Pentecost. Instead, the biblical titles Feast of *Shabua* and Pentecost are significant because they are both associated with timing, and the Bible emphasizes the DAY to celebrate this feast is Sunday, which is a specific DAY of the *shabua*, not a DATE.

THE SIGNIFICANCE OF UNDERSTANDING SHABUA

Understanding *shabua*-days enables us to determine the precise DAY (Sunday) when God came down in fire on Mount Sinai (precedent); when the Old Testament commemorative Feast of *Shabua* was celebrated (pattern); and when the corresponding New Testament fulfillment took place in Jerusalem on the day of Pentecost (prophecy). The key to determining the timing is knowing that a *shabua* is always "a complete time period of seven"; that *shabua*-days always begin on Sunday and end on the regular Sabbath; and that the Bible links multiple *shabua*-days together to mark time.

In chapter 1, we defined the biblical concept of *shabua* as "a complete time period of seven." In chapters 2 and 3, we reviewed the way in which individual *shabua*-days are used to determine biblical timing. In chapter 4, we examined the connection between *shabua*-days and the Seven-Day Feast. In this chapter, we saw how multiple *shabua*-days are linked together to determine when the Feast of *Shabua* is celebrated. Although the Feast of *Shabua* was the primary focus of this chapter, all Old Testament feasts, festivals, and holy days foreshadow New Testament events in a similar manner.

The interrelationship between the exodus, biblical feasts, Jesus, the church, and eschatology (the study of end-times events as described in the Bible) is uncanny. Volumes could be written about the significance and relevance of each of the three primary Old Testament biblical feasts (two spring and one fall). For more information on these feasts, read the books of Exodus, Leviticus, Numbers, Deuteronomy, and the Gospels. There you will see the way multiple Old Testament precedents and patterns are linked to prophecies fulfilled in the New Testament.

SHABUA YEARS, THE SEQUEL

In *Shabua Years*, the sequel to this book, we will examine *shabua*-years. It governs long-term timing in the Bible in the same way that *shabua*-days governs short-term timing. Many more examples of the ways in which the Old and New Testaments are linked through precedent, pattern, and prophecy will also be presented. In the same way as this book, *Shabua Years* relies on Scripture as the final authority on biblical topics, particularly those that are controversial. Some of the widely debated biblical topics examined in *Shabua Years* include the year of Creation, the rapture, the great tribulation, the second coming, the kingdom age, the millennium, and the new heaven and the new earth.

To be continued...

ENDNOTES

CHAPTER 1

1   Merriam-Webster. "About Us: Noah Webster and America's First Dictionary." https://www.merriam-webster.com/about-us/americas-first-dictionary.

2   Merriam-Webster. "Help: How many words are there in English?" https://www.merriam-webster.com/help/faq-how-many-english-words.

3   Blue Letter Bible. "H7620 - shabuwa` - Strong's Hebrew Lexicon (KJV)." https://www.blueletterbible.org//lang/lexicon/lexicon.cfm?Strongs=H7620&t=KJV.

4   Merriam-Webster. "Dozen." https://www.merriam-webster.com/dictionary/dozen.

5   Dictionary.com. "Dozen." Douglas Harper, Historian. http://www.dictionary.com/browse/dozen.

CHAPTER 2

1   Universe Today. "How Many Stars Are in the Milky Way?" by Matt Williams. Last updated December 11, 2016. http://www.universetoday.com/123225/how-many-stars-are-in-the-milky-way-2/.

2   Universe Today. "How many galaxies are there in the universe?" by Fraser Cain. Last updated November 1, 2016. http://www.universetoday.com/30305/how-many-galaxies-in-the-universe/.

3   NASA. "Hubble Space Telescope." www.nasa.gov/mission_pages/hubble/story/index.html.

4   Hubble Space Telescope. "The Hubble Deep Fields." Accessed June 19,1017. http://www.spacetelescope.org/science/deep_fields/.

5   Ibid.

6   NASA. "Hubble goes to the extreme to assemble farthest-ever view of the universe." September 25, 2012. https://www.nasa.gov/mission_pages/hubble/science/xdf.html.

7   Space.com. "How Fast Does Light Travel?: The Speed of Light" by Nola Taylor Redd. May 22, 2012. http://www.space.com/15830-light-speed.html.

8   Universe Today. "How Far Is a Light Year?" by Fraser Cain. July 2, 2017. https://www.universetoday.com/45003/how-far-is-a-light-year/.

9   NASA. "The Cosmic Distance Scale." https://imagine.gsfc.nasa.gov/features/cosmic/nearest_star_info.html.

10   Erasmus Darwin. *The Botanic Garden*. Volume 1. "The Economy of Vegetation." 1791.

11   Edgar Allan Poe. "Eureka."

12   Encyclopædia Britannica. "Aleksandr Aleksandrovich Friedmann" by The Editors of Encyclopædia Britannica. Last updated January 25, 2017. https://www.britannica.com/biography/Aleksandr-Aleksandrovich-Friedmann.

13   PBS SoCal. "Big Bang theory is introduced." Accessed on June 7, 2017. http://www.pbs.org/wgbh/aso/databank/entries/dp27bi.html.

14   Universe Today. "Hubble's Law" by Jean Tate. Last updated December 24, 2015. http://www.universetoday.com/40064/hubbles-law/.

15   Vision Learning. "Theories, Hypotheses, and Laws" by Anthony Carpi, Ph.D., and Anne E. Egger, Ph.D. Accessed on June 7, 2017. www.visionlearning.com/en/library/Process-of-Science/49/Theories-Hypotheses-and-Laws/177.

16   Nature. "The Beginning of the World from the Point of View of Quantum Theory." (127, 706), 9 May 1931. http://www.nature.com/nature/journal/v127/n3210/full/127706b0.html.

17   Biodiversity Heritage Library. "British Association for the Advancement of Science: Report of the Centenary Meeting." http://www.biodiversitylibrary.org/item/96080#page/700/mode/1up.

18   National Geographic. "Origins of the Universe." Accessed on June 7, 2017. http://www.nationalgeographic.com/science/space/universe/origins-of-the-universe/.

19   Space.com. "What Is the Big Bang Theory?" by Elizabeth Howell. June 22, 2015. http://www.space.com/25126-big-bang-theory.html.

20   Universe Today. "What Is a Singularity?" by Matt Williams. Last updated January 7, 2017. https://www.universetoday.com/84147/singularity/.

21   Universe Today. "Who is Stephen Hawking?" by Matt Williams. Last updated June 29, 2016. https://www.universetoday.com/123487/who-is-stephen-hawking/.

22   Science.HowStuffWorks.com "What existed before the big bang?" by Robert Lamb. Last updated May 12, 2010. http://science.howstuffworks.com/dictionary/astronomy-terms/before-big-bang.htm.

23   CERN. "LHC the Guide." February 2017. http://cds.cern.ch/record/2255762/files/CERN-Brochure-2017-002-Eng.pdf.

24 National Geographic. "Origins of the Universe."

25 Hubblesite. "How Old Is the Universe?" http://hubblesite.org/reference_desk/faq/all.php.cat=cosmology.

26 BBC. "About the Big Bang Theory." http://www.bbc.co.uk/science/space/universe/questions_and_ideas/big_bang/.

27 National Geographic. "Physics Nobel Explainer: Why Is Expanding Universe Accelerating." By Victoria Jaggard. October 5, 2011. http://news.nationalgeographic.com/news/2011/10/111004-nobel-prize-physics-universe-expansion-what-is-dark-energy-science/.

28 NASA. "The First and Second Laws of Motion" by Carol Hodanbosi. https://www.grc.nasa.gov/www/k-12/WindTunnel/Activities/first2nd_lawsf_motion.html.

29 National Geographic. "Physics Nobel Explainer."

30 Vision Learning. "The Scientific Method" by Anthony Carpi, Ph.D., and Anne E. Egger, Ph.D. Accessed on June 7, 2017. www.visionlearning.com/en/library/General-Science/3/The-Scientific-Method/45.

31 Vision Learning. "Theories, Hypotheses, and Laws."

32 IBT. "Forbes: Finding the Higgs Boson Cost $13.25 Billion" by Eric Brown. Dated July 5, 2012. http://www.ibtimes.com/forbes-finding-higgs-boson-cost-1325-billion-721503.

33 CERN. "LHC the Guide."

34 Encyclopædia Britannica. *Quark*: https://www.britannica.com/science/quark.

35 CERN. "LHC the Guide."

36 Ibid.

37 Merriam-Webster. "*Faith*." https://www.merriam-webster.com/dictionary/faith.

38 Space.com. "What Are Redshift and Blueshift?" by Elizabeth Howell. May 2, 2014. Accessed June 12, 2017. www.space.com/25732-redshift-blueshift.html.

39 BBC. "History of Life on Earth." October 2014. http://www.bbc.co.uk/nature/prehistoric.

40 "Erasmus Darwin" in *Dictionary of Scientific Biography*, ed. Charles Coulston Gillispie (New York: Scribner's, 1970-1976), III, 579.

41 Charles Darwin. *The Correspondence of Charles Darwin*: 1821-1836, Volume 1.

42 Ibid.

43 Encyclopædia Britannica. "Evolution." Francisco Jose Ayala. December 6, 2017. https://www.britannica.com/science/evolution-scientific-theory.

44 Charles Darwin. *On the Origin of Species*.

45 Understanding Evolution. "Evolution 101." University of California Museum of Paleontology. https://evolution.berkeley.edu/evolibrary/article/evo_01.

46 Ibid.

47 Space.com. "How Was Earth Formed?" by Nola Taylor Redd. October 31, 2016. https://www.space.com/19175-how-was-earth-formed.html.

48 National Geographic. "Mantle." August 11, 2015. https://www.nationalgeographic.org/encyclopædia/mantle/.

49 National Geographic. "Core." August 17, 2015. https://www.nationalgeographic.org/encyclopædia/core/.

50 NOAA: National Ocean Service. "How much water is in the ocean?" http://oceanservice.noaa.gov/facts/oceanwater.html.

51 NASA. "Comets: In Depth." https://solarsystem.nasa.gov/planets/comets/indepth.

52 Ibid.

53 NASA. "About the Moon." https://moon.nasa.gov/about.cfm.

54 New Scientist. "Planet Earth makes its own water from scratch deep in the mantle" by Andy Coghlan. January 27, 2017. https://www.newscientist.com/article/2119475-planet-earth-makes-its-own-water-from-scratch-deep-in-the-mantle/.

55 Smithsonian.com. "How Did Water Come to Earth?" by Brian Greene. May 2013. http://www.smithsonianmag.com/science-nature/how-did-water-come-to-earth-72037248/#4cMHeJ3aJEfTsEtY.99.

56 Live Science. "How Did Life Arise on Earth?" by Ker Than. September 1, 2016. https://www.livescience.com/1804-greatest-mysteries-life-arise-earth.html.

57 Live Science. "7 Theories on the Origin of Life" by Charles Q. Choi. March 24, 2016. https://www.livescience.com/13363-7-theories-origin-life.html.

58 Ars Technica. "Microsoft Experiments with DNA Storage: 1,000,000,000 TB in A Gram" by Peter Bright. April 27, 2016. https://arstechnica.com/information-technology/2016/04/microsoft-experiments-with-dna-storage-1000000000-tb-in-a-gram/.

59 Merriam-Webster. "Probability." https://www.merriam-webster.com/dictionary/probability.

60 Probability Theory. "Monkeys Typing Shakespeare or Even Just the Word 'Hamlet.'" http://probabilitytheory.info/content/item/8-understanding-combinations-and-premutations.

61 Vision Learning: Glossary. "Second Law of Thermodynamics" http://www.visionlearning.com/en/glossary/index/S#term-5352.

62 Encyclopædia Britannica. "Principles of physical science: Entropy and disorder" by Brian Pippard. https://www.britannica.com/science/principles-of-physical-science/Conservation-laws-and-extremal-principles#ref366463.

63 LibreTexts: Chemistry. "A System and Its Surroundings." April 13, 2015. https://chem.libretexts.org/Core/Physical_and_Theoretical_Chemistry/Thermodynamics/Introduction_to_Thermodynamics/A_System_and_Its_Surroundings.

64 Vision Learning: Glossary. "First Law of Thermodynamics." http://www.visionlearning.com/en/glossary/index/F#term-5351.

65 General Kinematics. "Copper Mining and Processing: Everything You Need to Know." July 17, 2014. https://www.generalkinematics.com/blog/copper-mining-processing-everything-need-know/.

66 The United States Mint. "The Minting Process Revealed." https://www.usmint.gov/kids/coinNews/mintingProcess/index.html.

67 Encyclopædia Britannica. "Human body." February 16, 2017. https://www.britannica.com/science/human-body.

68 Inner Body. http://www.innerbody.com/.

69 Live Science. "How the Human Eye Works" by Ker Than. May 5, 2016. https://www.livescience.com/3919-human-eye-works.html.

70 Encyclopædia Britannica. "Sex Chromosome." March 05, 2014. https://www.britannica.com/science/sex-chromosome.

71 Encyclopædia Britannica. "Human Reproductive System" by Richard J. Harrison. August 26, 2014. https://www.britannica.com/science/human-reproductive-system.

72 National Geographic. "How Many Cells Are in Your Body?" October 23, 2013. phenomena.nationalgeographic.com/2013/10/23/how-many-cells-are-in-your-body/.

73 Encyclopædia Britannica. "Human body." February 16, 2017. https://www.britannica.com/science/human-body.

74 National Human Genome Research Institute. "A Brief Guide to Genomics." August 27, 2015. https://www.genome.gov/18016863/a-brief-guide-to-genomics/.

75 CERN. "LHC the Guide."

76 Ibid.

77 Shyamala Iyer. "Building Blocks of Life." ASU – Ask a Biologist. September 27, 2009. https://askabiologist.asu.edu/content/atoms-life.

78 United States Census Bureau. "U.S. and World Population Clock." Accessed June 1, 2017. https://www.census.gov/popclock/.

79 National Human Genome Research Institute. "From the Blueprint to You." April 2003. https://www.genome.gov/pages/education/modules/blueprinttoyou/blueprintcoverto2.pdf.

80 Ibid.

81 The Metropolitan Museum of Art. "Egyptian Cubit Rods." by Nora E. Scott. http://www.metmuseum.org/pubs/bulletins/1/pdf/3257092.pdf.bannered.pdf.

82 Encyclopædia Britannica. "Cubit." March 6, 2016. https://www.britannica.com/science/cubit.

83 American Civil Liberties Union. "Joint Statement of Current Law on Religion in the Public Schools." https://www.aclu.org/other/joint-statement-current-law-religion-public-schools.

84 Merriam-Webster. "Faith."

CHAPTER 3

1 Encyclopædia Britannica. "Jewish Religious Year." January 15, 2018. https://www.britannica.com/topic/Jewish-religious-year.

2 Adoremus. "Eucharisticum Mysterium-Instruction on Eucharistic Worship." May 25, 1967. https://adoremus.org/1967/05/25/eucharisticum-mysterium/.

1 Encyclopædia Britannica. "Sunday." April 13, 2015. https://www.britannica.com/topic/Sunday-day-of-week.

CHAPTER 4

1 Encyclopædia Britannica. "Edict of Milan." March 29, 2016. https://www.britannica.com/topic/Edict-of-Milan.

2 Encyclopædia Britannica. "Easter." April 25, 2018. https://www.britannica.com/topic/Easter-holiday.

3 R Laird Harris, Gleason L. Archer, Jr., Bruce K. Waltke, eds., Theological Wordbook of the Old Testament (Chicago: The Moody Bible Institute, 1980). "Hodesh."

4 Encyclopædia Britannica. "Jewish Religious Year."

5 Stargazing.net. "29 Days of the Moon." http://www.stargazing.net/david/moon/index29days.html.

6 A lunar year is twelve lunar months (12 x 29.53059 days), a total of 354.36708 days.

7 According to NASA, one solar year (one full orbit of Earth around the sun) is 365.2422 days (https://pumas.gsfc.nasa.gov/examples/index.php?id=46).

8 Judaism 101. "Jewish Calendar." http://www.jewfaq.org/calendar.htm.

9   Encyclopædia Britannica. "Jewish Religious Year."

10 Theological Wordbook of the Old Testament. "Abib."

11 Timeanddate.com. "Jerusalem, Israel — Sunrise, Sunset, and Daylength, March 2018." https://www.timeanddate.com/sun/israel/jerusalem.

12 Judaism 101. "Pesach: Passover." http://www.jewfaq.org/holidaya.htm.

13 Judaism 101. "Pesach Seder: How Is This Night Different." http://www.jewfaq.org/seder.htm.

14 Flavius Josephus, *The Jewish War*, book 6, chapter 9 in *The New Complete Works of Josephus*, trans. William Whiston (Grand Rapids, MI: Kregel Publications, 1999), 906.

15 Judaism 101. "Pesach Seder: How Is This Night Different."

16 Judaism 101. "Pesach: Passover."

ABOUT THE AUTHOR

PAUL WOZNIAK, JD, earned his BBA from the University of Wisconsin-Eau Claire, his CFP designation from the College for Financial Planning, and his JD from Pepperdine University School of Law. During his second year in law school, Paul began to develop an interest in God's Word after attending a Bible study with fellow students. He gave his life to Jesus Christ later that same year. Shortly after graduating from law school, he began his successful business and tax practice.

After 25 years in business, Paul sensed God was calling him out of the corporate world. Since that time—more than a decade ago—he has been using his extensive experience doing technical research to meticulously examine God's Word. His thorough and systematic approach to the Bible involves the study of linguistics, history, culture, archeology, and the sciences as well as travel to Egypt, Israel, and Jordan to conduct field research.

Paul has attended and been involved in leadership at Mariners Church/South Coast Community Church in Irvine, California, for 37 years, where he has served as chairman of the Board of Elders and chairman of the Board of Trustees. He and his wife, Gail, have been married for 34 years and have five children, two by marriage: Conrad and his wife, Ashley; Jordan and his wife, Tayah; and Chelsea.

BOOKING INFORMATION

Paul formed Shabua and is writing the Shabua book series to teach the Bible and share his findings with others. His desire is to accurately present Scripture in a compelling way that will inspire both believers and nonbelievers to study the Bible. To request a presentation of *Shabua Days* or for Paul to speak at your event, please email us at requests@shabua.com.

Revalation

7 divisions —

1. Jesus In Heaven w/spirit of every believer living/dead

2. The church on Earth
   - 2000yr period — we're living in that age

3.

4. Rapture
   - believers on Earth or church age → in heaven

5.

6. — 8. tribulation on Earth
   - "non. believers."

9. church believers comes back w/ Jesus on Earth

10. 1000 year remaining. Rapture.

resurrected + live on earth people that accept chri

Satan bound for 1000 years

SHARE YOUR THOUGHTS

If you have enjoyed this book or it has impacted your life in some way, we would love to hear about it.

Please send all comments to:
Shabua
5405 Alton Parkway
Suite A-757
Irvine, CA 92604

Or email us at:
review@shabua.com

CONNECT WITH US

Go to shabua.com and subscribe to be notified about forthcoming books, upcoming events, and more.

Session 2
book 24-56
study 18-30
Portraits of Jesus

New Testament
Gospel
Old Test.

(targets Jewish david King)
Servant — Matthew
Mark
"Son of Man"
Man
Luke
"Son of God" — John
↓
Diety

CPSIA information can be obtained
at www.ICGtesting.com
Printed in the USA
FSHW011721040419

9 781949 014006